Trade Battles

Trade Battles

Activism and the Politicization of International Trade Policy

TAMARA KAY AND R. L. EVANS

OXFORD
UNIVERSITY PRESS

OXFORD
UNIVERSITY PRESS

Oxford University Press is a department of the University of Oxford. It furthers the University's objective of excellence in research, scholarship, and education by publishing worldwide. Oxford is a registered trade mark of Oxford University Press in the UK and certain other countries.

Published in the United States of America by Oxford University Press
198 Madison Avenue, New York, NY 10016, United States of America.

Library of Congress Cataloging-in-Publication Data
Names: Kay, Tamara, 1971– author. | Evans, Rhonda (Rhonda Lynn), author.
Title: Trade battles : activism and the politicization of international trade
policy / Tamara Kay, R.L. Evans.
Description: New York City : Oxford University Press, [2018] |
Includes bibliographical references and index.
Identifiers: LCCN 2017034866 (print) | LCCN 2017049840 (ebook) |
ISBN 9780190847456 (updf) | ISBN 9780190847463 (epub) |
ISBN 9780190847432 (hardcover) | ISBN 9780190847449 (pbk.)
Subjects: LCSH: Commercial policy—Citizen participation. | Commercial
treaties—Citizen participation. | North American Free Trade Agreement
(1992 December 17)
Classification: LCC HF1379 (ebook) | LCC HF1379 .K384 2018 (print) |
DDC 382/.3—dc23
LC record available at https://lccn.loc.gov/2017034866

9 8 7 6 5 4 3 2 1

Paperback printed by Webcom, Inc., Canada
Hardback printed by Bridgeport National Bindery, Inc., United States of America

For Neil Fligstein and Peter Evans

Contents

List of Figures

Preface

AT A UNIQUE moment in history when many people around the world have seemed to reject globalization, an analysis of the North American Free Trade Agreement (NAFTA) is critical to understanding how issues of free trade and in particular free trade agreements, fed into that discontent. When we began graduate school in the 1990s, there seemed to be near universal excitement about the possibilities of globalization. Global communications and processes would link people together around the world, collapsing time and space. New technologies would diffuse quickly to make life easier across the planet, and help mitigate global inequalities. Globalization was about promise and hope for the future.

There were voices of dissent and discontent, however, and they tended to focus on concerns that an unfettered global capitalism and neoliberalism would actually deepen and increase inequalities, and wreak havoc on a fragile planet that was already showing signs of environmental distress and a changed climate induced by human activities. A chorus of these voices came together around a critique of free trade. The focus of their ire was a trade agreement negotiated in the early 1990s that one activist referred to as the "icing on the neoliberal cake." For them, free trade epitomized how an expanding global economy further privileged the rich by securing protections for property and intellectual property rights while constructing most social goods—labor and human rights, environmental protection, among many others—as externalities subject only to the vagaries of the market.

In a nation founded on ideas of individual rights and liberties and deeply rooted in a culture of individualism, making arguments about collective rights and common goods is often difficult and ineffective. But activists viewed NAFTA as a profound threat to the continent's labor and human rights, and to the common health of its environment. At its core, the battle they waged against NAFTA challenged the privileging of individual rights in North America, and sought to preserve the collective rights and common good of its citizens (by which we mean members of the community, regardless of legal status). This aspect of their battle against NAFTA was quite radical, and yet it is usually overlooked in the historiography and in analyses of the trade agreement.

It was in large part activists' response to NAFTA—particularly their focus on collective rights and common goods—that drew us both into its strong orbit. It is no coincidence that our interests coincided and our orbits collided at Berkeley. We were both students of Neil Fligstein and Peter Evans who together had expertise in organizations, social movements, development, and political and economic sociology. Harley Shaiken, a labor activist and scholar who had served as an adviser to Representative Richard Gephardt during the NAFTA struggle, was leading Berkeley's Center for Latin American Studies. He was enthusiastic about nurturing our interest in NAFTA.

Out of the belly of Barrows Hall then, two dissertations centered on NAFTA were birthed (Malcolm Fairbrother (2006) soon after produced a third, completing the trifecta). One focused on NAFTA's negotiation and the emergence of ethical trade advocacy (Evans 2002), the other on the emergence of solidarity among key unions in Mexico, the United States, and Canada in response to NAFTA (Kay 2004). Although they had different foci, the two dissertations centered on quite similar questions about why and how activists responded to NAFTA with collective approaches—both in how they framed trade policy (as an affront to the common good), and how they fought against it (collectively across North America's borders).

Our common interest in NAFTA cemented our intellectual bonds, but eventually the hours of dinner conversations shifted away from work, leading us both to realize that our relationship no longer centered on a neoliberal free trade agreement. It was, in fact, rooted in a strong and profound friendship that has sustained us both through very exhilarating and very difficult moments in our lives. It is the kind of friendship that naturally and effortlessly generates family bonds—we are each "Auntie" to the other's daughter, who refer to each other as cousins.

It seemed only natural then, to put the relationship to the test. We decided to join together on an intellectual project, and what better one than NAFTA? In 2004 we began working on what became our 2008 *American Sociological Review* article on the greening of trade policy. As the endeavor did not destroy our friendship we decided to continue with the project and produce a book manuscript that fleshed out the nascent empirical and theoretical arguments of the *ASR* article. In the meantime, the second dissertation was completed as a book and published in 2011 by Cambridge University Press as *NAFTA and the Politics of Labor Transnationalism*. The seeds of the first dissertation remain in this book and have allowed us to produce what we hope are rich contributions to the literature and historiography on NAFTA.

It is easy, and perhaps tempting, to focus on the unique historical and political moment in which this book emerges and to miss how NAFTA actually shaped the decades leading up to it. As the final touches were made to this book, NAFTA became repoliticized. It was a central issue in the 2016 presidential primaries and election. Trade in general, and NAFTA in particular, is a dominant focus of the forty-fifth U.S. president.

Given how large the current political moment looms, it could easily distract from the larger and more general point of the book, which is primarily about democracy, not trade per se. For the last twenty-five years, trade has been a proxy for the decay of democratic institutions and practices—and an epicenter of the battles to preserve them. NAFTA then, provides a lens through which to examine how the state attempts to thwart democratic interventions in policy formation. At the same time, the NAFTA case reveals how activists skillfully develop and deploy strategies in order to mitigate the effects of state institutional closure and influence state policy. The argument therefore resonates regardless of the outcome of the 2016 election.

Another key takeaway from the book is the importance of addressing the needs of workers and communities dislocated by trade and other threats to their livelihoods, from technological shifts to energy policies. For the last twenty-five years politicians, pundits, and scholars have offered too little empathy and understanding—and few viable policy solutions—in the face of economic and technological changes that rip families and communities apart when work is relocated or made obsolete. The arguments that trade creates net jobs or lowers prices for consumers, and that limiting drilling is better for the planet, may be accurate, but they are little consolation to an individual worker (whether he or she lives in the United States, Mexico, or Canada) whose future evaporates when a factory moves or a mine is shuttered.

The impact on workers of our desire to improve growth and buy cheaper products, develop new technologies, reverse climate change, and preserve the planet's resources should not be dismissed or ignored. Workers have been and will always be at globalization's front line. Failure to address globalization's negative effects has significant economic consequences for workers and their communities, and significant political consequences, as we saw in the United States and the United Kingdom in 2016.

Ultimately the NAFTA story shows that globalization is not inherently positive or negative. The rules governing globalization determine who benefits and who is harmed by the plethora of processes that constitute it, from investment and economic flows and the proliferation of communications networks, to technology transfers and cultural diffusion. Fair trade activists realized this early on—they understood that NAFTA would lay the foundation for the rules governing the global economy that would ultimately affect workers, migrants, farmers, indigenous people, the environment, access to land, water, medicine, and even cultural production. It was to protect these collective goods and collective rights around which they built their struggle against NAFTA. Although they did not succeed in killing NAFTA, it was a much stronger agreement because of their efforts. And, with the exception of the agreement that transformed the GATT into the WTO, no president since has been able to get passed a free trade agreement of greater political and economic significance.

Acknowledgments

THIS BOOK IS the result of our education at Berkeley under the guidance of unparalleled scholars and mentors Peter Evans and Neil Fligstein, and it is to them that we dedicate this book. Their commitment to our intellectual and professional development has been incomparable. For over twenty years they have been unwavering in their support for us as scholars and as women. We also thank Kim Voss and Harley Shaiken for their tremendous support and encouragement. And of course, we are extremely grateful to all of the women and men who shared personal recollections with us for this project. We have learned a great deal from them collectively, and we hope that this book adequately reflects their dedication, perseverance, and vision.

Friends and colleagues offered invaluable advice on various aspects of the manuscript, and to them we owe an enormous debt of gratitude. They include: Bart Bonikowski, Joshua Bloom, Lance Compa, Frank Dobbin, Malcolm Fairbrother, Mala Htun, Kendra Koivu, Sara Niedzwiecki, Susan Ostermann, William Stanley, Jami Nelson-Nunez, and James Jasper. For research assistance and for running technical reconnaissance on the final manuscript, from checking citations to formatting figures, we thank Asad L. Asad, Aaron Benavidez, Anna Calasanti, Deborah DeLaurell, Nicole Arlette Hirsch, In Paik, Jason Spicer, and Rhea Wilson. Jane Jones deserves special thanks for editing a final version of the text and offering invaluable advice that resulted in a much stronger manuscript.

The editors and staff at Oxford University Press have been extraordinary, and we are so grateful for their stewardship of this book. We have had the great fortune to work with James Cook whose guidance and insights made the argument more cogent and the contribution more clear. We thank him and the reviewers for the time they devoted to the manuscript. We are deeply appreciative of all Emily Mackenzie did to shepherd the manuscript through until the end. Some data and ideas from the book were originally published as "How Environmentalists 'Greened' Trade Policy: Strategic Action and the Architecture of Field Overlap" in the *American Sociological Review* (2008), and "New Challenges, New Alliances: The Politicization of Unions in a Post-NAFTA Era" in *Labor History* (2013). This research is made possible in part by support from the Institute for Scholarship in the Liberal Arts, College of Arts and Letters, University of Notre Dame. We also thank Scott Appleby, Marilyn Keough Dean of the Keough School of Global Affairs, and John T. McGreevy, I.A. O'Shaughnessy Dean, College of Arts and Letters, at the University of Notre Dame for their support of the project and for providing a sabbatical that allowed us to complete the final draft of this book manuscript.

Our deepest thanks to our dear friends: Jason McNichol, Eileen and Arek Nathanson, the Dales, Aaron Belkin, the Haleys, the Mariniers, the Mintzs, the Talajkowskis, the Osirims, Valentina Cogoni, Elizabeth Gorman, Jennifer Hoult, Rebecca Milliken, Karriann Farrell Hinds, Sheila Holmes, Duana Fullwiley, Joshua Bloom, Jason Spicer, Tiffany Florvil, Nura Aly, Angelina Godoy, Isaac Mankita, Isaac Martin, Mary Ann Mrugalski, Karen Jersild, Glenn Leggett, Marshall Ganz, Anthony Chen, Prudence Carter, Rowan Flad, and In Paik.

Our love and thanks to our families: Andrew Levin, Lynda Levin, Joshua Levin, Caroline Levin, Nicole Evans, Sue Curran, Deborah Black, Molly Kenefick, Lynne Miller, Rachael Chappell, Indigo Blauch-Chappell, Canyon Blauch-Chappell, Felix Blauch-Chappell, Michael Kay, Erica Sherman, Karla Kay, and Rana Kay, and the entire extended Toro and Volpe families.

We are forever grateful to our husbands, Travis Winfrey and Harold Toro Tulla, whose unwavering love, understanding, and encouragement allowed us to turn the final page. Most of all, we thank our daughters, Anina and Mireya, whose births coincided with the initial writing of this book. They bring us incalculable joy and remind us every day how important it is to fight for the collective common good. We are grateful to all the activists we met while writing this book who engage that battle every day so that we may all live in a world that values and privileges human dignity and our delicate and beautiful planet.

List of Abbreviations

ACN	Action Canada Network
ACTPN	Advisory Committee on Trade Policy Negotiations
ACTWU	Amalgamated Clothing and Textile Workers Union
AFL-CIO	American Federation of Labor-Congress of Industrial Organizations
AFSCME	American Federation of State, County and Municipal Employees
ART	Alliance for Responsible Trade
BECC	Border Environmental Cooperation Commission
BEP	Border Ecology Project
CAFTA-DR	Dominican Republic-Central America Free Trade Agreement
CBO	Congressional Budget Office
CEC	Commission for Environmental Cooperation
CJM	Coalition for Justice in the Maquiladoras
CLC	Commission for Labor Cooperation
COG	Congressional Oversight Group
CQ	*Congressional Quarterly*
CTC/CTWC	Citizens Trade Campaign/Citizen Trade Watch Campaign
CTM	Confederation of Mexican Workers (Confederación de Trabajadores de México)
CUSFTA	Canada-U.S. Free Trade Agreement
CWA	Communication Workers of America
DGAP	The Development Group for Alternative Policies
DOW	Defenders of Wildlife
EC	European Commission
ECE	Evaluation Committee of Experts
EDF	Environmental Defense Fund

EO	European Ombudsman
EPA	Environmental Protection Agency
EU	European Union
FOE	Friends of the Earth
FTAA	Free Trade Agreement of the Americas
FTC	Fair Trade Campaign
GATT	General Agreement on Tariffs and Trade
GSP	Generalized System of Preferences
IAM	International Association of Machinists and Aerospace Workers
IATP	Institute for Agriculture and Trade Policy
IBEW	International Brotherhood of Electrical Workers
IBT	International Brotherhood of Teamsters
ILGWU	International Ladies' Garment Workers' Union
ILO	International Labor Organization
ILRF	International Labor Rights Fund
IPS	Institute for Policy Studies
ISDS	Investor-State Dispute Settlement
IUE	International Union of Electronic, Electrical, Salaried, Machine and Furniture Workers
JPAC	Joint Public Advisory Council
MAI	Multilateral Agreement on Investment
MFN	Most-Favored Nation
MODTLE	Mobilization on Development, Trade, Labor and the Environment
NAAEC	North American Agreement on Environmental Cooperation
NAALC	North American Agreement on Labor Cooperation
NADBank	North American Development Bank
NAFTA	North American Free Trade Agreement
NAO	National Administrative Office
NEPA	National Environmental Policy Act
NGO	Non-Governmental Organization
NRDC	Natural Resources Defense Council
NTC	National Toxics Campaign
NWF	National Wildlife Federation
OCAW	Oil, Chemical and Atomic Workers International Union
OECD	Organisation for Co-operation and Development
OSHA	Occupational Safety and Health Act

PRI   Institutional Revolutionary Party (Partido Revolucionario
                Institucional)
RMALC   Mexican Action Network on Free Trade (Red Mexicana De
                Acción Frente Al Libre Comercio)
SEDUE   Secretariat of Urban Development and Ecology
STRM   Mexican Telephone Workers' Union (Sindicato de
                Telefonistas de la República Mexicana)
TAFTA   Trans-Atlantic Free Trade Agreement
TPA   Trade Promotion Authority
TPP   Trans-Pacific Partnership Agreement
TTIP   Trans-Atlantic Trade and Investment Partnership
UAW   United Automobile, Aerospace & Agricultural Implement
                Workers of America International Union
UE   The United Electrical, Radio and Machine Workers of
                America
UFCW   United Food and Commercial Workers
                International Union
UMW   United Mine Workers
USTR   United States Trade Representative
WWF   World Wildlife Fund
WTO   World Trade Organization

Trade Battles

1
Introduction

THE IMPACT OF SOCIAL MOVEMENTS
ON INTERNATIONAL TRADE POLICY

IN 2016 ANTIGLOBALIZATION sentiment exploded in the United States and around the world. On June 23, British citizens voted to exit the European Union (EU) in a nationwide referendum. The campaign supporting British exit, or Brexit as it became known, centered on British political and economic sovereignty, and on anti-immigration rhetoric that primarily resonated in rural areas and post-industrial cities. In the months that followed, demonstrations and marches erupted across the United Kingdom to protest the Brexit vote and delay the formal exit.

Waves of massive protests also erupted across Europe that fall in response to impending votes on the Trans-Atlantic Trade and Investment Partnership (TTIP)[1] and the Canada-EU Comprehensive Economic and Trade Agreement. In September over ten thousand protesters converged on Brussels, marched through the streets, and gathered around two-story inflatable Trojan horses placed outside the European headquarters. The German paper *Der Spiegel* reported on the sustained movement the TTIP had generated across the country: "An unprecedented protest movement of a scope not seen since the Iraq war in Germany has pushed negotiations over the TTIP trans-Atlantic free trade agreement to the brink of collapse. The demonstrations are characterized by a level of professionalism not previously seen."[2]

A month later in October, over 40,000 people marched in thirty French cities, 7,000 demonstrators gathered in Warsaw, and hundreds in Madrid. Protesters across Europe carried placards and signs, dressed in costumes, and brought props, musical instruments, and pets. They carried through the streets of Berlin a 30-foot paper mache snake puppet with dollars in its mouth. In Spain protesters linked themselves together with huge yellow styrofoam chains symbolizing enslavement under the agreement. Brightly colored banners declared "these are not international treaties, these are coups!" and "we are people, not commodities."[3]

The scene in the United States in winter 2016 was similar. On the eve of the signing of the Trans-Pacific Partnership Agreement (TPP) between the United States and eleven other countries of the Pacific Rim, activists rallied for two days on February 3rd and 4th. They organized demonstrations in thirty-eight U.S. cities with a kickoff in Washington, DC's Lafayette Park. There, in front of the White House, protesters chanted in front of an enormous sign that read "TPP = Betrayal."[4] Another round of demonstrations erupted on April 1 across the nation. Constituents hand delivered anti-TPP April Fool's Day cards during rallies at the local offices of their members of Congress. Cards were also sent to the offices of members of the House of Representatives in Washington, DC.[5] Protests against the TPP were also ubiquitous around the world, erupting from Malaysia to New Zealand.

By the time the U.S. presidential primaries began in February 2016, two of the frontrunners in each party—the Republican candidate Donald Trump and the Democratic candidate Bernie Sanders—had articulated their strong opposition to free trade agreements, particularly the TPP. Democratic candidate Hillary Clinton, who had helped negotiate elements of the TPP as U.S. secretary of state, eventually disavowed her support for the final agreement as negotiated by President Obama.

Bernie Sanders and Donald Trump's anti-trade stance shared some similar elements. They both identified the origins of the U.S. trade policy debacle with the North American Free Trade Agreement (NAFTA), negotiated by Bill Clinton in the early 1990s and supported at the time by his wife, Hillary Clinton. Sanders and Trump claimed NAFTA was responsible for the loss of millions of U.S. manufacturing jobs and the gutting of key industries, particularly in the Midwest. Sanders had actually voted against NAFTA as a representative in 1993. They both saw the TPP as a disastrous continuation of the bad trade policy precedent set by NAFTA.

There was divergence, however, in their anti-trade rhetoric. Sanders focused on the loss of jobs, corporate power, wages, and the lack of labor and environmental protections in free trade agreements. Trump, in contrast, married his anti-trade rhetoric to a more broad anti-immigration discourse, with a focus on Mexican immigration. In this way, he constructed Mexico as a country that had unfairly benefited from NAFTA, and Mexicans as a people who took advantage of lax immigration laws to work in the United States, taking jobs away from Americans.[6] To remedy the former he called for a renegotiation of NAFTA, and to remedy the latter he called for strict immigration enforcement and the construction of a U.S.-Mexico border wall that he insisted the Mexican government would pay for. This xenophobic attack played out differently across the country. Although his assault on NAFTA resonated in the midwestern states hit hard by the steady loss of manufacturing jobs since the 1970s, his anti-immigration position was generally more popular in southwestern U.S. border states.[7]

After Trump won the primaries and became the Republican presidential candidate, he solidified his policy and rhetorical platform primarily around trade and immigration. His anti-free-trade stance diverged from decades of Republican support for free trade liberalization. His opponent, Democratic presidential candidate Hillary Clinton, moved to the left of her previous position and the traditional Democratic platform on trade. The opposition of both presidential candidates to the TPP, a free trade agreement crafted by a Democratic president and aggressively pushed by the Republican congressional leadership—indeed one of the only Obama policies it supported—was unprecedented in U.S. history. This turn of events was particularly surprising given that trade policy has historically been an issue of little salience to voters, meaning they generally do not prioritize their voting in response to politicians' trade policy positions, nor do they hold them accountable for their votes on trade legislation (Guisinger 2009).

The worldwide backlash against globalization in 2016 was complex and had many different dimensions that included anti-trade, anti-immigration, and xenophobic rhetoric and policies. In the United States, this backlash contributed to the unexpected victory of Donald Trump in the U.S. presidential election. On the Monday after the inauguration, President Trump reasserted his commitment to a drastic change in U.S. trade policy—he signed an executive order instructing U.S. officials to notify partners that the U.S. would not implement the TPP. By May, he had sent formal notice to Congress to begin new negotiations of NAFTA.

What drove the backlash against globalization that made the events of 2016 possible? We argue that the dynamics that drove this backlash began to foment over twenty-five years ago during a battle over a free trade agreement—NAFTA, the one that Donald Trump placed squarely at the center of his presidential campaign. The solidification of a neoliberal trade regime began with NAFTA's passage in 1993, catalyzing a resentment among working class voters in particular areas of the United States who were left behind by trade. Donald Trump tapped into that resentment. Trump's election was therefore a consequence, in part, of trade politics and policies that had their roots in the first trade battle that emerged in the early 1990s—the battle over NAFTA. This book is about how those trade politics and policies emerged and developed during NAFTA's negotiation, and how they continued to affect subsequent trade battles, reinforcing resentment among anti-trade activists, including many working class voters.

NAFTA, the First and Unexpected Trade Battle

The first puzzle about NAFTA is: How did a trade agreement generate so much public outrage and compel such an incredibly diverse array of activists to resist through massive mobilization and protest? In other words, how did trade policy in general, and NAFTA in particular, become politicized in the early 1990s? This is a compelling puzzle because surprisingly, in the decades prior to 1993, international trade policy was a nonissue. In the 1970s and 1980s trade did not generate discussion, much less public debate. It was not a topic of dinner table conversation anywhere in the world; it was an esoteric, technical international economic issue with little domestic policy resonance (Rupert 1995; O'Brien 1998). It was an issue largely left to economists and technocrats. Activists and nongovernmental organizations (NGOs) did not mobilize around it, demonstrate against it, or prioritize it in any way. NAFTA's passage was therefore expected to be a fait accompli. No one guessed that NAFTA would be terribly controversial.

In the early 1990s, however, trade—and specifically trade agreements—were beginning to capture all the tension and ambivalences about globalization, and NAFTA was its concrete manifestation.[8] Trade went from being an archaic issue with little political resonance before NAFTA to making headline news every week during NAFTA's negotiation and beyond. Activists, many of them working class and union members, forcefully pushed back against NAFTA's passage by engaging in disruptive action. During the height of the anti-NAFTA struggle in May 1993, activists organized a "National Week of Action." Thousands of protesters took to the streets across the continent. They held rallies in St. Louis, Vermont, Portland, Seattle, and Grand Forks, North Dakota.[9] A tractorcade drove across Colorado, and a march in New York City drew over a thousand, including union and environmental activists from Greenpeace, the Bronx Clean Air campaign, and auto and garment industry unions.

In addition to engaging in protests and other disruptive action, activists also actively worked to shift how the public and government officials viewed trade policy. They explicitly highlighted NAFTA's potential extra-economic effects—linking all kinds of rights issues (labor, environmental, human, indigenous, and so on) to trade. Activists changed the parameters and cultural stakes of free trade— it was not simply about losing jobs, but about destroying the environment, undermining consumer protection, expanding corporate power, and threatening indigenous people, among many other issues. Prior to NAFTA, there was no coupling of environmental rights and protections to trade.

But activists successfully linked labor and environmental protections to trade during the NAFTA struggle—and that cultural reframing stuck. We cannot now uncouple trade from labor, the environment, and a myriad of other issues. This is how North Americans *think* about trade today, and that framing diffused across the globe, with many labor and environmental organizations around the world adopting it and demanding labor and environmental protections in trade agreements that their governments negotiate.[10] That the labor-environmental trade linkage marked such a strong cultural shift is evidenced by how much resonance it has today. The debates about labor, environmental, and other protections in the TPP and TTIP started with NAFTA, and so it is critical to historically trace that cultural shift back to NAFTA.

The enormous contention around all trade agreements after NAFTA proves how successful this shift in political culture was, but it also highlights the impact of activists' struggle *even though they failed to kill NAFTA*—because they *changed* the terms of the debate *and* changed government trade negotiating strategies, effectively politicizing trade policy for the first time since World War II. Even more important, however, trade policy has become a target of activism post-NAFTA as it never was before it. Labor and environmental activists forged a sustained challenge to

U.S. trade policy that garnered a wide following and has been influential in the years since NAFTA's passage.

How did this happen? Specifically, how were labor and environmental activists able to politicize trade policy during NAFTA's negotiation? And, how did they develop and deploy a set of social movement strategies that have sustained a challenge to trade policies after NAFTA and set the stage for future trade battles? These are the central questions of this book. We argue that labor and environmental activists politicized trade policy by leveraging broader fissures in the trade negotiation process and creating a set of social movement practices around trade that had not existed before,[11] generating continued activism on trade policy in the years since.

This set of social movement practices included both institutionalized strategies (such as lobbying, letter-writing and call-in campaigns, filing legal challenges) and disruptive strategies (such as protests and demonstrations, marches, sit-ins) that leveraged broader cleavages across state and nonstate political arenas. Our theoretical framework is centered on the dynamics that shape mobilization across these arenas (as we discuss in more detail in Chapter 2). It suggests that the places where they intersect can create unique points of leverage for activists that can render particular targets more vulnerable and strategies more effective. Labor and environmental activists exploited these leverage points by mobilizing across them, which enabled them not only to politicize trade policy within state arenas (among legislators and trade policy officials) and among the public, but also to influence the content of NAFTA itself through its side agreements.

How did activists accomplish this? First, they had to construct a way to frame trade issues that would resonate with the public and also unite the perspectives of disparate and often antagonistic grassroots organizations. They "greened" trade policy by pushing a new labor-environmental rights frame—a discourse that linked environmental and labor rights to trade for the first time, and that presented health, poverty, and labor rights issues as they did environmental externalities—as problems that could not be resolved through market mechanisms, problems that were the very product of those market mechanisms.

The linkage helped broaden and unite the anti-NAFTA coalition by expanding the pool of potential supporters of the new labor-environmental rights frame and increasing the constituencies for whom the broader coalition claimed to speak. The new trade discourse enabled activists to appeal to an extensive swath of national and local organizations that had not previously participated in trade policy debates. Activists garnered public support for this new framing by promulgating it through a vast network of civil society organizations, including labor unions and grassroots environmental, consumer, and human rights groups. By greening trade policy and turning a previously technocratic concern into a highly visible populist issue, activists succeeded in politicizing trade in the public realm for the first time since World War II.

At the beginning of the NAFTA battle in 1991, labor and environmental activists' goal was not to kill the agreement, but rather to *improve* it by forcing the government to incorporate the new labor-environmental rights frame into NAFTA, and to include strong labor and environmental protections and enforcement mechanisms. This would not be an easy task; from the beginning of the 1991 fast-track fight under the George H.W. Bush administration, U.S. government negotiators resisted the linkage of labor and environmental concerns to trade and refused to even consider incorporating labor and environmental protections into the agreement.

Activists responded to this obstacle by mobilizing public hostility to NAFTA and harnessing that antagonism to influence legislators who would eventually vote on the agreement. By creating a significant threat to NAFTA's final congressional passage, they hoped to indirectly influence negotiators. The labor-environmental rights frame enabled legislators with different constituencies to take a stand in opposition to the agreement. This was particularly important for generally pro-labor Congress members whose constituents might lose jobs to NAFTA; appropriating a greening discourse enabled them to avoid a protectionist slant to their arguments as they tried to derail or modify the agreement.

As negotiations wore on, this strategy bore some fruit. Using a combination of disruptive tactics (including marches, protests, and political theater) that helped create a groundswell of public opposition to NAFTA, and institutionalized tactics to influence legislators, activists pressed the president and negotiators for concessions. And little by little, they relented: the United States Trade Representative (USTR) accepted and adopted the labor-environmental rights frame; changed the rules to allow environmental organizations to participate in USTR advisory committees, giving them a formal role in trade policy for the first time; and included labor and environmental protections in side agreements.

Activists' mobilization of new frames, resources, alliances, and rule changes across state and nonstate arenas actually changed the government's negotiating positions and influenced NAFTA's final form. In response to the threat that NAFTA would not pass, President Clinton adopted a suggestion made by key environmental leaders to negotiate for additional protections as a means to secure passage.[12] Activists helped ratchet up the protections in the side agreements, resulting in the first trilateral trade agreement to include a mechanism for the enforcement, however weak, of labor and environmental laws.[13] Without activists' political mobilization, NAFTA would likely have had no protections at all.

Of course, it is important not to overstate activists' influence on the actual content of the agreement itself. NAFTA did not prioritize labor and environmental protections, and created woefully inadequate enforcement mechanisms. Activists influenced NAFTA *primarily* by challenging the elite ideological commitment to trade liberalization, and opposing the routine machinations of how trade policy is accomplished in Washington. Using both institutionalized "insider" and disruptive grassroots "outsider" strategies, they created an oppositional trade movement that was more internationalist, more focused on the grassroots, and far more diverse in participation and message than anything that came before it. The fair trade movement they created helped alter public opinion and impacted congressional support for inclusion of environmental and labor provisions. Ultimately, it changed the way trade politics were performed in the United States and who was aware and engaged in politically contesting the space.

Mobilization, the State, and Institutional Opportunities

Labor and environmental activists' ability to mobilize around institutional leverage points during NAFTA's negotiation was possible, in large part, because they had some access to state institutions. The NAFTA case is illuminating because it shows that when the state provides even minimal access and information to civil society actors, it is easier for them to mobilize around institutional leverage points. Activists' access during the three key moments of NAFTA's negotiation (fast-track from March until May 1991, substantive negotiations from June 1991 until August 1992, and side agreement negotiations from March to August 1993) was not total. Indeed, the government generally tried to maintain a closed process. Activists' access to key documents and information, however, varied, depending largely on whether they were insiders or outsiders. During the fast-track struggle, only labor advisors and members of Congress had access to official texts of the agreement. After activists mobilized, some environmental organizations were also allowed to participate in substantive negotiations as official advisors with access to these documents (they were formally appointed and cleared in November 1991).[14] The government did not release the negotiating text to the public, although a draft was eventually leaked.

At different points in the negotiation (which we mean as the period from fast-track to final congressional passage), activists had access to other information, documents, and government officials. Labor and environmental representatives participated on USTR committees, and the USTR sought civil society participation and comment (primarily to gauge minimal conditions necessary for passage) by meeting with labor unions and environmental organizations. Activists on USTR committees also had information about counterproposals made by Mexico and Canada. Members of Congress held a plethora of hearings to solicit civil society input. They also had access to trade policy officials. Certain documents, such as an environmental review and integrated border environmental plan, were made public.

We show that the strategies activists used during the NAFTA struggle were shaped, in part, by their access to information and officials at key moments. Having access to information about where negotiators stood on different aspects of the agreement, what areas of contention existed, and what bottom-line demands were made by various stakeholders, allowed activists to develop and deploy specific framing, resource brokerage, and alliance-building strategies at key moments during the negotiations. Access to information and to state institutions allowed activists to assert their democratic interest and have an impact in an arena such as trade where they had not previously done so. Of course, this access and information was limited. Indeed, during NAFTA's negotiation activists repeatedly criticized the government's lack of transparency and their marginalization, particularly in relation to corporate actors. They successfully filed lawsuits to obtain more access and information. The lack of total access, however, almost certainly limited their ability to push for and achieve more labor and environmental protections in the agreement.

In the years after NAFTA's passage, activists' access and level of participation in trade policy varied, but the government in general continued to maintain a closed process in order to minimize pushback and thwart public opposition to trade agreements. During the Clinton administration the Multilateral Agreement on Investment (MAI), negotiated in secret, was almost completed before activists learned about it when the text was leaked. Activists had more access, input, and leverage under the Bush administration after the 2006 election when Democrats controlled the House and Senate. During the TPP negotiations the Obama administration treated texts of the agreement as classified information, and threatened that cleared advisors who revealed the texts to their colleagues and constituents could be prosecuted. Administration officials also prevented many members of Congress and their staff from accessing the text and commenting on it. USTR Michael Froman made it nearly impossible for citizens to influence TPP in meaningful ways.

Activists responded to the continued efforts of the government to thwart access by foregrounding issues of transparency—both in the negotiation process and in the trade agreements themselves. They realized that investor-state dispute settlement (ISDS) provisions could be a unifying issue to bring together broader constituencies to oppose trade agreements. ISDS provisions, like those in NAFTA's Chapter 11, allow corporations to sue governments for unlimited amounts in secret tribunals if a law or government action results in the loss of current or future profits. ISDS provisions and their threat to national sovereignty also resonated among the public. After NAFTA, there was a discursive shift among labor unions and environmental organizations. The majority of activists' discursive work during the NAFTA debate on Capitol Hill centered on linking labor and environmental protections to trade, and on highlighting labor and environmental rights and protections. In contrast, during the TPP and TTIP debates activists largely focused their critique on issues of transparency, participation, and democracy.

Our analysis of labor and environmental activists' ability to leverage across institutional arenas in order to politicize and shape trade policy during the NAFTA battle also raises important questions about its implications today. Key among them is that when the government closes institutional channels, it makes it much more difficult for social movements and other civil society organizations to influence policy. But it also raises the stakes. One could argue that by maintaining closed negotiating processes after NAFTA and refusing to respond to civil society concerns about the content of trade agreements, trade policy elites paved the way for the demise of the Free Trade Agreement of the Americas (FTAA), the World Trade Organization (WTO) Doha Round, and the TPP, as well as the election of Donald Trump. Indeed, it appears many working class voters in key Midwestern states who had been left behind by trade chose the anti-trade Republican candidate who promised to bring back their jobs and reinvigorate manufacturing, rather than the Democratic candidate who had supported free trade for most of her career and had helped negotiate the TPP. Of course, many working class voters simply stayed home and refused to vote.

Despite President Trump's anti-trade position, it is unlikely that he will prioritize strong labor and environmental protections that will be satisfactory to labor unions and environmental organizations in NAFTA and other trade agreement negotiations. As of this writing, labor and fair trade activists have noted that his USTR Robert Lighthizer has solicited their input and supports some of their suggestions. Trump's penchant for undermining state institutions and government agencies, undercutting his own appointees, and changing his policy positions, however, suggests the folly of predicting the final outcome of NAFTA.

The Argument: Why Trade, Why NAFTA?

Why should scholars and activists care about the politics generated over two decades ago by a free trade agreement? Obviously, the worldwide anti-globalization backlash in 2016 attests to the importance of trade as a political touchstone. Of course, it is important to distinguish between two very different strands that constituted that backlash: progressive movements that fought against what they viewed as the consolidation of corporate power through free trade agreements such as TPP and TTIP, and conservative movements that rallied nationalism and xenophobia in a bid to prevent job loss, close national borders, and thwart immigration. In the United States, the tendency of politicians and economists to largely minimize and ignore the real effects of trade on those it left behind, particularly the working class in the Midwest, left a gaping chasm of discontent and resentment that Donald Trump was able to identify and exploit.

In this book, we argue that the most compelling reason to examine the battle over NAFTA, however, is that its negotiation reveals a great deal about the relationship between the state and civil society. Since the mid-1980s, a literature that foregrounds the state's role as both a social actor and institution, and examines its effects on politics and policy, has emerged in the social sciences (see Evans, Rueschemeyer, and Skocpol 1985; Evans 1985, 1995; Morgan and Orloff 2017). Our analysis extends this literature by analyzing how the configuration of overlapping state and nonstate arenas affects the ability of civil society organizations to influence state policy. It shows how critical institutional opportunities are to activists' efforts to try to shape international policy; activists improved NAFTA—even though they ultimately failed to kill it—by leveraging across state institutional arenas *and* engaging in disruptive social movement mobilization. Significant shifts in trade policy came when activists—by rallying public and congressional allies—could impede the passage of trade agreements. The NAFTA case suggests that activists have a better change of influencing policy across state arenas that are less insulated, and in which there is less absolute power and less concentrated centers of authority.

Our framework therefore has broad implications for policy debates beyond trade; it contributes to a vibrant and burgeoning literature that tries to understand the role of civil society (including social movements) in shaping international policy of various kinds. Given that many areas of interest to sociologists—environmental degradation, labor rights, and economic development—are significantly affected by international trade policies, we seek to remedy the relative lack of sociological engagement with trade policy politicization and formation through a theoretical framework that helps explain how social movement activists can influence it.[15]

Perhaps most important, our research exposes the links between institutional opportunities and democratic practices. At moments when the state blocks institutional channels to activists—effectively employing democratic closure—their ability to try to improve trade agreements is severely hampered. Government secrecy around trade means that social movement activists do not see what is going on and cannot leverage broader cleavages, and therefore have few opportunities to influence trade policy.

The U.S. government's post-NAFTA efforts to maintain secrecy in trade negotiations is a testament to the impact of activists' politicization of trade policy beginning with NAFTA—labor and environmental organizations were so effective at making trade a contested public issue that the state continued to undermine democratic practices around trade and thwart activists' efforts to influence negotiations. This became entrenched in the post-NAFTA political culture, and was detrimental to civil society and democracy. But this entrenchment is even more insidious than anti-NAFTA activists could have imagined twenty-five years ago, because the strategy of the government is to situate trade policy in such a way that it is severed from civil society institutions. In effect, the state has severed economic policy from democratic intervention.

The NAFTA story then, should serve as a warning. Robust and effective state institutions are essential to democracy, as an abundance of research across the social sciences shows (Starr 2007; Tilly 2000). But transparent and responsive state institutions are equally essential to democracy (Baum 2011; Hurst forthcoming; Nonet and Selznick 2017; Kitschelt 1986; Diamond 1999). Undermining activists' ability to influence trade policy does not involve weakening state institutions directly; it simply involves closing them to civil society scrutiny and participation, thereby weakening them indirectly. There are clear implications not only for future fair trade movements but also for other kinds of civil society organizations that attempt to influence policy, ranging from social movements struggling to change international climate policy to refugee and immigration policy and international banking regulation.

The NAFTA lesson is illustrative and compelling: it is extremely difficult for activists to influence and shape government policies when institutional channels are blocked by the state. And when the state closes institutional opportunities for civil society participation—for example, by negotiating climate change agreements secretly—it leaves activists little recourse but to engage in disruptive tactics as the best chance for success. This dynamic actually intensifies politicization and polarization.

Politicizing International Trade Policy

In the early 1990s few could have guessed that an arcane trade agreement would catalyze the first struggle against neoliberalism that spread to Seattle, Quebec City, Mar del Plata, and beyond. But for many activists, NAFTA symbolized the first battle in the trade wars (for Canadians it was the second). It galvanized a broader anti-corporate globalization movement that has arguably been the most active and sustained international social movement of the last thirty years, and signaled a turning point in the politicization of trade policies (Rupert 1995; O'Brien 1998). NAFTA was a watershed moment, primarily because in the early 1990s activists recognized that trade policy was beginning to blur distinctions between domestic and international policy issues.

Economic integration through the Canadian–U.S. Free Trade Agreement (CUSFTA) and the Mexican maquiladora program encouraged companies to move manufacturing plants to areas with the lowest labor costs and least regulation on the continent.[16] In addition, General Agreement on Tariffs and Trade (GATT) rounds oriented toward decreasing non-tariff trade barriers made domestic regulatory laws in each of the three countries vulnerable to the scrutiny of trade lawyers and dispute mechanisms. The broad transnational coalitions that became firmly established during NAFTA negotiations were in part a result of structural forces at both the regional and global level that led activists from different social movement sectors—and different countries—to define their circumstances as linked.

Activists realized that the inability of nation-states to completely regulate industries and markets meant that regional and global integration would have economic *and* social consequences. Thus, the rules of North American trade would affect not only jobs and the conditions of work, but also the environment, consumer goods and services, health and safety, and human rights. NAFTA, then, ushered in a new kind of trade policy debate that linked economic and social rights, and national and international arenas; domestic issues now had an international component. Indeed research suggests that trade policy becomes increasingly politicized as it moves from a focus on border regulation (through tariff policy) to greater emphasis on the integration of economies through capital mobility and changes in domestic law (Howell and Wolff 1992; Preeg 1995).

The expansion of the trade arena to include health, safety, consumer, and environmental standards, among many others, laid the groundwork for a whole new group of actors to define their interests as entwined with the international trade system. North American trade and integration would impact not only domestic actors traditionally considered to be trade-affected constituencies, such as manufacturers and unions, but also previously unmobilized actors, such as environmentalists, consumer activists concerned with health and safety laws, and human rights organizations.

The new debate required new strategies and a new kind of struggle. For a broad swath of activists across issue areas, NAFTA signified the enshrinement of a low-wage, deregulatory strategy of economic integration into official policy across the continent. In response, activists created a fair trade movement to promote policies to protect the rights of North America's workers, consumers, environment, indigenous populations, farmers, and the poor from erosion by international trade laws and direct foreign investment. They argued that the rules of the global economy should have an ethical or moral dimension, and that regulatory protections should not be sacrificed in the name of economic integration.

It was not easy—and even potentially risky—to make claims based on collective rights and common goods in a political culture (particularly in the United States) rooted in individual rights and liberties. But activists viewed NAFTA as a profound threat to the continent's labor and human rights, and to the health of its environment. Their rhetorical battle against NAFTA, which prioritized the preservation of the collective rights and common good of its citizens,[17] was quite radical because it fundamentally challenged a culture of individualism and the privileging of individual rights across North America.

The fair trade movement they constructed also combined the most internationalist strands of the labor movement's calls for global recognition of workers' rights to organize, collectively bargain, and strike, with more recent critiques of trade policies' effects on environmental, consumer rights, and other regulatory law. Although the movement against NAFTA did not always function as a single coherent entity, and its members did not always view strategic and tactical goals identically, they united to build power to fight for a trade system that would support domestic efforts to promote labor, environmental, and social welfare broadly defined, and encourage economic integration with strong regulatory protections.

Politicization and Building Power-To

In November 1993, when NAFTA passed by a small margin, activists who opposed it were devastated. The vote was close (234 to 200 in the House), and up until the final hour they had expected to win. Ultimately, environmental and labor activists viewed NAFTA's passage as a defeat and were frustrated by the insufficiencies of its environmental and labor protections. Many pundits and scholars shared this view. Beginning in 1994, a steady stream of scholarship emerged, highlighting the failures of NAFTA and its labor and environmental side agreements, the continued assault on labor and environmental rights, and the ever-diminishing power of workers across the continent (see Bronfenbrenner 2007; Caulfield 2010). We agree with these assessments: NAFTA's side agreements are relatively weak, have led to few victories for workers' rights, and have generally not improved the conditions of workers and the environment across North America. Indeed, as we approach NAFTA's twenty-fifth anniversary, workers across the continent are arguably facing one of the worst political and economic crises of the last century, and our planet is being irrevocably altered by climate change.[18]

Amidst the fervent and justified reaction to NAFTA's shortcomings, how activists built power to fight during its negotiation is usually missed or ignored. In the case of NAFTA, activists did not win, and the side agreements by any objective measure were not a success if evaluated solely in terms of unions advancing their agenda against all odds and providing adjudicative mechanisms with teeth. However, North American activists' efforts were not completely futile. They did have a significant impact if measured in terms of politicizing trade, expanding and reframing the trade debate, forcing the government to include labor and environmental protections (however weak) into the agreement, and building a broad international coalition that spanned issue areas. In analyzing the impact of social movements on trade policy outcomes, we therefore adopt a more multifaceted approach that measures impact in terms of both "power-over" and "power-to."

These ideas emerge from Bernard Loomer's articulation of two kinds of power: unilateral versus relational (Loomer 1976). As Marshall Ganz explains, the former reflects a claims-making strategy that "requires creating the power to alter relations of dependency and domination."[19] The latter reflects a collaborative strategy "to generate more power to achieve common interests by creating more interdependency among the actors who share those interests."[20] Politicization, then, involves building this relational power, or power-to, including the ability to reframe issues and construct new discursive linkages between them (e.g., the link between trade and environmental protections), and the ability to build larger constituencies across organizations and movements, increasing the likelihood that activists can eventually change social facts and achieve power-over. As Jamie K. McCallum persuasively argues in his analysis of transnational labor struggles, "victory is not as simple as winning; it is about building the power to fight in the first place" (2013:159).

Activists built power-to during the NAFTA negotiations but did not achieve power-over because they lost their struggle when the trade agreement passed. However, they came very close to defeating NAFTA by mobilizing and lobbying in Washington, DC, and in home regions to threaten loss of votes and loss of organizational support for recalcitrant members of Congress. Indeed, on the eve of its signing, it appeared that NAFTA would not pass given its weaknesses on labor and environmental issues. Pro-NAFTA leaders expressed skepticism that the supplemental negotiations would overcome legislative divisions. The private view of most senior officials in the administration was that the president should jettison the accord and "cover his tracks."[21] Activists' ability to put the NAFTA vote in jeopardy was a considerable victory. Although President Clinton's final hour horse-trading secured the votes needed to pass NAFTA, the result of labor and environmental activists' ability to politicize and mobilize around trade was historic.

And, in NAFTA's wake activists redeployed their transnational networks in efforts to successfully achieve power-over in several cases. They regrouped and broadened as new free trade agreements such as the FTAA emerged on the political horizon, fostering an activism on trade policy throughout North and South America that is more internationalist, grassroots-oriented, and organizationally diverse than any trade mobilization that came before it. And, although they had few successes, their victories were significant. Activists killed fast-track legislation in the United States in 1997 and 1998. In 1998, the negotiations over the MAI among Organisation for Co-operation and Development (OECD) countries failed due to pressure from labor, environmental, and other civil society organizations, particularly those in France and Canada. And in November 2005 activists' efforts helped destroy the FTAA in Mar del Plata, Argentina, after over a decade of negotiations.

Arguably activists' greatest success was undermining the TPP. As the NGO Public Citizen declared on its website: "It was stopped by thousands of diverse organizations representing working people united across borders—fighting against corporate power and for the environment, health, human rights and democracy."[22] Although the TPP's demise was a direct result of President Trump's executive order, at the time the agreement did not have sufficient votes in Congress to pass. Activists had been quite successful in drumming up opposition in the United States and around the world. Of course, we can never know what its fate would have been if the election—and the opposition to trade agreements it generated (particularly among Republican members of Congress who generally supported trade)—had played out differently.

Utilizing a more nuanced measure of the impact of social movements on trade policy outcomes as both "power-over" and "power-to" allows us to more accurately assess the real impact of civil society organizations and social movements, particularly when they do not achieve material improvements or protections for workers and the environment, or even their stated goals.

The Enduring Significance of Trade Battles after NAFTA

Although a significant number of scholars have examined various aspects of NAFTA's negotiation, and a growing literature emerges around the TPP and TTIP negotiations, none of the current accounts provides a broad and rigorous analysis of how labor and environmental activists politicized trade and influenced the state's international trade policy during the NAFTA battle, or how and why some strategies have shifted in current battles over trade. Moreover, current research does not provide a more general theory that helps explain the dynamic relationship between social movement and state strategies, and trade policy outcomes over time.

Most scholars have focused on more narrow accounts of the negotiation process—often from a political science perspective. Recent books on TPP and TTIP focus on the geopolitics of the negotiations (Hamilton 2014; Morin et al. 2015). Similarly Baer and Weintraub's edited volume (1994) tackles the uniqueness of NAFTA's negotiation vis-à-vis North American political relations, and Bognanno and Ready's edited volume (1993) presents the different perspectives of relevant stakeholders (labor, industry, and government officials). Both were written before NAFTA negotiations were complete. Hermann von Bertrab (1997) offers his insights as part of the Mexican negotiating team, and William A. Orme Jr. (1996) focuses on NAFTA's historic integration process that transformed the political landscape of the continent.

Both Frederick W. Mayer's (1998) U.S.-focused look at NAFTA and Cameron and Tomlin's (2000) broader analysis recognize that domestic pressure shaped negotiating outcomes. Mayer moves beyond a two-level game theory approach by focusing on the role of interests, institutions, and symbolism to explain negotiation outcomes. Cameron and Tomlin, in contrast, seek to integrate theories of asymmetrical international bargaining by building on a two-level game theory approach and institution-based arguments. Neither book, however, focuses directly on the role of social movements, provides data on social movement actors' strategic decision-making, or develops a general theory of activists' strategy in relationship to state institutions.

Some political scientists have contributed to research on NAFTA by offering social movement rather than international relations analyses of the agreement. John Audley (1997) provides an excellent analysis of environmental organizations' struggle to influence the NAFTA negotiation but does not include a comparison with labor unions. And Jeffrey M. Ayres (1998) focuses his analysis primarily on the anti-CUSFTA and subsequent anti-NAFTA movement that emerged and developed in Canada. Jonathan Graubart (2008) examines how activists utilized NAFTA's labor and environmental side agreements after the agreement was in force. The sociological literature on trade is limited, although the scholars who have studied it have made significant contributions. Michael Dreiling (2001) focuses on the political mobilizations that emerged to fight for and against NAFTA. Tamara Kay (2011a and 2011b) analyzes NAFTA's effect on transnational relationships among North American unions. Francesco Duina (2006) offers a comparative analysis of the social construction of the European Union, Mercosur, and NAFTA. And Nitsan Chorev (2007) examines how trade policy changed from the 1930s to the 2000s in the United States, resulting in the triumph of liberalization.

There is also a broader literature on interest representation in trade deals, much of which adopts an international political economy perspective and is focused on the role of NGOs and social movements in global trade more generally. Riordan Roett's edited volume (1999) tackles Mercosur. Justin Greenwood (2011) examines the crucial role interests play in policymaking in general, and the European Union in particular. Hannah Murphy's case study of the WTO (2010) examines NGOs' ability to influence trade policy. Matthew Eagleton-Pierce (2013) looks at power and legitimation in relationship to the WTO, and Rorden Wilkinson (2014) examines how the WTO perpetuates inequalities among nations and how it could be improved to promote more equitable development. Erin Hannah (2016) offers a constructivist analysis of how NGOs affect trade policy in the European Union. Her edited volume with James Scott and Silke Trommer (2015) explores the role of expertise in trade policy formation. Ferdi de Ville and Gabriel Siles-Brügge (2015) examine the negotiation of the TTIP, and Silke Trommer (2014) looks at NGO and trade union influence on trade policy formation in West Africa.

Our book adds to this excellent extant literature on trade in North America and around the world by focusing on the empirical puzzle of how activists politicized and influenced trade policy during the first trade battle around NAFTA negotiations despite the activists' relative weakness in the trade policy arena. And we extend this literature by applying a theory of overlapping political arenas (or what is referred to in organizational and political sociology as "field theory") to the case of NAFTA. We show how, by exploiting leverage points across state and nonstate arenas and engaging in disruptive mobilization, activists politicized and influenced trade policy across the continent for the first time in history.

Although our analytical gaze is focused on North American activists and trade policy formation, our framework centered on the dynamics across political arenas can be applied to various trade battles around the world. But our framework also provides a foundation for a more integrative mapping of routine and disruptive strategies that can help explain more generally how social movements can influence policy within hostile state arenas. Indeed all states have overlapping arenas, although their organization and configuration vary. Our framework can therefore be applied to a wide range of cases in an effort to understand the dynamic relationship between movement strategies and political contexts.

Perhaps most important, we extend the current literature by highlighting how trade battles expose the linkages between institutional opportunities and democratic practices. When the state closes or severely limits institutional opportunities for civil society participation, it simultaneously severs policy from democratic intervention *and* leaves activists little recourse but to engage in disruptive tactics as the best, and in some cases, only chance for success.

This is not unique to NAFTA and to the U.S. government. Indeed the ability of activists across the globe to influence not only trade agreements, but also policy of various kinds, depends in large part on the willingness of their governments to keep state institutional channels open. For countries in which at least some of these channels remain open, the lessons of how anti-NAFTA activists leveraged across state and nonstate arenas remain very valuable. But the NAFTA case also reminds activists to remain vigilant. As in North America, their ability to apply pressure across state arenas can also be severely constrained if governments close points of leverage across them (as the Obama administration did during the TPP negotiations, and as the Trump administration did while the American Health Care Act of 2017 was being debated). This will change the options available to movements, likely pushing them to take more radical stances and privilege disruptive politics as their only means of influencing government policy.

Research Strategy and Book Organization

During the NAFTA battle, the government's response to activists' demands was documented through different iterations of negotiating texts and congressional testimony. Activists' strategies were shaped, in part, by their access to different kinds of draft documents and government negotiating positions. Having access to information about where negotiators stood on different aspects of the agreement allowed activists to develop and deploy specific framing, alliance and resource brokerage, and rule-making strategies at critical points. We are able to track this back and forth between activists and the government because the content of different versions of NAFTA's side agreements was shared with labor unions and environmental organizations.

To analyze this back and forth we employed a case study that allows us to flesh out strategic choices and events and incorporate actors' understanding of their impact into the analysis. We analyzed every article from *Inside U.S. Trade* (a total of 656), the only publication that provided weekly coverage of environmental and labor issues related to NAFTA.[23] Its reporting included drafts of leaked negotiated NAFTA texts and copies of letters to and from trade participants, as well as coverage of NAFTA-related press conferences, congressional hearings, trade-related speeches, and meetings between decision-makers and NGO advocates. *Inside U.S. Trade* offered unique and crucial data by providing day-by-day reporting of events. We supplemented *Inside U.S. Trade* coverage with all available *Congressional Quarterly* (CQ) articles, publicly released governmental documents, and articles from the major national newspapers relating to environmental and/or labor issues associated with NAFTA (a total of 328).[24]

We conducted content analysis of NAFTA congressional hearing testimony provided by environmental and labor representatives (a total of 143) to assess the discursive frames they employed to influence legislators. Hearing testimony was used because it was explicitly oriented to the legislative arena, and it enabled us to eliminate sample bias by analyzing the complete body of public statements of this type. We initially used open-ended coding to tease out stated concerns, whether linkages between environmental and labor issues were mentioned, and suggested solutions. Once the full range of responses for each of these variables was determined, the reliability of the coding was verified through two additional reviews by a single coder of each testimony. The validity of the coding schema was verified through interviews with labor and environmental activists themselves.

We obtained the full range of public documents from key environmental, labor, and other anti-NAFTA groups for the time period under study (a total of 1,225), including press releases, position papers, advocacy ads, op-eds, and internal memos through access to organizations' archives and activists' personal files. We conducted fifty-three in-depth interviews with at least one representative from each of the major U.S. labor unions and environmental organizations involved in the NAFTA fight so that we might obtain insight into activists' assessment of their strategic motivations and mistakes. We also conducted a separate set of over 150 interviews with U.S., Mexican, and Canadian labor leaders and union staff, government officials, labor activists in NGOs and labor lawyers.

To gauge public perception of the negotiations, we examined data from all fifty available major opinion polls concerning NAFTA during the time period from initial announcement through final passage. For an analysis of congressional voting patterns concerning labor and environmental issues, we reviewed ratings by the American Federation of Labor-Congress of Industrial Organizations (AFL-CIO) and the League of Conservation Voters for all senators and representatives of the 103rd Congress and compared them to the final NAFTA voting record. For an assessment of the receptivity of members of Congress to the claims of environmental and labor advocates, we also analyzed all 295 House and Senate floor speeches on NAFTA. Finally, we conducted a detailed content analysis of the provisions of the agreement.

The NAFTA story unfolds in eight chapters. Chapter 2 lays out our theoretical contribution centered on inter-field dynamics—meaning dynamics across overlapping political arenas—that offers a framework for understanding how social movements influence state policy. Readers who are not interested in field theory can skip this chapter and still follow the narrative as it begins in Chapter 3 (although it would be useful to peruse the fields relevant to NAFTA section at the end of Chapter 2). We decided to use the term "field" throughout the book because it is widely utilized and theorized across sociological literatures. To engage those literatures it is necessary to use the term in Chapter 2, and to revisit our theoretical contribution to field theory in the conclusion in Chapter 8. For readers who are not familiar with the concept of a "field," it can be used interchangeably with "arena." In order to avoid any confusion, we decided not to alternate between the two terms in the empirical chapters. Chapter 3 explores key political and economic conditions in North America that led to NAFTA's negotiation and examines the relations between labor unions and environmental organizations in the years prior to its proposal. Chapter 4 examines how labor and environmental activists initially came together and used framing and alliance-building strategies to broaden a labor-environmental rights frame during the fight over fast-track legislation in Congress. Chapter 5 analyzes how activists used outsider strategies and mobilized public pressure to increase legislative opposition to NAFTA during the substantive negotiations that followed passage of fast-track legislation. It also reveals how activists' pressure led to the negotiation of additional labor and environmental side agreements. Chapter 6 explores how activists used institutional channels to influence the side agreements. It reveals, through documented interactions, the cat-and-mouse game between activists and the state as they responded to each other's maneuvering and changed their strategies in relation to each other. Chapter 7 examines the government's continued effort to thwart activists' participation in trade policy after NAFTA, and how activists responded to subsequent trade agreements. The conclusion, Chapter 8, suggests how the book's theoretical and empirical findings can inform our understanding of the relationship between states and civil society more generally, and teases out the implications of this study for future research on different kinds of politicization and policy formation. It also examines the implications of trade battles for democratic practices and movement mobilization.

2

Theorizing Social Movement Influence on the State

THE QUESTIONS THE NAFTA battle raises—how did activists politicize and influence trade policy—lie at the heart of cutting edge research among sociologists and political scientists who study how civil society organizations, specifically social movements, influence the state and state policies. Two decades of research suggests that three variables are the best predictors of social movement influence on political outcomes: a movement's organizational form, strategies, and the political context that it confronts. Because there is too much variation in how these factors combine and interact to be able to devise a recipe for success across all movements, research has turned to examining the interaction of these factors in specific contexts, which some scholars suggest is the most fruitful direction for future research. As Amenta and colleagues comment on the current direction of scholarship: "There are no specific organizational forms, strategies, or political contexts that will always help challengers. Instead, scholars should be looking for specific forms of organization and strategies that are more productive in some political contexts than in others" (2010:296).

The Relationship between Strategies and Political Contexts

Questions of how strategies and political contexts interact therefore are critically important for social movements research. For the last thirty years, political opportunity theory and its variants have provided the dominant framework for understanding this relationship. They posit that changing political contexts explain variation in the level and success of insurgency. Doug McAdam, in his classic explanation of the rise and success of the civil rights movement, argues that macro-level shifts in opportunities, including the northward migration of African Americans, general salience of civil rights among the public, and international political pressure, explains why activists' mobilization and influence increased from 1961 to 1965 (McAdam 1982).

Despite its ubiquity, political opportunity theory has faced serious criticism. As even its original proponents point out, the concept of political opportunity is vague and broad (see Gamson and Meyer 1996; Goodwin and Jasper 1999; Meyer 2004). Others suggest that it fails to explain how activists gauge the openness of a political opportunity structure, or how their strategic choices affect a structure's permeability (see Kingdon 1995; Goodwin and Jasper 1999). Recognizing the value of political opportunity theory, however, scholars have engaged in compelling work that attempts to extend and expand it. They have studied how activists adapt strategies to particular political contexts (Ganz 2000; Martin 2010; McCammon 2012), and how political contexts determine strategies (Bernstein 1997; Walker et al. 2008).

Other scholars have attempted to reconceptualize political opportunity theory, calling attention to its inability to adequately account for "the fundamental interaction of social practice and structure" (Bloom 2015:392).[1] Joshua Bloom (2014, 2015; Bloom and Martin 2013), calls for a re-theorizing of political opportunity as the leveraging of insurgent practices across institutional cleavages, as he explains: "Meso-level institutional cleavages serve as opportunities for insurgent practices, mediating any macro-structural effects. In this sense, political opportunity is an institutional cleavage, that is, an institutionalized conflict or sustained antagonism between routinized interests of influential social groupings or authorities" (2015:395).

Bloom's theory is quite useful for understanding how insurgent movements that seek to disrupt business as usual exploit fissures in institutional structures to mobilize effectively and influence policy changes. Because opportunities exist across broad institutional cleavages that are constantly changing and getting reconfigured, the trick for activists engaged in disruptive movements is to develop practices—or cultural routines that combine historically particular forms of action and rhetoric— to challenge authorities across these cleavages. As Bloom explains, his "insurgent practice theory" directly addresses three of the key weaknesses in political opportunity theory:

> First, conditions do not independently favor insurgency by a group. Analyzing context effects requires taking insurgent practices into account. Second, macro-structural effects on insurgency are mediated by meso-level institutional cleavages. Considering opportunities at the meso level allows much more precise explanation of the timing and influence of specific insurgencies. Third, context effects are interactive rather than independent. Opportunities determine the effects of insurgent practice rather than causing insurgency directly. (2015:396)

Bloom's framework is unique because it brings together context and strategy in a way that is predictive of the kinds of insurgent practices that are more likely to be successful across a given institutional cleavage. Moreover it helps explain how and why, when a cleavage is reconfigured, a particular practice becomes ineffective. In the case of the civil rights movement, for example, activists effectively challenged authorities using sit-ins. When the state demanded integration, the practice no longer leveraged institutional cleavages, and was therefore no longer effective. The goal of insurgent movements, and the key to their success according to Bloom, is to develop and deploy insurgent practices across institutional cleavages.

Insurgent versus Institutionalized Practices

In his reconceptualization of political opportunity theory, Bloom focuses on insurgent practices. He neither discusses nor theorizes institutionalized practices, or those that seek redress by engaging official—usually state—channels such as lobbying, filing lawsuits, electoral politics, etc. Scholars have long differentiated between activists' use of routine political advocacy and disruptive or contentious direct action; interest group scholarship in political science focuses on what is generally termed "insider" and "outsider" politics (see Kollman 1998; and Browne 1998),[2] and social movement scholars delineate between institutional and contentious politics.

Although there is a plethora of research tracing interest groups' and social movements' use of different tactics, scholars have not adequately dissected the relationship between strategies that engage the state and its authority, and those that attempt to challenge it disruptively. As Bloom (2017) explains, a key problem is the focus on individual group membership rather than on mobilization practices:

> The classical distinction revolves around the position of contending groups. *Members* are said to command sufficient resources and so advance their interests using institutionalized or "contained" means. Conversely *challengers* are largely excluded from access to institutionalized power, and seek to advance their interests by disrupting business as usual. But it turns out that the generalizable differences in kinds of mobilization actually concern the form of practice, not determined by group membership. Members of the same social group—and even the same individuals—can participate in either or both types of mobilization simultaneously. The more salient distinction in mobilization dynamics is not driven by *who* is mobilizing, but by *how* they are mobilizing.[3]

The extant literature also provides little theoretical guidance about when each of these types of strategies or practices is more advantageous and in what political context. Social movement theorists tend to reify disruptive and insurgent activity and therefore miss its complex relationship with routine institutionalized practices. This is problematic given that almost no movements have historically utilized insurgent practices to the exclusion of all others. In reality, activists often employ a variety of strategies simultaneously, both institutionalized and insurgent, marked as insider and outsider. During the civil rights struggle, for example, sit-ins and freedom rides were carried out in combination with lawsuits and lobbying. Moreover scholars' emphasis on disruptive behavior paradoxically undermines the notion of political opportunity structure because political openings actually minimize the need to employ insurgent action by providing less costly avenues for pursuing policy goals.

Field Theory, Social Change, and Agency

Theoretical approaches that foreground institutional fields are quite useful in pushing forward a more integrated framework for understanding the dynamic between social movement strategies and political context in general, and how social movements influence policy using both institutionalized politics and insurgent action in particular. Throughout the book we use the term "institutional field" (hereafter "field"). Although we could easily substitute "arena" for "field," we decided to use the latter because it is widely utilized and theorized across sociological literatures (see Martin 2003; Davis et al. 2005; Fligstein and McAdam 2012).

The field concept emerges from two theoretical traditions: Bourdieu's work on social fields, and in organizational theory. For Bourdieu, the social spaces that constitute fields—art, economics, etc.—represent the structures of different components of social life through which power is constituted, contested, and reproduced as individuals pursue common interests (Bourdieu and Wacquant 1992; Swedberg 2006). For organizational theorists, a field is constituted by like organizations that directly interact or are indirectly oriented to each other, and that "in the aggregate, constitute a recognized area of institutional life . . . " (DiMaggio and Powell 1991:674–665). Although there are different ways to constitute fields,[4] most organizational scholars focus on the dynamics of a single field and define it to map onto existing categorizations of industries or sectors (see Meyer and Scott 1983; DiMaggio and Powell 1991). When policy questions are addressed, then, industry-specific regulatory agents and other state actors who influence that substantive industry are all aggregated within a single field (see Laumann and Knoke 1987).

Here we adopt Fligstein and McAdam's more broad definition of fields as "constructed social orders that define an arena within which a set of consensually defined and mutually attuned actors vie for advantage" (2012:64). Incorporating the concept of a constructed social order is important, because it delineates fields not only by networks of actors, but also by specific institutional logics and discrete norms. The idea of a set of consensually defined and mutually attuned actors is particularly important—a field adheres as a coherent entity only to the extent that the actions of actors operating within it are motivated, shaped, and constrained by the features of that field.[5] Defining fields in terms of actors who constantly vie for advantage also recognizes the inherent dynamism of fields—change is constant and actors can use their skills to stimulate it in various ways.

Organizational scholars generally focus on what happens *within* individual fields. For example, research has focused on the creation of new fields, competing logics inside fields, and the effect of outsiders on fields (see Clemens 1993; Scott et al. 2000; Armstrong 2002; Schneiberg and Soule 2005; Lounsbury 2007; Duffy, Binder, and Skrentny 2010). Their research provides a theoretical foundation for understanding social movement influence by: (1) emphasizing the networked nature of the political terrain, in which relationships between "hubs" within a field predominate and in which hierarchies of actors exist; (2) highlighting the social constructedness of the terrain, in which widely shared beliefs may limit the parameters of political debate and shape the perception of what is possible; and (3) underlining the importance of informal norms and formal regulations that restrict and channel action. Although fields have different internal logics, all are organized such that actors, beliefs, and rules matter.

Organizational scholars recognize that changes occur within fields, and frequently examine how actors (and social movements) devise strategies to influence a given field. What is not well theorized in the organizations and social movements literatures, however, is how activists can forge novel sources of power by leveraging *across* fields. Despite extensive scholarship on internal field dynamics, there has been little work on the dynamics *between* and *across* individual fields.[6] Fligstein and McAdam highlight this problem: "Virtually all of the previous work on fields, however, focuses only on the internal workings of these orders, depicting them as largely self-contained, autonomous worlds" (2012:18). It is surprising that organizations scholars have, for the most part, limited their analyses to *intra-field dynamics* given that social actors and organizations—including elements of the state itself—*almost always* straddle multiple fields in which the organizing principles, networks of actors, and institutional characteristics differ.

Laumann and Knoke's (1987) "organizational state" provides a useful starting point for thinking about the points of leverage that straddle fields. Rejecting the unitary state that, at the time, was at the center of most international relations theories, Laumann and Knoke conceived of the state as a complex grouping of multiple overlapping policy fields (which they call domains)[7] that include both state and nonstate actors and organizations.[8] This conceptualization foregrounds the relevance of actors outside a field and the influence hierarchies within it rather than perpetuating a simple division of insiders and outsiders. The policy domain/field concept extends social movement ideas about elites and challengers; not all nonstate actors are challengers because they may hold "hub" positions within a given field. Conversely, politicians can be "challengers" to a dominant ideology within a policy field.

Although Laumann and Knoke's model illuminates the routine functioning of policy decision-making, it does not offer theoretical purchase on how social movement activists engage fields, or examine the mechanisms that allow them to achieve policy outcomes across fields. They argue that most policy fields are characterized by stability, in which a core group of actors dominates the determination of policy problems and governmental solutions. Only a very small number of decisions become the subject of public controversy, which, Laumann and Knoke argue, is "the result of poorly understood processes whereby key actors come to contest the symbolic framing in which 'routine' decisions had heretofore been made."[9] It is this issue of politicization that lies at the heart of the NAFTA battle, and that remains insufficiently understood.

In contrast to Laumann and Knoke, Fligstein and McAdam foreground the instability of fields. Indeed, at its core, their analysis of fields offers a more general theory of social change and agency. They locate possibilities for both in the relationship *between* fields: "The main theoretical implication of the interdependence of fields is that the broader field environment is a source of routine, rolling turbulence in modern society. A significant change in any given strategic action field is like a stone thrown in a still pond sending ripples outward to all proximate fields" (2012:19). They explain the important connections between fields, particularly those between nonstate and state fields:

> the long-term prospects for stability and change in a field are affected at least as much by threats and opportunities that arise outside of the field—usually in proximate fields or the state—as those within the strategic action field itself. To accurately capture the dynamics of any given field the analyst must, in our view, understand the internal structure and workings of the field and the broader set of relationships that tie any given field to a host of other strategic action fields (including various state fields). (p. 169)

Fligstein and McAdam extend Laumann and Knoke's conception of the state as overlapping policy fields by suggesting a way to understand how actors come to contest or politicize issues in fields: it is how skilled social actors use their position in fields, the resources available to them, and their connections to others in and outside the field that determines their ability to reproduce a field or alter it. This framework is very useful for thinking about how social actors (including social movement actors) can influence state policy. Fligstein and McAdam's formalization of a theory of state and nonstate fields expands upon Laumann and Knoke's initial model, and builds upon our 2008 conceptualization of the state as: "an aggregation of multiple fields that overlap with non-state fields" (Evans and Kay 2008:973).

Reconceptualizing Political Opportunities in Relationship to Intersecting Fields

Although Fligstein and McAdam consider how fields can be interconnected (distant and proximate, dependent and interdependent, nested and hierarchical) and therefore where sites of stability and stasis across them might lie, they do not specifically locate sources of leverage in the places where fields intersect. Indeed, they focus on crises within fields as sites of transformation and opportunity: "Challengers may find an opening (what social movement theorists call a "political opportunity") to force changes on the existing order. They may ally themselves with other dominant groups, invaders from other fields, or state actors to help reconstitute a given field" (2012:112). We extend their theory by showing how points of intersection *across* state and nonstate fields can be leveraged strategically by activists to achieve specific policy outcomes. And, we go one step further, suggesting that political opportunities emerge from how both state and nonstate fields intersect, which creates unique points of leverage that render particular targets more vulnerable and strategies more effective. In conceptualizing political opportunity structures as leverage points across institutional fields, we weave together useful strands of the social movement and organizations literatures to build a framework that extends our understanding of the dynamic between social movement strategies and political context.[10]

Bloom's understanding of political opportunities as institutional cleavages, then, is very similar to our conceptualization of them as leverage points across institutional fields, as we discussed in earlier work: "Our framework allows social movement scholars to reconceptualize political opportunity structures not simply as 'windows' that are randomly opened or closed to movement activists (requiring clairvoyance to detect and exploit), but rather as dynamic configurations of overlapping fields that can be leveraged strategically to achieve specific policy outcomes. Political opportunity structures are constituted where fields interlock. Key allies, powerful new frames, and resources for disadvantaged actors are found at the intersections where structural contradictions are highest" (Evans and Kay 2008:988).

When fields intersect, transformation in one field can occur because of the leverage derived from the way that it interlocks with other fields and as a result of networked actors operating in multiple fields.[11] The concept of inter-field leverage places *strategy* at the center of analysis because activists' influence on policy results from their ability to skillfully use leverage across fields. This is implicit in social movement analyses of organizational capacity-building, resource mobilization, and alliance building. But it is also a result of intersecting status hierarchies and spheres of influence that derive from interpersonal relationships, control of key resources, and ideological affinity. Fligstein and McAdam are explicit in their characterization of fields in these terms: "The links between fields are shaped by a number of factors: resource dependence, mutual beneficial interactions, sharing of power, information flows, and legitimacy" (2012:59).

Our focus on inter-field dynamics therefore allows us to show how activists utilize framing, resource mobilization, and coalition-building—all of which are core concepts in social movement scholarship—to leverage across fields. Our goal is to show how a field overlap framework helps to illuminate and specify the dynamics of these widely discussed movement strategies and mechanisms of political contention (McAdam, Tarrow, and Tilly 2001). We do not attempt to supplant these strategies with wholly new ones. Rather we attempt to expand our understanding of their relationship to political contexts. We suggest that their success and failure depends on how they are deployed across fields to exploit leverage points or, in Bloom's schema, institutional cleavages. What we are suggesting with our theory of field overlap, and what Bloom is offering with his theory of insurgent practice, is that leverage points always exist; success results from matching strategies/practices to the unique configuration of those points of leverage, unlocking the potential to transform power dynamics. Therefore, in addition to looking for specific strategies that succeed in some political contexts and not others as Amenta and colleagues urge (2010), we should also examine why only specific combinations of strategies (both insider and outsider) succeed in any given political context.

In showing how activists try to politicize issues and influence policy across fields, we thus foreground four strategies for: (1) shifting the framing of an issue across fields, (2) changing the rules across fields, (3) brokering resources across fields, and (4) building alliances and coalitions across fields. Framing strategies enable skilled actors to strategically adapt frames in one field in order to facilitate their resonance, adoption, or reconceptualization in another field. They can build upon existing frame concordance between fields or translate conceptual understandings from one field to another, thereby reconceptualizing key political ideas or discursive parameters across fields and transforming the collective understanding of available political options.

The most fundamental changes occur when rule-making strategies are used to transform the rules bounding a preexisting field, which can advantage previously disadvantaged groups and transform influence hierarchies. Actors that lack influence within a field can draw upon relationships with others more influential in it to gain direct access to the field, increase their legitimacy within it, or indirectly influence decision-making. This captures the importance of alliance-building strategies and highlights the potentially transferable nature of influence; relationships outside of specific policy contexts can become an effective political resource, and legitimacy within one field can facilitate access to another. Skilled actors can also employ resource brokerage strategies by utilizing financial and/or political resources to gain influence or power in another field by inducing trade-offs, explicitly buying access, providing discourse-shaping information, etc. Social movement scholars have long recognized the importance of resources for political mobilization. Here, however, we emphasize the importance of resources that can be rallied externally and leveraged across fields.

Our framework helps explain how activists, who by definition begin from a position of relative political weakness, can have influence within a hostile field by leveraging resources across overlapping fields. State officials can have considerable statutory power in one state field and negligible influence in another. Activists may gain access to a state field in which they are marginal because of their influence in a nonstate field. The tendency of influence to permeate across fields results from institutional configurations that create intersecting status hierarchies, spheres of influence, and ideological affinities.

Using the NAFTA case, we show how activists can exploit sites of intersection with one field to change the parameters in another, use their position in one field to gain access to an intersecting field, use resources as leverage in another field, and expropriate legitimating discourse from one in pursuit of goals of another. By exploiting these points of leverage, activists can construct new policy issues—such as trade—as subjects of public controversy and try to influence how the decisions surrounding them are made. Understanding strategic action in relationship to overlapping fields, then, helps us illuminate and better understand the processes underlying politicization. When we look at the contexts in which trade policy actors operate, for example, it quickly becomes apparent that they often stand at the intersection of multiple fields oriented to overlapping but not identical goals. Rather than draw a boundary around all the actors and institutions engaged in trade policy to define it as a single trade field, we believe it is more analytically useful to think of those actors as embedded in distinct yet intersecting fields that address trade issues in the context of broader problem-solving directives and that operate according to distinct institutional logics in the pursuit of those goals.[12] We now turn to a description of the fields, or arenas, relevant during the NAFTA negotiations.

Fields Relevant to NAFTA

The NAFTA battle included discrete time periods punctuated by decision points that brought different fields, actors, and points of leverage into play. Figure 2.1 provides a timeline of key events in NAFTA's history for readers to reference as they move through the text. We show how four key fields affected trade policy outcomes during the NAFTA struggle in the United States: the U.S. legislative field (herein the legislative field), the U.S. trade policy field (herein the trade policy field), the transnational trade negotiating field (herein the transnational negotiating field), and the grassroots politics field. Although the president, in coordination with his/her cabinet and members of his/her Economic Policy Council, possesses authority over the development of trade policy, Congress continues to legislate the parameters in which the president is allowed to operate.

NAFTA announced
Sept 20, 1990

Bush Announces Intention to Negotiate Trade Agreement with Mexico.

Cananda Joins Negotiations
Jan 23, 1991

Fast Track Request
March 1991

Fast Track Approved
May 1991

Substantive Negotiations
June 1991 – August 1992

Bush Signs Substantive Agreement
Dec 17, 1992

Supplemental Negotiations
March 1993 – August 1993

Supplemental Negotiatiations Concluded
August 1993

Supplemental Agreements Signed
Sept 14, 1993

Clinton Elected
Nov 3, 1992

Clinton Begins Term
Jan 20, 1993

NAFTA Passed by U.S. House and Senate Nov 17–20, 1993

NAFTA Goes Into Force
Jan 1, 1994

1991   1992   1993   1994   1995

FIGURE 2.1 NAFTA Timeline

The *legislative field* includes Congress, staff, and nonstate congressional advisors. Under the Constitution, Congress determines the conditions under which trade negotiations occur and ratifies trade agreements. Fast-track privileges (first introduced in the Trade Act of 1974), granted by Congress enable the Office of the USTR to negotiate changes in domestic law while restricting congressional ability to amend elements of an agreement; members can only vote up or down on the agreement as a whole. The distinction between power and influence is crucial in this context; although under present rules rank-and-file members of Congress lack the power to affect the details of international trade negotiations, they collectively maintain influence over the negotiation process through their nullifying power. Trade policy field members need to ensure that their actions do not tip the required numbers of legislators against the agreement; the win-set therefore includes the constellation of possible positions that will retain the support of the requisite majority. With most trade agreements, it is the point of ratification that provides the legislature as a whole with leverage. The degree of constraint experienced by negotiators will in part vary according to the ratification point; a priori ratifications provide greater latitude to negotiators than do ex post facto ratifications.[13]

The *trade policy field* includes the Office of the USTR and its staff, approximately a thousand nonstate members of official advisory committees, negotiators from various government offices, and members of Congress and staff involved in trade-related committees. Negotiating authority centers on the USTR, which operates as part of the executive branch and conducts negotiations on behalf of the president. USTR has ambassadorial and cabinet rank. The USTR includes negotiators with a variety of technical specialties, and it has historically operated with the broad mandate to promote trade liberalization. The USTR coordinates U.S. trade, and commodity and investment policy among the different departments responsible for trade issues, and helps develop U.S. trade strategy.[14]

During NAFTA negotiations, ten members of Congress were appointed as congressional advisers to international trade negotiations. The House Ways and Means Committee and the Senate Finance Committee were regularly briefed on USTR activity and consulted for advice, and they provided crucial input on negotiating drafts. In addition, Congressional committees that are regularly involved in specific trade-related matters include: the House Banking and Financial Services, Commerce, and International Relations Committees, the Senate

Foreign Relations, Banking, and Agriculture, Nutrition, and Forestry Committees. The trade policy field therefore spans both the executive and legislative branches, even though the USTR officially negotiates on behalf of the president.

The NAFTA case illustrates the importance of conceptualizing the state as an aggregation of multiple fields that intersect with nonstate fields because the trade policy field has a unique corporatist structure that has institutionalized the participation of private companies and labor unions in trade policy development. Business and union leaders regularly meet with officials from the USTR to provide input and advice through a three-tier advisory system mandated by Congress. The first tier—the Advisory Committee on Trade Policy and Negotiations (ACTPN)—comprises executives appointed by the president who collectively represent key sectors of the U.S. economy affected by trade issues. The second tier consists of policy committees, such as those for investment and services, that provide policy advice concerning general policy areas. Finally, the third tier includes technical, sectoral, and commodity group committees that provide information about the effects trade policies will have on specific sectors. During NAFTA negotiations the Labor Advisory Committee consisted of approximately eighty union members and represented a broad range of organized labor groups.[15] Not only do such seats provide routinized access to USTR negotiations, but they also legitimize the position of those nonstate actors as participants within the field itself.

Participation in the USTR advisory system, however, is heavily weighted in favor of representatives from the largest U.S. companies. Participants in ACTPN during NAFTA negotiations included the heads of major U.S. corporations. At least ten of the forty-five companies represented on ACTPN at that time had facilities or subsidiaries in Mexico,[16] and only two representatives were labor leaders. The configuration of the trade policy field thereby institutionalizes the influence of large corporations on trade policy through the hierarchy of USTR advisory committees.[17]

The *grassroots politics field* encompasses the public arena distinct from the state in which mobilization to affect state policy outcomes occurs. Action within this field includes a broad range of activity, both routine and contentious: press conferences, mass marches, petition signings, sit-ins, and political theater. But although mobilization in the grassroots politics field may ultimately be oriented to influencing state decision-makers, the field's defining characteristic is the public nature of that mobilization. It therefore expands the reference group by which government decision-makers measure their actions. It is within this field that collective identity and mobilization potential is collectively constituted, either through coordinated activity or political response (i.e., voting blocs). We refer to mobilization in the grassroots politics field as "popular politics" to distinguish it from the direct "advocacy politics" that occurs in the U.S. trade policy and legislative fields.

The *transnational negotiating field* includes the negotiators and staff empowered to represent their nations in trade negotiations. During NAFTA negotiations it included U.S., Mexican, and Canadian trade policy representatives. The field underlines the relationship between action in domestic and international fields; negotiators are influenced by the actors, rules, resource considerations, and policy frames of their own domestic trade policy fields, those of their counterparts, and those within the field itself.

Leveraging across Fields during NAFTA's Negotiation

Unlike most scholarship on trade that focuses broadly on overall negotiating outcomes, we narrow our analysis to how activists politicized trade during the NAFTA battle, and how they shaped key but limited outcomes: linking labor and environmental rights and protections to trade, changing the rules to win formal recognition and participation of environmental organizations on trade advisory committees, and demanding that labor and environmental protections, however weak, be included in the agreement. Because our analysis seeks to understand how social movements influence state policies, we do not engage the very diverse and broad trade policy literature that largely focuses on international relations and inter-state negotiations. We view our contribution here to the social movements and organizations literatures (and even more specifically, in bridging key elements of them), rather than to trade policy theory.

It is also important to note that although what happens in individual fields is important to the NAFTA story, our focus here is on the processes that occur across multiple fields. This does not mean that we ignore activities within fields that are critical to understanding trade politicization. We explore, for example, how anti-NAFTA organizations built their coalition within the grassroots politics field, and we address how obstacles within the legislative field made it difficult for activists to achieve more. We argue, however, that the data shows that the best explanation of how activists politicized and influenced trade outcomes lies not in what transpired in any one field, but rather, in the dynamics across them.

3

Trade Politics prior to NAFTA

THE CONFIGURATION OF the trade policy field and the characteristics of its intersection with the legislative and transnational negotiating fields were formed during decades of political contention and negotiation in the years preceding NAFTA's introduction. The trade policy field was dominated by a political elite who blamed the Great Depression on high tariffs and believed that the key to postwar stability was a more integrated global economy led by the United States. In the years following the onset of the Great Depression, these trade policy officials created an elaborate U.S. policymaking system designed to support continuous reductions in barriers to trade. They helped establish a global framework to reduce or eliminate trade barriers under GATT. And to further shield Congress from constituent pressures to enact protectionist measures, they utilized a fast-track mechanism (a provision of the Trade Act of 1974) that gave the president authority to negotiate trade barrier reductions without congressional amendments. The combination of a committed network of trade policy field actors and rules that facilitated a reduction in trade barriers was effective. By the 1970s, world trade had been significantly liberalized, and at home there was very little opposition to this policy approach.

As global trade expanded, however, support for it began to slip in the legislative field. The deteriorating plight of import-affected industries in the 1970s and 1980s, the unfair trade practices of some of the United States's global competitors, an overvalued dollar, and rising trade deficits took their toll. The majority of members of Congress were still unwilling to fundamentally tamper with the rules constituting the trade policy field, but they did begin to use influence (derived from their ultimate ability to pass trade agreements) to press for trade policies that were more fair. Members of Congress prodded U.S. trade policy officials to work more aggressively to open foreign markets to U.S. companies, and to provide for greater assistance to import-affected industries. As the NAFTA talks opened, leaders in the trade policy field knew that they would have to take practical steps to assuage the misgivings of leaders in the legislative field to ensure NAFTA's passage. They would be introducing new non-tariff related provisions into the agreement, and it would be the first agreement between the United States and a developing country.

Meanwhile, in the transnational negotiating field, trade officials from all three North American countries were converging on a policy consensus. Changing ideological winds and compounding economic weaknesses (in Mexico, harrowing economic crises) propelled both Canada and Mexico toward a closer economic relationship with the United States. At the same time, problems with GATT moved the United States to pursue a regional trade alternative. The timing was propitious; nonetheless, the Canadians and Mexicans entered NAFTA talks with some trepidation. Following implementation of a bilateral U.S.-Canadian free trade agreement in 1989, Canada had fallen into a deep recession, while free-trade "reforms" in Mexico had imposed severe hardships on the Mexican people. Both countries were willing but wary.

Liberalized trade policies (and a series of peso devaluations) also brought a proliferation of maquiladoras to the U.S.-Mexico border region, and the resulting strains and predations roused labor, environmental, consumer, farm, and human rights groups on both sides of the border. Rules created in the transnational negotiating field directly impacted their domestic policy options. Thus, as the NAFTA talks opened, a whole new group of actors in the grassroots politics field began to understand that their terrain now intersected in a concrete way with the transnational negotiating field. With the exception of the unions that participated in the USTR advisory committees, however, none of these groups had a history or an established role in the trade policy field. And although a number of new trade actors began to mobilize in the decade prior to NAFTA's introduction, the creation of new actors affected by trade policy in the United States was not sufficient to develop a new social movement on trade. Indeed it took NAFTA to propel them as a force into trade politics. It also took NAFTA to catalyze a more sustained and formal alliance between labor unions and environmentalists. We begin with an examination of the changing structural conditions prior to NAFTA in each of the four fields, then examine the roots of a discursive link between labor and environ-mental rights in relation to trade, and the creation of nascent networks oriented to trade policy.

Pushing Trade Liberalization in the Trade Policy Field

Although the laws that govern the trade policy field and the bodies that oversee trade policy have developed over time and with sometimes con-tradictory intent, the attributes of the trade policy field are not a mere accident of history. The rules that established its modern contours and the characteristics of the intersection between it and the legisla-tive field were established to facilitate specific outcomes—namely trade liberalization. The divided governance structure with executive control over policy development and congressional authority over passage, the corporatist inclusion of business and labor leaders through the USTR advisory structure, and a fast-track procedure that limits input from the legislative field all encourage certain types of trade policies and in-hibit others (see Goldstein 1993; Destler 1995). Throughout the post-Depression era, supporters of trade liberalization have dominated the trade policy field, and have instituted rules alleviating countervailing pressures.

The modern trade policy field has largely been shaped in response to the Depression and the subsequent role of the United States in spearheading the development of a new international trading system. Before the Depression, Congress had primary responsibility for de-termining tariff levels on goods entering the United States. The Constitution explicitly empowers Congress to govern international trade and, for most of its history, Congress enthusiastically argued over the merits of competing tariff proposals. The debates centered not on the question of whether tariffs were good for the nation, but rather on whether the political parties differentiated themselves over the question of how high tariffs in different industries should be set. Taxing imported goods was thought to be an effective way to encourage nascent industries and shield markets from severe market dislocations. Perhaps most significantly, tariffs were also an important means of obtaining federal revenue.

The last major development of tariff levels by Congress occurred in the now-infamous Smoot-Hawley Tariff of 1930. What began as a modest increase in tariff rates to assist producers at the onset of a depression ballooned into a highly protectionist bill. The Smoot-Hawley tariff was subsequently blamed for facilitating the collapse of global trade and sinking the nation deeper into depression. Many were concerned that the economy had become too complicated for Congress to handle specific tariff levels. With the Depression as a backdrop, Congress altered the institutional mechanisms for setting U.S. trade policy by abdicating in its 1934 trade act much of its power over tariffs to the executive branch. The act extended control over trade, within specified limits, to the administration. The president and his/her staff became responsible for trade negotiations themselves, and for the development of the specifics of U.S. foreign economic objectives. Using their ability to alter the rules, legislators lessened their own direct power, and therefore altered the composition of actors and the configuration of the trade policy field (Destler 1995).

This shift in power had significant consequences for the development of trade policy. Whereas Congress viewed trade primarily as a domestic political issue, successive presidents came to use trade policy largely as a foreign policy tool, particularly for containing communism (Nelson 1996:167). Key congressional committee members responsible for trade matters continued to be crucial actors within the reconfigured trade policy field, and the need for congressional passage of trade agreements still provided a pressure point, albeit a reduced one, for industry and labor lobbyists to affect trade policy through action in the legislative field.

The 1934 act also established the principle of reciprocity in tariff reductions or other import restrictions. Under the act, the president could negotiate bilateral agreements with other nations to mutually reduce tariffs. Tariffs could be reduced up to fifty percent without Congressional involvement. The president could also decide to extend negotiated tariff reductions to all nations under the most-favored-nation (MFN) principle. Low-tariff access to the lucrative U.S. domestic market proved an effective prod for negotiating concessions from other nations. The regulatory and institutional changes made to the trade policy field meant the days of unilateral tariff increases through Congress were effectively over.

As World War II drew to a close, a commitment to multilateral trade liberalization became more fixed within the trade policy field. Not only were previous economic approaches discredited by the worldwide depression, but also a causal connection was posited between open commercial policies and peace between nations. Trade liberalization overwhelmingly dominated the trade policy field, and the administrative actors in it became leading proponents for a global trade regime that was multilateral, liberal, and nondiscriminatory. To that end, the United States helped establish GATT in 1948, a multilateral agreement that created a framework of reciprocal trading rights and obligations, as well as systematic reductions in trade barriers. Each signatory nation agreed to extend MFN status to all other signatories and to establish a trade dispute mechanism with independent arbiters. During the next fifty years, GATT's scope was broadened in seven successive rounds of negotiations, eventually involving more than eighty participating countries and nearly thirty additional nations under special arrangements. Together, these countries account for nearly 80 percent of the world's trade. Under GATT, tariffs worldwide decreased from an average of 40 percent in 1947 to less than 5 percent by the 1990s (Rosenberg 1994; Kaplan 1996).

An Eroding Consensus on Liberalized Trade in the Legislative Field

Until the 1970s, trade was generally perceived as a "dull, 'no-win' issue" among U.S. legislators (Destler 1995:81). Although protectionism was unacceptable within the trade policy field and generally unpopular in the legislative field, free trade was not widely popular among the general public (Destler 1995:81–82). Taking a strong public stance for freer trade was therefore not useful politically. Members of Congress believed the lesson from Smoot-Hawley—that congressionally-set tariffs would inevitably be high tariffs—and accepted their more limited role in the trade process both to serve the greater good of freer trade and to shield themselves from the political pressure of protectionist-minded constituents (Nelson 1996). Indeed, delegating primary responsibility for trade to U.S. trade policy officials in the executive branch enabled members of Congress to support trade liberalization through institutionalized channels while claiming that their direct power was limited (Destler 1995).

The liberalized trade approach that dominated U.S. foreign economic policy in the decades following World War II came under increasing pressure in the early 1970s, and the breakdown of consensus for trade liberalization in the legislative field began—albeit with continued dominance in the trade policy field. Expanding manufacturing capacity in Europe and Japan created greater competition for U.S. producers in a number of industries, and trade deficits exploded.[1] The breakdown of the Bretton Woods exchange system[2] and the first oil shock during this period signaled a heightened vulnerability to economic events beyond U.S. borders (Bayard and Elliot 1994:12). Unemployment levels increased, productivity levels declined, trade deficits ballooned, and inflation surged. Technological and legislative changes facilitated the transfer of capital overseas, leading to plant relocations. As these economic dislocations created pressure to back away from a trade liberalization agenda, countries increasingly used subsidies and other discretionary policies to evade the limits set by GATT. Moreover the heterogeneous community of GATT nations often did not achieve agreement on contentious issues, making it harder to enforce GATT rules. These transformations strained congressional commitment to liberalized trade, as industry and union pushback against U.S. trade rules became more vociferous and more frequent in the legislative field.

Thus increased friction developed at the intersection between the two fields, as did increased threats in the legislative field to use its rule-making power to limit further liberalization efforts in the trade policy field. The tensions between officials in the trade policy field and legislators intensified as trade balances deteriorated. Although members of Congress ultimately refused to enact major protectionist legislation or revoke the executive branch's authority over trade (with the exception of the GATT Kennedy Round when they checked President Johnson's expansion into non-trade barriers), they tried to compel trade officials to shield domestic industry from the most egregious harm from imports through influence that stemmed from the implicit threat of altering the trade policy field.

Over the next two decades, unions also changed their overarching trade stance from one that favored trade liberalization to a position critical of U.S. trade liberalization policies. Industry and union leaders in affected industries responded to the growing crisis by pressing Congress to ameliorate worsening trade deficits. They pursued grievance mechanisms, voluntary export restraint agreements, and more sweeping legislative changes. Legislative resolutions included calls for explicit quotas and domestic content laws and against renewal of trade preferences for developing countries. Industry and union leaders argued that the government should shield hard-hit U.S. industries and workers from major short-term dislocations to ensure a stable and equitable market system, and urged the president and the USTR to open foreign markets to U.S. producers.

During the 1970s and 1980s the numbers of industries seeking assistance from the government expanded dramatically. Moreover new industries sought aid, including mature manufacturing sectors such as steel and automobiles that had substantial export markets. Although steel unionists joined with steel manufacturers to press for voluntary restraint agreements and other supports, the United Auto Workers (UAW) initially split with the auto manufacturers and emphasized growth through the continued opening of foreign markets (Nelson 1996). As economic dislocation spread across the manufacturing sector, however, unions began to back away from their earlier commitment to liberalized trade. Many AFL-CIO affiliated unions demanded greater U.S. intervention in trade disputes, and unions in industries harmed by imports joined coalitions for specific legislative and procedural campaigns. They began to push the AFL-CIO to reconsider its complete commitment to liberalized trade.

By the late 1970s, some members of Congress started to question legislative abdication of trade authority, particularly because increased public concern was making trade an issue with some political advantages (Destler 1995:81). Although officials in the trade policy field maintained their support for trade liberalization, those in the legislative field began to question its efficacy, and their support faltered. The postwar pact on liberalized trade among the political elite was beginning, in small but crucial ways, to break down.

Concerned members of Congress stressed the importance of reciprocity in U.S. trade policy. Using their indirect influence on the trade policy field through the implied threat of rule changes and ratification failures, they insisted that U.S. trade policy officials not offer any trade concessions unless they were matched by equal dispensations from other nations. They advocated that access to the U.S. market be linked to the opening of a similar market to a comparable U.S. producer and that the threat of loss of that market be used as a threat to ensure balanced trade. And they suggested that countries running large trade surpluses with the United States should be required to increase exports of U.S. goods as a precondition to increased trade. Finally, concerned members of Congress argued that ensuring fair trade required the United States to sanction countries that kept their domestic markets closed or improperly subsidized their exports (Goldstein 1993:178–179).

Ultimately during this period, members of Congress tinkered with the system without fundamentally altering it; they made numerous threats to reassert their primacy over trade policy, only to then reverse themselves. Members who participated in both the legislative and trade policy fields maintained a solid commitment to trade liberalization. Although the discursive commitment to trade liberalization continued to dominate within Congress, the consensus had broken down and the hegemony of trade liberalization in the legislative field ended. No alternative trade philosophy emerged, however, that engendered comparable support in the legislative field.

Although Congress pushed to aggressively promote the interests of U.S. companies in foreign markets, members did not fundamentally change the institutional parameters that had so successfully fostered a global trade liberalization regime. Limitations in the global trade regime and increasing pressures to open foreign markets by actors in the legislative field and oppositional actors in the trade policy field did, however, lead to an increased focus on regional trade. The result was a move among trade policy field actors from a multilateral strategy to a more targeted focus on increased access to foreign markets for U.S. goods.

A Shift to Regional Trade in the Transnational Negotiating Field

In the 1980s when President Ronald Reagan suggested the creation of a free trade zone extending across the Americas, few would have imagined that a trade agreement even among North American nations was possible. Mexican officials were wary of excessive U.S. influence, and Canadian leaders were actively working to reduce their country's reliance on the U.S. economy. That these three nations would come together a decade later in a far-reaching trade and investment agreement, and that primary resistance to the agreement would be centered in the United States, would have been nearly impossible to predict at the time. Changing economic and political circumstances created the conditions for what before had seemed unachievable in the transnational negotiating field. Trade policy actors from each country, who had earlier perceived their interests as being in conflict, began to converge on a shared vision of an integrated regional trade policy.

The shift among trade policy field actors to a more forceful equitable trade stance was complemented by a move away from strict multilateralism in favor of a more mixed bilateral and multilateral trade policy. When President Reagan originally called for a free trade agreement with Mexico during a campaign speech in 1979, the Mexican government was highly antagonistic to the proposal, and it went nowhere. But as the Reagan administration grew more frustrated by the difficulties of making further changes under GATT, the possibility of securing trade agreements with individual countries grew in importance. Trade policy field actors began to pursue a dual strategy of continuing to work for multilateral trade liberalization while negotiating bilateral agreements. Moreover, the strengthening of the European Union and of Japan's role in Asia increased the importance of pursuing bilateral strategies within the Americas and deepening economic coordination of the region.

Regional economic integration, however, was very unpopular in Mexico. When Reagan first proposed a regional trade agreement in 1979, Mexican president José López Portillo told Reagan's campaign manager: "our children, and probably our grandchildren, would never see the day" of a U.S.-Mexican economic union (Orme 1993:24). López Portillo argued that Mexican nationalism and the importance of a peasant and labor coalition to the corporatist government precluded the possibility of such an agreement. Even as late as 1988 when Mexican president Carlos Salinas de Gortari entered office, he declared that a NAFTA-style treaty was unfeasible given Mexican wariness of the United States (Pastor and Wise 1994). Salinas did, however, pursue economic liberalization policies in Mexico, a process that began under his predecessor Miguel de la Madrid in order for Mexico to join the GATT in 1986.[3] The Salinas administration privatized larger public enterprises, including the phone company, two major airlines, and steel and copper companies. Salinas also denationalized the banking system in 1990. The combination of trade liberalization, fiscal restraint, market reform, and dampened wages finally appeared to stabilize the Mexican economy.

But after unsuccessfully attempting to solicit European foreign investment during a trip in February 1990, Salinas finally called for U.S.-Mexican free trade negotiations—only two years after he disavowed the idea. Salinas faced resistance, however, particularly from many small and medium-sized businesses that would be hurt by increased trade (Fairbrother 2007). His administration neutralized opposition and built support for an agreement by linking reforms into one package (Pastor and Wise 1994) and convincing many smaller firms that freer trade would be good for economic efficiency and political stability in general. NAFTA, then, marked the culmination of Salinas's efforts to radically transform Mexico's economic, and to some extent political, structures. Changes in actors within the regime, along with an altered discursive understanding of how best to improve Mexico's economy, led to a shared embrace of regional trade liberalization by the relevant actors in the Mexican and U.S. governments.

Like Salinas, Canadian prime minister Brian Mulroney charted a new course for Canada's domestic and foreign policy that facilitated NAFTA's passage. Whereas previous administrations sought to mitigate Canada's reliance on the United States as a trading partner,[4] Mulroney and his Progressive Conservative party tried to overthrow Canada's deep-rooted protectionism and embrace closer economic and political ties with the United States. He declared that "[g]ood relations, super relations, with the United States will be the cornerstone of our policy" (cited in Bothwell 1992:140). Mulroney's vision included deregulation, deficit reduction, dismantling of government enterprise, and foreign investment.

In 1985 Mulroney decided to pursue a free trade agreement with the United States in an effort to coalesce his neoliberal economic strategy and create a stronger U.S. partnership (Bothwell 1992). His decision was also motivated by a desire to shield the nation from rising U.S. protective legislation and countervailing and anti-dumping duties on a number of successful Canadian export industries.[5] The United States had relied increasingly on these measures in what many Canadians viewed as disguised protectionism. Canadian leaders hoped to establish a common set of rules and a common definition of subsidy that would enable a more predictable trade relationship with the United States.

CUSFTA which went into effect on January 1, 1989 was hailed as "the most comprehensive and ambitious trade negotiation ever pursued between two sovereign nations" prior to NAFTA (Hart 1991:122). CUSFTA committed Canada and the United States to eliminate all tariffs between the two countries over a period of nine years. Customs duties, duty-drawbacks, and restrictions on imports and exports were to be completely phased-out. The agreement also included provisions on intellectual property, government procurement, and services, among others. CUSFTA however, was not without its Canadian critics who expressed concern about Canada's ability to maintain its cultural heritage and generous social policies in the face of greater economic integration with the United States. And in 1990 when the economy went into deep recession, critics blamed CUSFTA for Canada's economic woes. It was therefore with considerable trepidation that Canada entered into NAFTA negotiations.

Trade Increases Concerns and Activists in the Grassroots Politics Field

In the decade prior to the NAFTA negotiations, rules being made in the transnational negotiating field were increasingly constraining activists while simultaneously changing the economic and environmental realities for communities along the U.S.-Mexico border. Issues that had been purely domestic, such as collective bargaining, farm price supports, and environmental safety, were becoming international in scope as a result of efforts to reduce non-tariff barriers to trade. Moreover the rapid expansion of the maquiladora program in northern Mexico raised significant labor and environmental concerns and undermined collective bargaining within the United States (Bronfenbrenner 1997). Labor activists north of the Rio Grande found themselves grappling with Mexican policy considerations while trying to address domestic labor concerns. In response to changes in the points of intersection between the trade policy and grassroots politics fields, activists began to establish alliances with previously unaligned (or even antagonistic) actors.

At the global level, rules in the transnational negotiating field were increasingly constraining what activists could do, and further calls to ramp up trade liberalization were met with heightened concern by activists who had not previously worked on trade policy. Free trade proponents called for GATT to harmonize domestic standards to facilitate the flow of goods and services across the globe. The Uruguay Round negotiations in 1986 launched an ambitious agenda that included harmonizing key elements of domestic agriculture, environmental, and food safety policies and eliminating domestic laws considered trade-restrictive. High on the list was the removal of agricultural price supports and subsidies. Countries would be able to apply more restrictive standards if they considered cost-effectiveness, applied the measure "least restrictive to trade," and avoided unjustifiable distinctions. However, countries seeking to apply more restrictive standards would need to justify their decision with relevant scientific and technical information (Charnovitz 1993:274; Wathen 1993).

GATT negotiators' turn to non-tariff trade barriers and their concern with the trade effects of domestic laws exposed a wider array of domestic actors to changes in GATT rules and rulings than those involved in economic sectors affected by imports, exports, or direct foreign investment. Non-tariff barriers therefore extended the distributive effects of trade (see Frieden and Rogowski 1996) to create additional non-economic, or extra-economic effects. Thus, instead of only creating economic winners (aided by exports) and losers (impeded by import competition), new trade policies would also create regulatory winners and losers.

As trade policy field officials began to blur distinctions between domestic and international policy issues, activists operating across a broad range of social movement sectors realized that many domestic issues now had an international component. These changes in trade rules had significant consequences for the points of intersection and leverage across fields: they altered frames around the policy preferences of domestic actors, catalyzed the mobilization of additional actors and the disintegration of old alliances, and created new alliance-building possibilities oriented to trade and integration issues. While the effects of regionalization within North America were altering the balance of power between industrial capital and labor, the expansion of the trade arena to include health, safety, consumer, and environmental standards laid the groundwork for a whole new group of actors to define their interests as entwined with the international trade system. The rest of this chapter details labor unions and environmental organizations' response to these changes in the decades preceding NAFTA, and traces the seeds of their ideological convergence on trade issues that eventually took root in a more formal alliance to oppose NAFTA.

Labor Unions: From Trade Liberalization to Protection

Although unions' positions on trade have historically varied by industry, the AFL-CIO and individual unions generally supported trade liberalization policies in the period between World War II and the late 1960s (Cohen 1988; Milner 1988). The strength of the U.S. economy in the postwar period favored an open policy position for unions more broadly. The relative lack of global competition to U.S. economic preeminence and large gains in productivity created a period of stability and enabled workers to achieve real improvements in their standards of living.

As economic changes wreaked havoc on U.S. jobs and industries in the 1970s, however, the AFL-CIO's overarching frame on trade began to shift from solid support of trade liberalization to criticism regarding U.S. trade policy. Import competition from Japan supported by low labor costs and more flexible industrial relations strategies threatened U.S. jobs, and labor activists grew increasingly concerned about plant closures, job loss (particularly high-wage manufacturing jobs), and a rise in anti-union strategies. In 1975, the AFL-CIO reviewed its trade-related policies and its executive council demanded that the United States president curb imports that were causing unemployment and trade deficits and restrict exports of raw materials and technologies that could damage the national interest.[6] The council argued that Congress should examine all trade agreements that might affect jobs and industries, and the president should limit the flow of export capital overseas (Galenson

1996:132). The council also complained of domestic job loss as a result of direct investment by U.S. firms in foreign countries.[7] Thus, by the onset of NAFTA negotiations, labor had occupied the role of the primary oppositional actor in the trade policy field for more than a decade.

While the AFL-CIO haggled in the legislative and trade policy fields over trade policy, a small group of labor activists operating outside of the AFL-CIO agenda began work in the early 1980s to link trade law to international labor standards. Concerned with human rights violations in developing countries and the movement of U.S. jobs to countries with lower labor standards, these activists sought to protect what the International Labor Organization (ILO) established as core international labor rights, including the right to form unions, bargain collectively, and strike. And because they had no influence in the trade policy field, they targeted the legislative field by lobbying members of Congress.

The activists achieved some success by applying pressure to change the institutional rules of the transnational negotiating field. In 1984 they lobbied for and eventually obtained a provision of GSP that linked a country's access to preferential tariff rates on its recognition of basic labor rights. Although the Reagan administration only weakly enforced the provision, it was an important legislative victory. After activists presented strong evidence in 1987 that workers' rights had been violated, trade policy field officials were forced to deny GSP tariff preferences to Paraguay, Nicaragua, Romania, and Chile (Marshall 1990:70). Activists scored an additional success with the reauthorization legislation for the Overseas Private Investment Corporation in 1985, which forbid corporations from insuring business risks in countries that did not grant workers' their basic rights (Marshall 1990). The small group of activists formed a permanent organization, the International Labor Rights Fund (ILRF), just as the NAFTA issue was coming on the scene. Their continued work had important consequences for the development of the new anti-NAFTA coalition and its focus during the NAFTA negotiations.

The AFL-CIO was not antagonistic to these activists' efforts. Indeed the federation worked to obtain unilateral labor standards in the 1983 Caribbean Basin Initiative.[8] Pushing for labor standards, however, was not a central component of the AFL-CIO's legislative agenda. Instead, the AFL-CIO and its affiliates devoted considerable energy and resources in the legislative field to fighting for greater domestic industry assistance. Although individual unions were instrumental in obtaining redress provisions for their industries, the AFL-CIO was on the losing side of the majority of trade legislation battles during the 1970s and 1980s. They opposed aspects of the dominant liberalization frame in the trade policy field but did not successfully use their leverage in the legislative field to create meaningful change in U.S. trade policy. In general, labor unions were only able to generate enough support to influence the initiation of legislation or redress investigations. But with few exceptions, they could not overcome the continued commitment of a majority of members of Congress to trade liberalization and their unwillingness to fundamentally alter the rules governing the trade policy field.

Environmentalists: From Marginal Trade Actors to Key Players

Although labor unions had been involved in trade policy for decades prior to NAFTA, for environmental organizations trade largely remained off the issue agenda—and off the radar. Environmentalists understood the profound interconnection of environmental problems and their impacts across the globe, and with treaties on hazardous waste and endangered species recognized the possibilities of transnational environmental degradation. However, they remained removed from trade agreement issues and negotiations. Indeed the issue of environmental policy being undermined by trade agreements was not relevant in the first international discussions on the relationship between trade and environmental policy that occurred in the wake of the United Nations Conference on the Human Environment in 1972. Economists worried that countries that enacted strong pollution controls would undermine their trade competitiveness. In response, in 1972 the OECD developed the Polluter Pays Principle to encourage prices to truly reflect production costs, including environmental costs, and to keep pollution abatement costs in the private rather than the public sector. The OECD and GATT both established procedures for consultation on disputes on trade and environmental issues, but they were not used. Moreover the GATT working group on trade and the environment did not meet until 1991—over a year after environmentalists in the United States began to engage trade issues (Pearson 1993).[9]

As the farm crisis began to unfold in the mid-1980s, the significance of trade policy for the environment started to become clear. Farm activists that tried to push policies to protect farmers—particularly small family farms—faced repeated obstacles in Washington. Although some politicians supported their policy suggestions, they were untenable under proposed Uruguay Round GATT rules. Activists responded by educating themselves about GATT and forming farm advocacy organizations. Mark Ritchie, widely regarded as the earliest advocate outside of the labor movement in the United States to get involved in trade policy, spent a year in Europe learning about GATT in greater detail as a trade policy analyst for the State of Minnesota (years later he served as Minnesota secretary of state from 2007 to 2015). He realized that he needed to both expand the scope of his trade policy work and involve people beyond the small family farm network who could focus more exclusively on trade issues.[10] In 1986 Ritchie founded the Institute for Agriculture and Trade Policy (IATP).

Although relations between farm and environmental activists had been historically contentious at times, Ritchie believed it was crucial to include environmentalists who could both provide considerably more clout to the nascent movement and amplify family farm concerns. As Ritchie explained: "For me, there was an upper limit to how many places you could go talk about agriculture, but there was an unlimited number of places you could go talk about the environment."[11] With some foundation money, he hired two environmental activists to assist him, and together they started the Fair Trade Campaign (FTC). The FTC was established as a campaign with a grassroots rather than a legislative agenda. FTC participants saw it primarily as a vehicle for educating activists about trade-related issues that might affect their local work. They focused on developing a broad-based coalition in opposition to GATT in the grassroots politics field. Ritchie's decision to hire two environmental activists, both of whom had worked for the National Toxics Campaign (NTC), was intentional. Don Wiener, an early FTC activist, described NTC's model of developing leadership among local environmental activists: "It very much started from the bottom up and it was very much focused on addressing the needs of the different groups and their local battle, explain to them fairly precisely as we were beginning to learn about these fair trade agreements."[12]

The FTC also served as the initial catalyst in mobilizing national environmental leaders on issues of trade policy; they educated environmental representatives about the fundamentals of trade policy and illuminated the dangers unrestricted trade posed to the environment. For example they revealed that provisions of the GATT Uruguay Round draft that could impact U.S. environmental laws were lodged in the agriculture sections of the agreement draft. Some national environmental leaders quickly grasped the potential dangers of trade agreements to the environment (Shrybman 1991; Speck 1990). As Ritchie explained:

> The good news is that because the GATT had been ignored for so long, people inside became over greedy. And so what they were proposing and what they were doing, and the disputes they were litigating and so on, just kind of hit a thousand buttons from little wine producers in Oregon to dolphin lovers and old ladies who defend whales—on and on. But because they were so greedy and kind of outrageous, including really going after environmental laws, it made it possible for me to go around and knock on a lot of doors and say, "Oh by the way."[13]

In addition to mobilizing leaders of environmental NGOs and grassroots activists, the FTC also forged nascent alliances among farm and environmental activists. They staged anti-GATT protests, advocated in support of California's Big Green initiative, organized an educational trip to Europe, and worked to garner support from a plethora of organizations. The leaders of the National Wildlife Federation (NWF) were receptive. They recognized the need for ongoing dialogue on the relationship between trade and the environment, which was conceptually novel at the time. In 1990, NWF therefore began hosting the Working Group on Trade and Environmentally Sustainable Development in its DC office that included national environmental representatives from organizations such as the Natural Resources Defense Council (NRDC) and the World Wildlife Fund (WWF), along with international advocacy groups such as the Development Group for Alternative Policies (DGAP) (Wathen 1992).

Although the FTC ultimately achieved some success, the organization initially faced an uphill battle generating large-scale grassroots support. It was difficult for activists to garner both widespread media exposure and support for their cause given the complexity and obscurity of trade policy for most Americans at the time. Craig Merrilees, then in charge of the FTC's media strategy, described the initial difficulties the FTC faced: "I just can't emphasize enough how obscure this issue was in the beginning, and how impossible it seemed to move this beyond a real policy-wonk, you know, project, and to translate this into real terms with a real consequence for people outside the Beltway."[14]

As Ritchie's work became known among environmental activists, the breadth of organizations involved in it began to grow. In 1990 while working on strengthening food safety laws and attending congressional hearings on meat inspection and pesticide standards, including the Delaney Clause,[15] Lori Wallach of Public Citizen (a Washington, DC-based consumer advocacy organization) realized that strengthening the food law on carcinogenic substances would conflict with proposed Uruguay Round GATT rules. An article in a chemical manufacturing industry magazine revealed the seriousness and intensity of the potential threat, as she explained:

> And then, after three or four public hearings, there was an article in [an] industry publication I had to read called *Food Chemical News*, that literally reported a meeting of a large national association of chemical manufacturers that had a high-level administration official saying to the heads of all these chemical companies something like, "We really urge you not to launch a major fight right now, in trying to kill the Delaney Clause, because we'll be able to accomplish this through GATT and [the proposed U.S.-Mexico agreement], and be much more subtle, less politically damaging. Why, your fingerprints won't even be on this."[16]

Determined to investigate further, Wallach contacted Ritchie for help, convinced Public Citizen leaders to allow her to devote more time to the issue, and began attending NWF's working group meetings. At Wallach's urging, Public Citizen joined the emerging NGO debate about the social welfare consequences of trade liberalization policy, and ultimately helped spearhead the anti-NAFTA struggle. Thus even at this early stage new relationships among organizations that were differentially positioned politically emerged—all were outside of the trade policy field, but had greater or lesser degrees of grassroots resources and influence within the legislative field.

Intermittent Labor-Environmental Alliances prior to NAFTA

Although the leaders of environmental organizations began to think about the impact of trade on the environment during the late 1980s, it would take NAFTA to propel them into more formal working alliances with labor unions. Prior to NAFTA, interactions between labor unions and the environmental movement were at times contentious. It is a popular misconception that relations between labor unions and environmentalists have been consistently conflictual (Dewey 1998; Kazis and Grossman 1982; Mayer 2009; Obach 2004). Although conflicts occurred, and often captured media attention, cooperation has also been important, though less visible. According to Dewey, labor organizations and union members "demonstrated relatively strong support for many environmental initiatives prior to 1970" and played a significant role in garnering widespread public awareness of issues—particularly among the working class—in the environmental movement of the 1960s (1998:45). The interests of the labor and environmental movements are not inherently antithetical. Historically, however, they have not completely coincided. As Obach notes, for movements "in which there are some overlapping and some conflicting interests, predicting intermovement ties becomes more difficult" (2004:8). A brief history of labor-environmental interactions helps situate the different areas of issue overlap that emerged prior to NAFTA and provides a more accurate picture of the complex relationship between organized labor and environmentalists.

Although early conservationist efforts are often seen as the precursor to the environmental movement, the work of public health and labor activists also laid the foundation for environmental mobilization, particularly in the workplace (Gottlieb 2005:35). Indeed at the turn of the twentieth century well before the environmental movement began, labor and public health activists worked to eliminate hazardous substances in the workplace and from the broader environment. They also launched a radical critique of labor practices, which paved the way for the implementation of reform agendas and anti-sweatshop legislation (Gottlieb 2005:102).

Industrial illness was on the rise in the 1920s and 1930s (Rosner and Markowitz 1987); however combating it was hindered by a lack of information about its prevalence (Mayer 2009:29). By the late 1960s, medical discoveries linking hazardous work conditions to health outcomes helped bolster workplace activism (Mayer 2009). The United Mine Workers (UMW) helped pass the Occupational Safety and Health Act (OSHA) of 1970. Workers were not only involved in issues of public health as it pertained to work environments, but also in issues of public health that affected their communities. Unions raised concerns about the potential hazards of chemicals released into the environment; both the Clean Air Act of 1970 and the Clean Water Act of 1972 passed with the support of organized labor. Autoworkers pioneered working class engagement with environmental concerns in Michigan, pushing for the creation of more outdoor recreational space in the urban environment, the conservation of natural resources, and pollution control (Montrie 2008). The UAW sponsored the first Earth Day in 1970.

Environmentalists have also supported labor unions and workers' rights. In 1973 when the Oil, Chemical, and Atomic Workers International Union (OCAW) called a strike and launched a national boycott against a major oil company over workplace health and safety issues, eleven leading environmental organizations immediately pledged their support (Gottlieb 2005; Obach 2004). Environmental organizations also supported OCAW members during a conflict with a German chemical corporation. In 1984 the company reduced wages and benefits, fired 3,700 employees, and tried to undermine the union. When negotiations ended in a lockout, the OCAW waged a national campaign against the company, claiming that it showed little concern for workers' health and safety, and for the local environment. The OCAW argued that the union's presence ensured greater safety and cleaner operations, reducing the impact on the surrounding environment (Mayer 2009). The resolution of the dispute depended upon the involvement of environmentalist organizations, including the Sierra Club, Greenpeace, and the German Green Party, which united with the OCAW around health and environmental issues to ultimately win the battle against the company (Minchin 2003).

Although labor and environmental activists found common ground intermittently up until the 1980s, they also came into conflict. By the mid-1970s the environmental activism of key unions such as the UAW declined or ceased (Montrie 2008:93). Concerned that stricter emissions standards would adversely affect workers' jobs, the UAW split with environmentalists and other unions to oppose the Clean Air Act of 1970, and again in 1977 when the act was amended to incorporate stricter standards and a wider scope. The UMW strongly opposed 1990 amendments creating provisions on acid rain.

Beginning in the 1970s environmentalists' struggle to preserve forests and certain species such as the spotted owl in the Pacific Northwest pit them against workers in the timber industry—ten thousand of whom lost their jobs due to forest preservation measures. Some more radical environmentalists gained widespread media attention for their extreme tactics, which included blocking trucks and sabotaging logging equipment. The clash was popularly interpreted as a class war—the result of the incongruent interests of working-class loggers and middle-class environmentalists (Obach 2004). These controversies crystallized for the public a "labor versus environment" discourse and "shaped the perception that blue-collar workers are made to pay the price for environmental protection" (Obach 2004:57).

As this brief history shows, the relationship between environmentalists and labor unions prior to NAFTA is more complex than is usually presented in the media. Some scholars attribute the conflicts among the two groups to class divisions[17] (Rose 2000; Samuel 2009), others emphasize the effects of broader political and economic conditions and institutional pressures (Mayer 2009; Obach 2004; Stevis 2002), and still others point to the organizational structures of the movements themselves (Brulle and Jenkins 2008; Obach 2004). It is clear, however, that in the decades prior to NAFTA conflict often emerged when environmental regulations or protection threatened jobs. As the next chapters show, although potential job loss was a key component of unions' opposition to NAFTA, it did not stymie their efforts to build alliances with environmentalists. Indeed for the first time they found enough common ground to develop a discourse linking both labor and environmental rights to trade *and* to move beyond intermittent coalitions. The alliances the labor and environmental movements formed in response to NAFTA laid the foundation for a long-term relationship that ultimately persisted long after the NAFTA battle ended (see Kay 2015).

The Beginning of Labor-Environmental Convergence: Maquiladoras

The framing transformation that preceded labor-environmental alliances during NAFTA's negotiation had its roots in northern Mexico along the U.S. border as changes in direct foreign investment and the international rules governing trade between the two countries shifted the policy interests of domestic nonstate actors on both sides of the border. In 1965, the Mexican government decided to boost the economy by introducing an export-oriented assembly industry program that allowed foreign companies to build assembly plants (known as maquiladoras) in staggering numbers along the U.S.-Mexico border.[18] Items 806 and 807 of the Tariff Schedule of the United States allowed goods assembled in these border plants in Mexico with a certain share of U.S. components to be imported into the United States with duty paid only on the value added (Sklair 1993). The plan resulted in increased trade and integrated production. Total U.S. imports saw a tenfold increase between 1970 and 1987, surging from $40 billion to $400 billion, while imports under 806/807 "increased more than thirty-fold, from about $2 billion to over $68 billion" (Sklair 1993:11). Many high-tech manufacturing plants in Mexico proved to be as productive and therefore as competitive as their U.S. and Japanese counterparts (Shaiken 1990, 1994), providing an additional incentive for companies to take advantage of 806/807. By 1988 the program included approximately 1,500 factories and employed more than 350,000 workers (Hufbauer and Schott 1992).[19]

A number of key U.S. manufacturers shifted a percentage of their productive capacity to northern Mexico, transferring primary production to Mexican plants and using U.S. sites for final assembly and warehousing. By 1991, more than half of the largest one hundred U.S. companies operated maquiladoras. The rise of the maquiladora system profoundly affected the organization of production for the U.S. market in industries such as electrical and electronic goods, textiles and apparel, furniture, automobiles, and transportation equipment (Hufbauer and Schott 1992). Although U.S. companies also moved production to other countries, the rapid increase in maquiladoras signaled both the integration of northern Mexico into the U.S. manufacturing sector and an explicit competitive strategy of low labor costs through low wages and weak worker protections.

In Mexico, real wages for manufacturing workers fell precipitously during the 1980s, plunging 40 percent from 1982 to 1988 (Shaiken 1995:26). And wage rates in maquilas actually compared unfavorably with rates in other Mexican manufacturing plants; hourly compensation in maquiladora plants in 1985 averaged 276 pesos, compared to 538 pesos in non-maquiladora plants (Hufbauer and Schott 1992).[20] Maquilas operate under an industrial relations system of "a highly controlled labor movement and few other alternatives"; only 10–20 percent of maquiladora factories were unionized, and most that were unionized were run by the Institutional Revolutionary Party (PRI)-controlled Confederation of Mexican Workers (CTM) (Shaiken 1995:26).[21] Workers attempting to organize independent unions faced intimidation, threats, and even violence.

By the 1980s the rapid expansion of production sites by U.S. firms to the Mexican border began to alter the balance of power between management and unions in the United States. Workers faced layoffs as plants moved to Mexico, and companies used threats of plant movement to reduce wages and benefits (Bronfenbrenner 1997). As these forces coalesced, they elevated the importance of international trade and investment policy and agreements for U.S. unions, which were increasingly disadvantaged at the bargaining table. Although the policy agendas of manufacturing unions had included trade for decades, their international work was generally separate from and subordinate to domestic activities related to collective bargaining, working conditions, and worker safety. As journalist David Brooks, the U.S. correspondent for the progressive Mexican daily newspaper *La Jornada* explained:

> There was a growing realization among very few people in the labor movement, but still very important ones, that the process of economic integration, . . . [was] all of a sudden affecting in a direct way domestic interests of labor—everything from runaway shops to how you negotiated a contract. Where ten years before that, in the early 80s or something, the third thing on the bargaining table would be by the company to move a percentage of production to Mexico, and by the end of the 80s, it was the first thing on the table. All of these things all of a sudden started having real consequences on membership, on contracts, on all aspects, and forced what had been relegated before to the international departments [to become] of pivotal interest to people involved in domestic policy. And so it was actually taken away to a large extent from the international folk who had kept sort of a separate universe.[22]

Labor activists who focused on domestic issues found themselves profoundly and fundamentally affected by economic changes made possible through rules established in the trade policy field.

Increased economic activity across the U.S.-Mexico border also had non-economic or extra-economic consequences by straining the environmental, health, and public infrastructure of the border region. A dramatic increase in factories in northern Mexico brought large numbers of workers to the area.[23] The inadequate infrastructure resulted in insufficient wastewater treatment, unsafe drinking water, and poor living conditions (Pastor 1992). U.S. companies operated under more lax environmental, health, and safety controls than they did in the United States, which led to problems on both sides of the border. Water contamination, air pollution, and the inadequate disposal of hazardous waste affected the health and well-being of Mexican and U.S. border residents. At least half of U.S. maquiladoras generated hazardous waste that was not usually disposed of properly (Kopinak 1993).[24] Activists on both sides of the border had difficulty ascertaining the health risks plants posed because Mexico did not have a right-to-know law.[25] And maquiladora workers generally faced long hours for little pay without the ability to organize for better working conditions.

The situation on the border revealed the linkages between labor and environmental problems for a growing cadre of activists who increasingly saw that their solutions required advocacy across issue areas and across borders. It thus helped catalyze new and somewhat overlapping advocacy networks among them. Their collective response began in 1988 when key activists and organizations in the United States and Mexico hatched a plan to bring together civil society organizations in the United States and Mexico (and later Canada) to discuss North American economic integration. Yearly Mexico-U.S. Dialogos (Dialogos) exchanges, as they were called, included official and independent Mexican unions, U.S. and Canadian labor unions, environmental organizations, farming groups, and human rights activists, among others.

Dialogos was the earliest trinational group to deal with the perils of regional economic integration, and it intensified awareness among environmental and labor activists about each other's work along the border. Evidence of issue overlap quickly appeared in key organizations. The AFL-CIO, for example, ran stories in its newspaper *AFL-CIO News* detailing the environmental problems of maquiladoras.[26] And in 1989 the AFL-CIO trade department produced a report titled "The Maquiladoras: The Hidden Cost of Production South of the Border" that highlighted and examined environmental problems in the factories, including toxic poisoning, the lack of adequate wastewater facilities, pollution of water supplies, toxic dumping, and the denial of fundamental health and safety protections for maquiladora workers.[27] AFL-CIO representatives on the ground who were involved in local grassroots organizing against plant malfeasance, and their new contacts in local environmental organizations (such as Arizona Toxics Information, the Border Ecology Project, and the Texas Center for Policy Studies) provided the majority of the information in the report. These local organizations emerged in the 1980s to address environmental degradation and sustainable development in the border area. They conducted research and public education campaigns, advocated specific policy changes, and pushed for full public disclosure and participation concerning the environmental consequences of border plants. They also foregrounded the need for coordinated, transnational action.

Labor-environmental issue overlap became institutionalized in 1989 when forty environmental, labor, and religious organizations formed an informal alliance that became the Coalition for Justice in the Maquiladoras (CJM). CJM focused on improving conditions for maquiladora workers in the factories and in their communities by establishing a code of conduct for maquiladora industries and pushing for independent unionization, higher health and safety standards, and increased wage levels.[28] Many progressive Mexican organizations and even some U.S. organizations were wary of joining the CJM because of the AFL-CIO's participation; the labor federation's history of anticommunist activities (particularly in Latin America),[29] and tendency to employ racist rhetoric and policies to scapegoat foreign workers and immigrants for job losses in the United States concerned potential partners. According to Browne and Sims (1993), at least one "U.S. group turned down the Coalition's invitation to join for fear of damaging its working relations with Mexican counterparts."[30] A Mexican union leader described the position of some Mexican labor activists: "The work with maquiladoras was difficult because many people didn't want to work with American coalitions."[31] To assuage reluctant partners, AFL-CIO representatives subsumed the federation's role as the labor movement leader and reached out to groups wary of their dominance and international Cold War reputation. An AFL-CIO official instrumental in creating CJM explained how he tried to win over potential partners by confronting the federation's problematic past and articulating a commitment to change:

> I played a major role in building the Coalition and going out and meeting with organizations and encourag[ing them] to join this Coalition in 1989, '90, '91. But when I would go and talk to groups, I would say look . . . I realize the AFL-CIO has a terrible history of what I think is certainly bordering on a racist attitude towards Mexican workers and we have this tremendous history in terms of our international involvement in Latin America, which is deplorable. And there is a commitment to developing a program which is a departure from the past and that we need to develop a program that educates our members about the need to work with brothers and sisters, workers in Mexico, in order to fight a common enemy. And that's how people were willing to join a coalition in which the AFL-CIO played a major role. . . . I saw a need that in order to do this work it was necessary to be self-critical of the AFL-CIO, and in order to build this work that that was necessary. And it happened. So I think . . . that's the position that ultimately the AFL-CIO took, in support of that kind of approach.[32]

The role key AFL-CIO activists played on the border was critically important in linking labor to environmental concerns and building bonds of trust with small local environmental organizations.

Setting the Stage for the NAFTA Struggle

In the decades prior to NAFTA's introduction, elites within the trade policy and legislative fields successfully liberalized trade policies and largely faced little opposition to this approach at home. By the mid and late 1980s, elites within Canada and Mexico had also changed their stance—some albeit reluctantly—on trade with the United States. Simultaneously, the broader Washington Consensus policy agenda in which free trade was partnered with the roll back of capital controls and investment and financial regulation, establishment of new protections for intellectual property and foreign investors, privatization and deregulation of the service sector and budget austerity—was increasingly embraced by many in the trade policy and legislative fields. Ironically this constellation of pro-free-trade, pro-neoliberal forces that swept across the continent and broadened the scope of trade policy to include these non-tariff related provisions, helped constitute a new set of actors with a stake and interest in the development of trade policy in the United States. As North American economic integration moved forward and with the 1986 launch of the Uruguay Round—which also broke from the past GATT rounds to include non-tariff issues in trade pacts—and as negotiators expanded the scope of their authority deeper into domestic law, the stakes for these new actors became even higher.

The expansion of the scope of what was included in trade negotiations and thus the constitution of new actors affected by trade policy in the United States was necessary but not sufficient to develop a new social movement centered on fair trade. Indeed a new fair trade movement required the imagination and dedication of activists who worked to bring together representatives from disparate sectors. The nascent networks they constructed in the 1980s helped develop the discursive foundation for an environmental-labor rights linkage and became the building blocks through which mobilized coalitions fought for fair trade during the NAFTA battle and beyond.

4

Politicization and Framing

LINKING ENVIRONMENTAL AND LABOR RIGHTS

THE POLITICAL WRANGLING over fast-track began immediately after President Bush announced on September 25, 1990, his intention to negotiate a trade agreement with Mexico.[1] In the early 1990s when the NAFTA battle began, both labor and environmental activists had to look outside of the trade policy field in an effort to influence the negotiating principles of its key negotiators. Although labor unions maintained positions as official government advisory group members in the trade policy field, and their fair trade frame linking trade and labor rights was acknowledged in it, they were nevertheless marginalized by negotiators. Environmental organizations had no role in the trade policy field at all, and the conceptual linkage between trade liberalization and environmental degradation did not exist within it. Indeed when NAFTA was introduced it was generally assumed that it would pass with minimal resistance and any opposition would come from labor representatives and their congressional allies.

Both labor unions and environmental organizations had influence in the legislative field, however, and Congress had a critical point of leverage over U.S. trade policy—it had the power to extend or revoke the president's fast-track authority. Although the fast-track grant passed by Congress in 1988 had a five-year term, it included a standard provision allowing any member of Congress to introduce a resolution in 1991 to cut short the fast-track delegation halfway through that term. This leverage point between the legislative and trade policy fields created an opening for grassroots activists to try to change the rules in the latter; by working with congressional allies, they could impact the negotiating positions of officials in the trade policy field.

The two strategic hurdles environmental activists and their congressional allies faced throughout negotiations were enormous: first, there was no discursive linkage between trade and environmental rights or protections. They therefore had to get actors in the legislative field to recognize and include environmental issues in the trade debate. This effort would be easier if they worked with labor activists to develop an oppositional frame against NAFTA that linked labor and environmental rights and served as the ideological foundation for building a groundswell of opposition in the grassroots politics field that could be leveraged into the legislative field.

Second, if they succeeded in expanding the trade discourse in the legislative field, they had to figure out a way to apply pressure on the trade policy field so that negotiators would recognize and include environmental protections in the trade agreement itself. This was no easy task because negotiators drew a firm line in the sand as the debate began: they stated clearly and unequivocally that environmental issues had no place in NAFTA's negotiation. In addition, environmental negotiating objectives could only be added at key moments. There was no mechanism to add them to Congress's fast-track authority delegation, for example, because the resolution's language was preset in the statute and only could terminate fast-track, not change its terms.

In this chapter, we explore how environmental activists tackled the first hurdle by utilizing framing strategies to legitimize environmental critiques of trade liberalization and then to construct an expanded labor-environmental rights frame with labor activists that strengthened both movements' anti-NAFTA message. We look at how anti-NAFTA organizations built their coalition within the grassroots politics field and promulgated the new labor-environmental rights frame across a wide spectrum of organizations within it. We then examine how environmentalists dealt with the second hurdle by using their alliances with other members of the anti-NAFTA coalition and members of Congress to gain legitimacy and concessions in the trade policy field.

Constructing a New Frame in the Grassroots Politics Field

To build a case against NAFTA, activists had to construct a way to frame trade issues that would resonate with the public as well as key members of Congress, and would also unite the perspectives of disparate and often antagonistic grassroots organizations. They would also have to make concrete the effects of agreements usually discussed in abstract and highly technical language. The challenge they faced was significant; activists had to get average people to care about international trade policy, an issue that generated almost no public interest before. And they had to rally labor and environmental activists so that they would be willing to mobilize around it, commit scarce resources to it, and even engage in disruptive action. They had to politicize trade policy for the first time since WW II.

The opportunities for changing frames in the legislative field were considerable, however, because fair trade was already a powerful oppositional frame in the field. Pushed primarily by labor unions in the decades prior to NAFTA, it centered on national economic interest and the promotion of a level economic playing field for U.S. unions and industries against foreign competitors. It focused on job loss and protecting U.S. workers from companies that moved abroad, thereby eliminating high-paying blue collar jobs and undermining unions. Although the legitimacy of the fair trade frame was well established, opponents often attacked its focus on jobs and labor rights as protectionist. And progressive activists, including some environmentalists, derided its overly self-interested nationalist stance.

To change the dominant framing of trade was a formidable task. Challenging existing symbolic framing involves "collective framing" work, in which actors mobilize a new consensus around a modified or broader understanding of policy concerns and possible outcomes (Snow and Benford 1992; Klandermans 1988). A collective action frame "is an interpretive schemata that simplifies and condenses the 'world out there' by selectively punctuating and encoding objects, situations, events, experiences and sequences of actions within one's present or past environment" (Snow and Benford 1992:137). Collective framing work involves constructing meaning; it allows political entrepreneurs to accentuate and name grievances, construct larger frames of meaning, and draw new connections around which new coalitions can be built (see Klandermans 1988; Snow and Benford 1988, 1992; Melucci 1989; Tarrow 1994; McAdam, Tarrow, and Tilly 2001).

Such coalition building can be limited to actors within a particular field, or it can extend more broadly across fields. With NAFTA it encompassed multiple fields, as activists targeted decision-makers in both the legislative and trade policy fields to promote an expanded array of trade concerns. But activists also worked in the grassroots politics field to pressure political elites to modify their support for trade liberalization. At different points during the negotiation, the construction of an expanded labor-environmental rights frame helped link organizations by giving coherence to the coalitional participation of groups with differing agendas, levels of engagement, and philosophical outlooks. Labor and environmental activists were at the front lines of the discursive struggle.

Building a Coalition to Combat NAFTA within the Grassroots Politics Field

The first to actively sound a warning and organize a broader mobilization among NGOs against the free trade agreement were Canadian activists who had fought against CUSFTA—even though Canada was not involved in the proposed negotiations at the time. In October 1990, a contingent of Canadian activists went to Mexico to stir up interest among local labor, environmental, and human rights activists. Then, in November, Canadian representatives met activists from U.S. organizations, including the ILRF, environmental working groups, and the IATP.[2]

At the meetings, the Canadians laid the groundwork for the establishment of a North American network of NGO activists focused on trade issues that would operate in both the grassroots politics fields in each country and in the legislative field in the United States. Participants realized how important and politically charged the negotiations would be, and that they provided an opportunity to build common interests among progressive activists across the continent.[3] Canadian activists' prior mobilization against CUSFTA through the Action Canada Network (ACN)—created specifically to fight the free trade agreement—became the model for the Mexican and U.S. coalitions' development and organizational structure, which led to the creation in the United States of Mobilization on Development, Trade, Labor and the Environment (MODTLE),[4] and the Mexican Action Network on Free Trade (RMALC). At the U.S. meeting, representatives also proposed a trinational, cross-sectoral congressional forum on the effects of trade liberalization on social and environmental welfare.

The development of informal networks in turn created multiple "discursive nodes" that enabled a further elaboration and dissemination of an expanded perspective on trade policy among NGO activists. At the center of these nodes were: (1) D.C.-based and border environmental organizations that worked collectively to establish the legitimacy of assessing trade policy in terms of its environmental consequences; (2) the AFL-CIO, which disseminated position papers and talking points among labor unions; and (3) an anti-NAFTA coalition (herein referred to collectively as the anti-NAFTA coalition) made up of a wide variety of constituencies (e.g., consumer, farmer, etc.) that brought together national and local labor and environmental organizations through large umbrella networks, including the FTC (which focused on grassroots organizing), MODTLE (which functioned as a think tank and focused on research and transnational mobilization with counterparts such as RMALC and the ACN), and the Citizen Trade Watch Campaign (CTWC)[5] (which focused on DC lobbying and included industrial unions, key members of the family farm movement, and consumer and environmental groups).[6] Figure 4.1 details these networks during the fast-track fight and also provides information on the major labor unions and environmental organizations that coordinated activity along sectoral lines—some of which simultaneously participated in the anti-NAFTA coalition.

It is important to emphasize that not only is framing work rarely coordinated from a single, unitary point (Melucci 1988), but it is also rarely completely uniform. Framing occurs both through the explicit collaboration among organizations in crafting a condensed interpretive schema and through the discursive output of individual organizations that may produce their own collective action frames or further reduce, refine, and adapt the encoded frames established by others. Because these groups neither possessed identical values nor were equivalently positioned within the hierarchies of the trade policy and legislative fields, they inevitably focused on or highlighted different aspects of the new labor-environmental rights frame.

Greening Trade Discourse

Before labor and environmental rights and protections could be coalesced into a coherent frame, activists had to construct a linkage between trade and environmental issues centered on a critique of environmental degradation in relationship to trade. Environmental sociologists and prominent political theorists have characterized environmentalism as an "ascendant social force" (Buttel 1997:50)[7] that fills a vacuum left by the decline of the labor movement and social-democratic politics in the post-Fordist era, and described a "greening" of left political and cultural movements (see Beck 1992; Giddens 1994; Buttel 1997; DeLuca 1999).[8] Although their

CITIZEN TRADE WATCH CAMPAIGN (CTWC)

(D.C. Lobbying)
Public Citizen
American Federation of State, County and Municipal Employees (AFSCME)
United Food and Commercial Workers International Union (UFCWU)
FOE
National Family Farm Coalition
National Farmers Union
Sierra Club
ACTWU
ILGWU
IAM
IBT
CWA
IUE
UAW
Community Nutrition Institute
National Consumers League

FAIR TRADE CAMPAIGN (FTC)
(Grassroots Network)
IATP
Jobs with Justice
Clean Water Action
Pesticide Action Network
Industrial Labor Union Locals
Local Environmental Groups

MOBILIZATION ON DEVELOPMENT, TRADE, LABOR AND THE ENVIRONMENT (MODTLE)
(International Network)
ILRF
Economic Policy Institute
Institute for Policy Studies (IPS)
United Methodist Church
DGAP
UE
NWF
(Linked with RMALC and ACN)

ENVIRONMENTAL ORGANIZATIONS[1]

National Wildlife Federation
Natural Resources Defense Council
World Wildlife Fund
Nature Conservancy
National Audubon Society
League of Conservation Voters
Defenders of Wildlife
Environmental Defense Fund
Sierra Club
Friends of the Earth
Border Environmental Project
Arizona Toxics Information
Texas Center for Policy Studies

NATIONAL LABOR ORGANIZATIONS[2]

AFL-CIO
ACTWU
ILGWU
IUE
AFSCME
IBEW
IAM
IBT
CWA
UFCW
United Steelworkers of America
UAW

[1] With the exception of the Border Environmental Project, Arizona Toxics Information, and the Texas Center for Policy Studies, the organizations listed are DC-based. The three non-national organizations are located on the border with Mexico and collaborated with national environmental organizations in the formation of environmental policy positions that would affect the border region. Bold signifies organizations chosen to participate on USTR advisory committees.
[2] This list includes unions affiliated with the AFL-CIO that were most involved in the NAFTA fight. The UE was at the center of the struggle but is not affiliated with the AFL-CIO.

FIGURE 4.1 Coalitions and Networks during the Fast-Track Fight

arguments tend to underemphasize the heterogeneity and overemphasize the efficacy of the environmental movement,[9] the greening concept applies aptly to the development of a new labor-environmental rights frame during the NAFTA struggle: the frame represented a true greening of trade discourse. Not only were environmental issues linked for the first time to U.S. trade policy within the field itself, but activists also used an environmental lens to filter and legitimate other social welfare claims as they relate to trade.

Environmentalists have long questioned the optimistic assumption that economic development is inherently progressive, and criticized the forces of economic growth, capital accumulation, and industrial development.[10] Disagreements exist between environmentalists who believe that sustainable economic development is possible and those who argue that the "treadmill of production"[11] inevitably leads to environmental degradation. But it is a widespread environmental critique that unfettered market forces lead to environmental externalities that aren't handled well by the market itself. Environmental critiques of the effects of economic integration, global commodity chain production, and industrial development are difficult for neoliberal advocates to counter. The problems of excess carrying capacity and economic externalities lack the relativist claims of poverty and other social welfare issues. And although free trade supporters disagreed about the extent of the border problems and the best solutions, they found it difficult to argue that no problems existed, or that Mexicans alone created them.

This greening of trade discourse attained its most potent effect in the linkage of environmental and labor concerns by focusing on a downward harmonization of standards. The use of the maquiladora region as the embodiment and physical manifestation of a future under NAFTA, and the specter of pollution havens and a race to the bottom of environmental regulation provided the logical cornerstone for a larger argument about a decline in social welfare conditions more generally. The greening of trade discourse brought the imprimatur of scientific language and concepts, and an increasing legitimacy to an internationalist perspective that enabled activists to fight the protectionist label that had been attached to opposition in the trade policy field. As a Greenpeace activist explained in his congressional testimony: "Greenpeace believes that international trade is not an end in itself, that trade institutions must be accountable, and that trade must be subordinated to concern for the environment and to authentic, people-centered, socially equitable development."[12]

Perhaps more important, activists' use of environmental framing to elucidate an expanded critique of U.S. trade policy provided a potent wedge against neoliberal trade claims. An environmentalist critique exposed the contradictions of a laissez-faire approach. Early activists who formulated an environmental critique of trade extended arguments about the subordination of environmental needs to economic interests and the harm that results when collective environmental goods are left to the inexorable logic of market mechanisms alone.

An activist with Defenders of Wildlife (DOW) highlighted the linkages between trade and environmental dangers: "From an environmental standpoint, free trade should be a means to an end and not the end itself. We all have much work to perform if a successful environmental protocol is to be established. In order to realize the impressive potential of NAFTA, traditional rules of international trade must be reformed to fully and completely integrate environmental, conservation, health, and safety concerns."[13]

Activists thus highlighted how dictates of the market result in environmental damage that is external to market processes, and argued that economic integration in North America through NAFTA would enshrine a system of environmental degradation. The use of an environmental lens, particularly focused on conditions in the border region, highlighted market failures in terms that could be seen, tasted, and touched, and that affected both U.S. and Mexican citizens. Activists also used the environmental lens to criticize the structure of the trade policy field itself, arguing that institutional attributes designed to promote trade liberalization as utilitarian were in fact undermining citizens' welfare for the benefit of corporate profit.

In contrast to labor, the lack of a self-interested constituency has often been viewed as a liability in mobilizing around environmental issues (Audley 1993). However the lack of such a constituency combined with the universality of environmental claims was a source of rhetorical strength in the development of the new labor-environmental rights frame. The widespread public support for environmental issues prior to NAFTA's introduction also provided the frame a receptive audience. In 1989, 66 percent of Gallup poll respondents said they were "extremely concerned" about the pollution of sea life and beaches, and 50 percent extremely concerned about air pollution. In 1992, during the early stages of NAFTA's negotiation, the Gallup organization classified approximately 20 percent of Americans as hard-core environmentalists, who called themselves strong environmentalists.[14]

For Labor, a More Progressive Trade Discourse

The greening of trade discourse emerged not simply out of the insertion of environmental organizations into the trade debate. Indeed labor unions and labor activists not officially allied with the labor movement or the anti-NAFTA coalition embraced the discursive linking of labor and environmental rights and highlighted environmental degradation on the border. Moreover unions' fledgling interactions with environmental organizations *and* more progressive labor activists working on the border and on international labor standards and rights helped shift the official labor movement toward a more progressive discourse on labor and trade.

This labor discourse expanded the decades-old fair trade frame (centered on a level economic playing field for U.S. unions and industries against foreign competitors) by adding a moral and internationalist component that emphasized the linkage among North America's workers and prioritized transnational solidarity (Kay 2005; 2011a; 2011b). The discourse had its roots in core values of the early labor movement. Indeed when it was formed in 1864, the International Workingmen's Association (or First International as it became known) articulated the need for a global working class movement and international solidarity. Progressive unionists and workers have invoked this core value since the nineteenth century during different struggles, including activists working on international labor standards in the decades prior to NAFTA's introduction. But a new generation of labor activists with an international focus synthesized these older frames with the emerging focus on the shared cross-border problems stemming from trade liberalization forces.

For some within the AFL-CIO and its affiliates, the adoption of a more progressive discourse reflected instrumental concerns that focusing solely on jobs would alienate the public and potential allies. But for others, many of whom had participated in the civil rights movement, the farm workers' struggle, and various Latin American solidarity movements, the decision reflected moral concerns that scapegoating foreign workers contradicted the supposed values of an international labor movement. By 1990, many of these civil-rights-trained leaders had assumed positions of power within unions, replacing cold warriors or mitigating their influence (Voss and Sherman 2000). Their impact on adopting a more progressive labor discourse during the NAFTA struggle was therefore quite significant.

But perhaps even more historic were their efforts to put the discourse into practice by building relationships with Mexican unions, particularly independent unions not affiliated with the government's ruling party. Although North American unions had contact with each other for decades prior to NAFTA through various institutions and organizations (e.g., the World Federation of Trade Unions, the International Confederation of Free Trade Unions, and international trade secretariats, among others), these interactions were not equitable, were not based on efforts to create and nurture long-term programs based on mutual interests, and usually only involved union leaders and elites.[15] Moreover the AFL-CIO's questionable anticommunist activities and some affiliates' tendency to blame foreign workers and immigrants for the loss of "American" jobs, tainted relations among North American unions.[16] When asked about the AFL-CIO's involvement in transnationalism prior to NAFTA, a leader in the federation's international department explained:

> Basically there was nothing, or very little before NAFTA. The AFL was involved with the Confederation of Mexican Workers[17] and worked mostly through the International Labor Organization on issues not related to the U.S. or Mexico, but on other Latin American countries, problems. . . . The transnational activities that existed prior to 1990 were not really linked to national unions, but rather were carried out by progressive locals, or dissident northern movements, and did not involve long-term relationships usually.[18]

The relationships progressive union activists forged in the early 1990s were new and unique in North America, and they were bolstered by a more progressive labor discourse that prioritized cooperation over competition (Kay 2005; 2011a; 2011b).

Despite labor's more progressive discourse, its position on trade was repeatedly undercut rhetorically by utilitarian pro-free trade arguments. Free trade advocates—who acknowledged that there will always inevitably be losers under liberalized trade regimes—repeatedly attributed labor leaders' complaints about the effects of trade on their industries to self-interest, and criticized as protectionist their efforts to fight job losses. Environmentalists' new greened discourse on trade and the environment was more immune to the protectionist critique, but its novelty meant that it had little legitimacy and traction in the trade policy, legislative, and transnational negotiating fields.

A Fully Developed Labor-Environmental Rights Frame

As the NAFTA struggle unfolded, labor and environmental activists began to develop and rally the labor-environmental rights frame that had its origins in their collaborative work along the U.S-Mexico border. They twinned environmental and labor concerns through claims that incentives to move plants to Mexico as a result of less regulation could result in downward labor and environmental regulatory pressure in the United States. The linkage was a win-win for environmentalists and labor unions. For environmentalists, frame adaptation allowed them to piggy-back on labor influence; it heightened the political relevance of environmental issues by rhetorically linking them with the default oppositional trade frame, that is, a more progressive version of fair trade. As John Audley of the Sierra Club explained: "whether we were actively conscious of it or not, political power existed when we were, either loosely or formally [allied] with labor, in terms of legitimizing our work . . . I mean, our work to defeat NAFTA at the time was based largely in our ability to form a coalition with labor. A standing alone environment would not have beaten anything related to trade."[19] Labor activists used environmental concerns to expand the authority of their oppositional position and blunt criticisms of protectionism.

Together, environmental and labor activists, with their consumer, family farm, and faith group allies, fought the general protectionist label that had been attached to opposition in the trade policy and transnational negotiating fields. The rhetorical linking of labor and environmental arguments undercut this label in two ways. First, the linkage helped broaden and unite the anti-NAFTA coalition by expanding the pool of potential supporters of a new oppositional frame and increasing the constituencies for whom the coalition claimed to speak. The broadened trade discourse enabled activists to appeal to an extensive swath of national and local organizations that had not previously participated in trade policy debates. Such widespread appeal was crucial to activists' efforts to mobilize activity in the grassroots politics field to pressure actors in the legislative field. Moreover the concordance between labor and environmental discourse enabled legislators with different constituencies to take a stand in opposition to the agreement. This was particularly important for generally pro-labor members of Congress whose constituents might lose jobs to NAFTA; appropriating a greening discourse enabled them to avoid a protectionist slant to their arguments as they tried to derail or improve the agreement.

Second, the weakness of environmentalists politically became a substantial benefit to labor advocates rhetorically. The simultaneous bane and the strength of the environmental movement lies with a moral authority that comes from addressing issues that affect all citizens broadly without representing specific constituents. The vulnerability of labor activists to the charge of self-interest was moderated by the inclusion of environmental elements that transcended the traditional trade constituencies; environmental framing took the debate outside the realm of the purely economic. Suddenly, the bounds between who wins under liberalized trade and who loses became blurred. As then secretary-treasurer and future president of the AFL-CIO Tom Donahue emphasized, wage and labor rights concerns are more vulnerable to criticism of relativism, whereas environmental issues can clearly be measured with one yardstick: "When people look at wages in other countries, it's difficult to convey how low these wages actually are. Encephalitis horror stories people understand, because it's not relative. Environmental issues found greater resonance, even though I hate to admit that."[20]

As discussed in more detail later, however, two distinct groups of environmentalists split around labor-related issues. Although environmentalists generally agreed on the framing of environmental problems associated with the unregulated advancement of trade liberalization in the region, those participating in the anti-NAFTA coalition supported linking environmental concerns to labor, and those outside the coalition did not. The latter thus essentially acted as free riders within the legislative and trade policy fields; they benefited from the political influence of labor unions in threatening the passage of the agreement, while attempting to distance themselves from the protectionist label attached to labor. The remainder of this chapter examines how labor unions and environmental organizations utilized the newly formed labor-environmental rights frame during the initial stage of NAFTA's negotiation.

Part I: Rallying the Labor-Environmental Frame in the Legislative Field

During the period between the initial announcement of intent to negotiate NAFTA and the vote on fast-track, activists rallied the labor-environmental rights frame in a variety of contexts and venues. Labor unions and environmental organizations used the frame in the grassroots politics field in publications and outreach to members and affiliates, and in their media campaign directed at the general public. They also began to push the frame in the legislative field through lobbying and in congressional testimony. The NWF, for example, highlighted the potential environmental dangers of increased trade with Mexico in a position paper distributed on November 17, 1990, that discussed the impact of the maquiladora operations on the border environment, "unregulated expansion" of foreign investment industries, the problems associated with shared water resources, expanded use of fossil fuels, and the additional extraction of natural resources more generally.[21] The position paper was the first by a national environmental organization to highlight the environmental consequences of unregulated maquiladora expansion in Northern Mexico. It provided technical and framing resources for congressional allies initially questioning the environmental dimensions of the proposed agreement.

Activists rightly criticized the secrecy of NAFTA's negotiations, but they used every opportunity for access. Despite the Bush administration's lack of interest in their input, they availed themselves of all institutional inroads to meet with USTR officials and submit formal comments. But the main venue to air their grievances, critiques, and suggestions was through a series of congressional hearings. Because the Democrats controlled both the House and the Senate and many committee chairs were critical of NAFTA, between May 21, 1990, and May 24, 1991 (prior to and then during fast-track negotiations), twenty congressional hearings were held on the free trade agreement—over one per month—and labor and environmental activists participated in all of them.

We analyzed all 143 testimonies provided by labor and environmental actors during the twenty congressional hearings testimony. The analysis centered on hearing testimony because it was possible to ensure all records had been obtained, and because the testimony was oriented to both trade policy and legislative field members. Analysis of the data compiled reveals the success of the labor and environmental linkage in the legislative field. Of the twenty hearings, fully 55 percent dealt with environmental and/or labor issues. The most significant finding is that 82 percent of hearings that dealt with environmental and/or labor issues addressed them *together*. Although none focused exclusively on environmental concerns, only 18 percent addressed labor issues alone. Labor and environmental rights quite quickly became the default oppositional frame in the legislative field, and the two issues became coupled conceptually. This is a remarkable finding given that the linkage between trade and environmental issues was a novel and controversial one at the time.

Activists' Testimony in Congressional Hearings

Although there was some variation in how activists deployed the labor-environmental rights frame depending on the topic of the hearing, the time period, and the particular committee, the frame developed early and remained relatively consistent throughout the initial year of the NAFTA debate and even beyond during NAFTA's negotiations. Content analysis of the hearings testimonies shows that key themes—maquiladora environmental and labor violations, and the threat to consumers from lack of regulation and oversight of health and safety standards—emerged to illustrate and support the labor-environmental linkage. Activists widely adopted these themes regardless of their active participation in the anti-NAFTA coalition, reflecting the widespread dispersion of the new frame.

The primary theme that coalesced labor and environmental issues utilized the maquiladora region as the embodiment of the long-term consequences of a potential unregulated free trade agreement, including poverty, health problems, dangerous working conditions, and environmental degradation along the border. A leader of the FTC explained his use of the maquiladora theme: "I wanted to make the border the focus for the conflict between the rhetoric of free trade and the reality of the maquilas and the myth that free trade led to prosperity and led to environmental improvements."[22] Border conditions crystallized in time and place a number of highly complex arguments about the relationship between developed and developing countries in trade regimes and downward harmonization of production standards. The border region provided, with graphic visual images and startling statistics, a concrete example of the effects of rapid and unregulated industrialization on producer and consumer nations.

Environmentalists and labor leaders argued that maquiladoras damaged the environment both directly through lax environmental controls, and indirectly through taxing the infrastructure and ecological balance of the region. They argued that because the United States and Mexico had different regulatory structures, economic integration would lead to a race to the bottom by providing incentives for governments to dismantle worker and environmental protections. An official with the NTC and the FTC testified:

> The Administration is blind to these problems because their trade and environmental policies are guided by ideologues who preach against the evils of government regulation, and who despise public accountability of private corporations. The Administration is simply not capable, on its own, of imposing the tough environmental regulations on U.S. corporations that are in Mexico, precisely because they want to avoid paying decent wages, provide worker safety protection, adopt sound environmental policies and—heaven forbid—pay their fair share of taxes.[23]

Labor leaders in particular used the possibility of moving to Mexico to evade environmental laws in the United States to highlight the far more common corporate practice of relocating to Mexico to reduce labor costs. The AFL-CIO quickly picked up the themes of the harmonization of environmental standards downward, environmental degradation on both sides of the border, and negative environmental consequences for Mexican workers. These themes are evident in the earliest AFL-CIO testimonies before congressional committees, and other unions employed them as the full-blown campaign developed. Mark Anderson, then director of the AFL-CIO's Task Force on Trade, captured the discursive linkage in his testimony:

> Beyond the question of wage differentials, the vast differences in regulatory structures and social protections cannot help but create serious difficulties for U.S. production. In one sense, the establishment of a U.S.-Mexico free trade area would be, in commercial terms, no different than if one drew a circle around the city of Chicago and said, for example, that inside that circle U.S. minimum wage or child labor laws wouldn't apply, occupational health and safety regulations need not be observed, workers compensation and unemployment insurance need not be paid, and environmental protection laws could be ignored. All these standards and others like them impose costs on U.S. producers. We as a nation, however, have decided those costs are necessary to improve the standard of living of all our citizens. In Mexico, there are no such costs to be borne.[24]

Anderson also described in detail the movement of Southern California's furniture industry to Mexico to avoid environmental laws, and a consulting company's advertisements touting the advantages of doing business in the Mexican border region without OSHA, Environmental Protection Agency (EPA), and Air Quality Restrictions.[25]

Labor activists often offered shocking imagery that was more graphic and less focused on the scientific language of environmentalism than the rhetoric used by environmental activists. They argued that corporations exploited maquiladora workers who were left impoverished and with little recourse to change their fate. Linking environmental and labor problems caused by maquiladoras also allowed labor and environmental activists to counter the pro-trade claim that trade liberalization inevitably leads to rising standards of living more generally.[26] While free trade advocates espoused win-win scenarios in which the more efficient allocation of capital resources resulted in improvements in the standard of living for all citizens, activists countered that not only was it possible to envision lose-lose alternatives, but also that concrete examples already existed at the border. An activist with Arizona Toxics highlighted in his congressional testimony the poor living standards along the border: "If public and occupational and environmental health in fact are not addressed in a free trade agreement as an integral part of that agreement, it seems to me that free trade does not mean a higher standard of living as we have heard proponents claim. But what it really means is a return to the Dickensian squalor of the early Industrial Revolution, much of which we already see on the border."[27]

Activists also attacked the popular assumption that consumers are the biggest winners in trade liberalization. They argued that consumers could be among its biggest losers: the dangers of unregulated pesticides and carcinogens and inadequate safety regulation far outweighed the money consumers might save by purchasing cheaper products. Activists argued that trade negotiators had expanded the scope of trade policy to such an extent that they would profoundly affect conditions outside the trade arena as it had traditionally been defined. As Lori Wallach and Tom Hilliard of Public Citizen explained:

> Environmental and consumer safety laws are not market mechanisms, but public health measures. The U.S. government has an inherent duty to protect consumers from poisonous substances, and that duty does not depend on the economic value of trade concessions offered by foreign countries. While trade agreements could have

beneficial effects for consumers by lowering prices and increasing competition, if such agreements also take away consumer safety and health protection or expose such laws to later challenge by trade courts, the bottom line is a net loss for consumers.[28]

They therefore constructed environmental externalities *and* deregulatory harm as new costs to consumers. Moreover they reversed the traditional economic reduction of citizens to cost-minimizing consumers and instead accentuated the importance of consumers as citizens. Thus activists opened up the trade discussion in the broadest sense by forcefully arguing that trade was not merely an issue of the bottom line. It was an issue with which a broad swath of consumers and environmentalists should be concerned. And it was an issue that more citizens should engage to ensure the government protected citizens' health and safety.

The portrayal of corporations as motivated by interests antithetical to the needs of ordinary citizens, consumers, and workers put a different spin on the traditional class rhetoric of the labor movement. To deny the class issue would be to negate or silence the anxiety of ordinary working Americans in a time of recession and economic uncertainty. The ability to broaden that message to incorporate a greater number of Americans enabled activists to build upon traditional frames of the labor movement without being limited by the demographics of the traditional labor base. Although workers' losses could always be offset by others' gains, reconstituting the majority as those protected by environmental regulations enabled activists to counter the utilitarianism at the root of free trade ideology.

Shifts in the Legislative Field, Intransigence in the Trade Policy Field

During congressional hearings and with the innovation of coalitional lobby visits to hundreds of members of Congress in which labor, environmental, consumer, family farm and faith groups jointly criticized NAFTA, activists made tremendous headway politicizing trade policy and constructing a labor-environmental rights frame that resonated in the legislative field. But trade policy officials made it clear from the beginning that they would not eliminate deregulatory or non-tariff related provisions that became known when a draft NAFTA text eventually leaked, and also would fight to limit the inclusion of labor and environmental issues in particular into the agreement. They also attempted to dissuade members of Congress from tying labor and environmental standards to it.[29] This position reflected the Bush administration's general perspective. As reported in *Inside U.S. Trade* in January 1991:

> The USTR official sought to dissuade the legislator from trying to press for expansion of the free trade agreement agenda to include labor and environmental issues, a congressional source said. The official noted that some progress in those areas was being made in other fora and indicated that the Administration did not believe Mexico would consent to discussing such issues within the framework of the FTA.[30]

The message was the same in the transnational negotiating field leading up to the fast-track fight. When asked by reporters the parameters of the negotiations, Mexican secretary of commerce and industrial development Jaime Serra Puche responded: "Environmental issues and investment in Mexico's oil industry will not form part of the free trade talks. . . ."[31]

The intersection between the trade policy and legislative fields, however, created a point of leverage where rules could be altered and alliances brokered across them. It provided a pressure point for activists in the United States who otherwise would have been shut out from the trade policy field. At this point, institutional channels were partially open only to union advisors on official USTR committees. Environmental, consumer, and other organizations did not have this access and therefore had limited information except when it was leaked. The Bush administration was statutorily required under fast-track to consult with various congressional committees, and to release an official statement of objectives and intent when it gave notice on the fast-track resolution. In a December 1990 letter to Rep. Don Pease, USTR Carla Hills tried to assure him that congressional members would have a voice in the process:

> As we proceed with our free trade initiative, we will continue our long-standing policy of consulting with the Congress and all our private sector advisors. These consultations are all the more critical in light of the "fast-track" approval procedures, because the Administration needs to ensure Congressional concerns are reflected throughout the negotiations. . . . we have kept the House Ways and Means Committee fully informed of our intentions and

have sought guidance every step of the way. My staff and I have already met several times with the Members and staff on the Committee. In addition, we have discussed the initiative with many others in the House and Senate. . . . I have made and will continue to make every effort to work with you and your colleagues on developing a trade policy that benefits our nation and our people. I want to reiterate that on this and all other trade issues, I welcome your advice.[32]

Hills also recognized in her letter the unique point of leverage across fields created by the need for congressional approval of fast-track authority.

By the time the fast-track battle unfolded, activists and their congressional allies had scaled a critical strategic hurdle by expanding the default understanding of the trade debate within the legislative field to include environmental and labor issues. What began as a seemingly hopeless effort gained traction leading up to the fast-track fight as activists used framing strategies to advance a new labor-environmental rights frame. This enabled environmental activists in particular to wield influence in the legislative field far beyond their resources or their position in the legislative influence hierarchy. By drawing upon environmental policy resources and preexisting alliances, and by piggybacking on labor's legislative strength, environmentalists succeeded in legitimizing the environmental critique of trade liberalization and transformed themselves into legitimate trade actors in the looming fast-track fight and subsequent NAFTA struggle.

Activists' second challenge was to gain legitimacy and concessions in the trade policy field in which they had no formal or official role, and demand the inclusion of environmental issues in the negotiations. They also hoped to eliminate any NAFTA provisions that undermined environmental protections and goals. Despite the USTR's promise to work with labor and environmental organizations, activists continued to face stiff opposition from the administration.

Part II: Demanding Legitimacy and Concessions in the Trade Policy Field

A battle over continuation of fast-track authority, which trade policy officials were relying on to facilitate NAFTA's passage, came up before negotiations had even begun. Once President Bush formally requested fast-track extension on March 1, 1991, Congress had sixty legislative days to determine whether to submit a resolution of disapproval, which would cut the 1988 delegation off mid-way. The need for trade policy field officials to ensure fast-track continued, quickly brought U.S. domestic politics to the fore, as Congress's rule-making authority provided a mechanism to force concessions in the trade policy field around NAFTA negotiations. The fast-track resolution Congress could deploy would not provide for changes to the legal negotiating objectives. It only could sunset fast-track. But, fast-track's explicit linkage to the prospects that the proposed free trade agreement would be passed catapulted discussion of the negotiating agenda out of the trade policy field and before a Congress controlled by Democrats. And key Democrats were increasingly wary of the Bush administration's NAFTA agenda and trade liberalization agenda more generally—and had the power to cut short trade pact approval procedures designed to facilitate trade liberalization.

The prerequisite of fast-track not being cut short gave Congress the opportunity to directly signal its win-set parameters for ratification to the administration. Because of the intersection between the legislative and trade policy fields, activists excluded from the trade policy field (specifically the USTR advisory system) could mobilize in the legislative field to influence trade policy outcomes. And new labor, environmental, and consumer allies could draw on different legislative networks to both expand influence within the legislative field and broker alliances across the trade policy field. In the case of NAFTA, then, the a priori ratification through a fast-track non-extension resolution created the circumstances for a rapid mobilization of nonstate actors potentially affected by the agreement. And it enabled members of the legislative field to thrust environmental issues into the debate and legitimize new trade actors at the outset; they signaled to trade policy officials that labor and environmental issues in particular needed to be addressed in order to ensure passage of the agreement.

Although the fast-track non-extension resolution option offered activists a unique and unexpected opportunity to inject themselves early on into the free trade agreement debate, it provided them and their legislative allies with a relatively short time frame in which to do so. To start with, a prospective fast track non-extension vote could only be allowed if a member of Congress introduced the exact required language authorizing a set period or the resolution would not be privileged and thus not subject to a vote. But introduction of such a resolution also required a sense that it could be passed because a lopsided vote in favor of continuation of fast-track delegation for its full 1988–1993 term would signal a lack of concern with the direction of NAFTA talks. They had to mobilize quickly.

Activists began to exploit institutional leverage points across the legislative and trade policy fields very soon after the October 1990 meeting with their Canadian counterparts. A month later on November 20, a loose grouping of U.S. environmental, labor, family farm, and human rights organizations[33] met to discuss challenging fast-track as a way to force legislative and trade policy field officials to include environmental and labor issues in the trade agreement. In an early coordinated effort, members of the Working Group on Trade and Environmentally Sustainable Development organized a trinational public forum titled "Opening Up the Debate" in January 1991.[34] The organizers designed the forum primarily for the staff of the pivotal House Ways and Means Committee, one of the key committees that straddles the legislative and trade policy fields.

The forum championed the elaboration of trade critiques to include environmental issues and used the network connections of some working group members to extend legislative alliances to others.[35] It featured speakers from Mexico, the United States, and Canada and included workshops on a wide range of social welfare concerns: human rights, health and safety, maquiladoras, immigration and labor mobility, transboundary pollution, child labor, consumer protection, social charters, agriculture, sustainable development, and debt relief. U.S. Congress representatives Marcy Kaptur and Terry Bruce moderated panels.

The event was a success both in terms of coalitional development and political impact; more than four hundred trade policy field actors attended the event.[36] Although most of the participating organizations (termed a "motley crew" by the *Wall Street Journal*, from which MODTLE later derived its name) lacked substantial political clout in the legislative field, they attracted notice. An organizer of the event explained the importance of the diversity of participants:

> Most of the people that attended were trade lawyers, who had a powerful interest in not opening up the trade debate. Members of the Ways and Means Committee, trade economists and others in the trade community such as [economist Jagdish] Bhagwati thought that any linkage of labor and environmental standards was an illegitimate intrusion—that it was disguised protectionism. It was strategically important to the coalition to keep the debate as open as possible to counteract the perception that they were

being protectionists, even though we were going to be accused of it anyway.[37]

The widespread turnout and diversity of participants helped generate further interest in trade issues and building of relationships with Mexican and Canadian activists among DC-based NGOs.[38] In the wake of the event, several members of Congress—some with key positions straddling the legislative and trade policy fields—expressed support for labor and environmental issues. Senator Max Baucus, the chair of the Finance Committee's Subcommittee on Trade, supported the inclusion of labor and environmental issues in negotiations, as did House Ways and Means member Rep. Robert T. Matsui. Senator Donald Riegle specified the need for markers of success, including a "very careful, specific laying down of labor and environmental standards," as lower standards could create an incentive for the movement of factories overseas.[39] Arizona congressman Jim Kolbe said in a House Ways and Means hearing: "As we move forward to negotiations, the environment is certainly the number one issue that I think will be on everyone's mind."[40] Even members of Congress broadly supportive of trade liberalization did not feel that environmental concerns fundamentally contradicted their trade goals.

Key legislators also turned to environmental organizations to obtain technical information, frame strategies concerning the agreement's potential problems, and lobby support.[41] For example, in February 1991 eighteen House members sent President Bush a letter making their support for the continuation of fast-track contingent on an environmental review of the agreement and assurances through action that "environmental concerns will be properly addressed in the proposed trade agreement" and that "the U.S. and Mexico must give great weight to the full range of environmental concerns during both negotiation and implementation of any trade agreement. . . ."[42] The letter reflected the NWF's November 1990 position paper on the environmental impact of U.S.-Mexican economic integration, particularly the environmental and public health hazards of maquiladoras. The NWF and Friends of the Earth (FOE) supported the letter. . . .[43]

Politically, the event signaled to those in the trade policy field that environmental issues could expand the scope of domestic debates on trade. As a staffer at Greenpeace commented: "There has been a real explosion of organizations outside the labor movement who have called for social and environmental protections in the trade deal." He went on to conclude that the forum and press conference following it had had some impact on the public stance of trade policy field officials:

> The Forum and the Feb 6 press conference seem to have had some impact, as the position of the US Trade Representative changed Feb 6 from "Environment & labor rights are not trade-related issues and will not be discussed in negotiating the FTA," to a more conciliatory "We will seriously consider the concerns of the labor and environmental lobbies." Could be nothing more than rhetoric. But some congressional offices are calling us for suggestions on how to frame proposals to include environmental concerns in the [free trade agreement]."[44]

The congressional reverberations from the forum also suggested a potential receptiveness among legislators to broker alliances in order to oppose a trade agreement without environmental protections. *Inside U.S. Trade* reported the difficult position the Bush administration was in, noting the coherence among activists from different sectors, and that some members of Congress had embraced the linkage of trade and social justice issues after the event. Congress's constitutional role in trade, combined with Democrats' control of both chambers, meant both policy and political leverage for change was possible. And members of the trade policy field worried about the implications for passage of a fast-track non-extension resolution. USTR Hills warned: "opposition groups [are] forming even as we speak . . . There are those who would be quite happy to take away our fast-track authority and in so doing cripple us."[45] Hills's concerns were warranted; after the forum event alliances quickly multiplied. At Public Citizen's Capitol Hill office a week later, environmental organizations that unequivocally opposed fast-track joined with labor unions, consumer, faith and family farm organizations, and a senior staffer of a senior House Democrat to discuss initiating a legislative campaign to actively challenge fast-track continuation.

Once Democratic representative Byron Dorgan introduced the nonextension resolution, the visibility and outspokenness of environmental and labor activists complicated the USTR's efforts to minimize their attempts to expand the scope of negotiating aims. The USTR suggested that its firm stand on excluding environmental and labor concerns might not be possible to maintain. As the upcoming fast-track cut off loomed in the House, officials in the trade policy field worried that ties between labor and environmental organizations could prevent their effort to negotiate the type of agreement they sought. They therefore used Bush's EPA head William Reilly as a conduit between environmental organizations and trade policy officials, hoping that they could be won over.[46] Reilly, former president of the WWF, pushed for the inclusion of environmental issues in the trade negotiations. He also initiated his own advisory group to develop policy recommendations to overcome conflicts between negotiators and environmentalists. Because it had no staff working on environmental issues, the USTR was forced to rely on the EPA's Office of Policy Planning and Evaluation and International Divisions.

According to his staff, Reilly saw the linkage between trade and the environment as a way to increase the political authority of the EPA.[47] Reilly developed a good relationship with USTR Carla Hills that allowed his staff to attend interagency meetings and offer advice to officials responsible for policy development. On February 19th, the eve before Hills testified before various congressional committees, she met privately with six environmental organizations, including NWF and FOE, to search for a compromise position.[48] Reilly's networks and alliances in the grassroots politics field increased his influence among trade policy officials seeking to mitigate environmental and trade linkages.

The next day on February 20th, Democratic members of the Senate trade committee invoked the labor-environmental rights frame when they forcefully questioned USTR Hills about the possible movement of U.S. plants to Mexico to take advantage of lax labor and environmental enforcement. During the House Ways and Means trade subcommittee hearing, they raised concerns about the viability of an agreement without environmental and labor protections.[49] In an effort to dissipate congressional concerns, the USTR quickly backed away from its initial position that environmental and labor concerns had no place in trade negotiations. Hills acknowledged a need to work with organizations concerned with environmental problems and labor standards. As reported in *Inside U.S. Trade*: "U.S. Trade Representative Carla Hills this week said it 'behooves' the Administration to reach out to groups that have expressed increasing concerns over environmental protection, labor standards and drug trafficking in Mexico and determine what is the best way to deal with these issues."[50] And on March 1, the day President Bush officially requested fast-track authorization, Hills further suggested that a concurrent environmental treaty with Mexico be explored.[51] Activists had finally created a wedge vis-à-vis the USTR, and they intended to exploit it. Their efforts prior to the fast-track vote left them well-positioned; U.S. negotiators in the trade policy field were now in danger of losing fast-track privileges and operating under greater negotiating constraints. They recognized that they had to make some concessions or risk losing fast-track, and activists' legitimation of the inclusion of environmental protections in the agreement ensured that they would.

Democratic Legislators Demand the Inclusion of Labor and Environmental Protections

As soon as President Bush requested fast-track authorization, activists stepped up pressure in the legislative field to demand labor and environmental protections in the agreement. Rep. Dorgan introduced a non-extension resolution, which guaranteed a privileged vote under fast-track rules. Democratic Whip David Bonior and Reps Marcy Kaptur and Duncan L. Hunter (a Republican) joined Dorgan in lending support for the resolution that would cut off fast-track for NAFTA. Within Congress, the most important players for fast-track's continuation were all members of the Democratic Party: House Ways and Means Committee Chair Dan Rostenkowski, Senate Finance Committee Chair Lloyd Bentsen, and House Majority Leader Richard Gephardt. As the heads of the two congressional committees directly responsible for oversight of trade, Rostenkowski and Bentsen were powerful and influential members straddling the legislative and trade policy fields. They also had created the 1988 fast-track legislation and had a history of supporting the trade agenda espoused by business interests. Although Gephardt did not have a direct role in trade policy formation, he maintained considerable influence over the votes of his party members in the legislature. As continuation of fast-track was more in question in the House than in the Senate, Rep. Gephardt's influence could affect the outcome.[52] Gephardt maintained a fair trade position and was a vocal critic of the administration's trade policies. He had a close alliance with the AFL-CIO, and was also a potential presidential candidate who tried to avoid a protectionist taint. Bonior and Kaptur were close to grassroots labor and environmental activists as well as national unions.

The fast-track positions of these three members of Congress reflected the growing division within the Democratic Party on trade issues. In contrast to Gephardt, Bentsen and Rostenkowski firmly supported trade liberalization and used their positions as participants in both the trade policy and legislative fields to broker a compromise between decision-makers in them. They searched for the least-restrictive means to satisfy congressional concerns and ensure fast-track continued. On March 7, 1991, in an effort to preempt Gephardt and establish a position that would likely win in the House, Rostenkowski and Bentsen wrote a letter to President Bush requesting that he create a trade policy action plan that responded to labor and environmental concerns.[53] They advised him to address "the disparity between the two countries in the adequacy and enforcement of environmental standards, health and safety standards and worker rights"—albeit in the most narrowly defined way by limiting the scope of discussion to worker retraining and environmental and labor standards (Cameron and Tomlin 2000:73). In an April 23 meeting with President Bush to discuss the potential action plan, Rep. Rostenkowski emphasized that the president would "have trouble passing" the final agreement if he reneged on his promise to provide comprehensive trade adjustment assistance to displaced workers.[54]

Rep. Gephardt sent a letter to the president on March 27th that outlined the conditions required for him to vote to continue fast-track, which mirrored the AFL-CIO's department of economic research talking points on the agreement and reflected the labor federation's general embrace of a full range of social and environmental welfare concerns in it, including labor and environmental protections.[55] Working with environmental organizations, Rep. Wyden compiled a set of environmental criteria laying out the minimum needed for the administration's action plan.[56] He favored a two-track program in which environmental issues directly related to NAFTA be handled in the trade talks themselves, while other bilateral environmental concerns be handled in parallel discussions. Wyden suggested that the plan include a pledge to document existing border problems and guarantee the inclusion of environmental leaders in the U.S. negotiating advisory groups. He also asked for independent and enforceable dispute mechanisms for handling ongoing environmental problems.[57]

Also in March, EPA chief Reilly brokered a private meeting between NWF president Jay Hair and USTR Hills, which led to NWF's submission to the USTR of a set of "sustainable development" principles that should be followed during negotiations.[58] NWF finally had direct access to a key official in the trade policy field. Among the NWF's demands was the creation of "an environmental negotiating group that would be part of the NAFTA talks."[59]

Divisions among Environmental Organizations

NWF's willingness to engage the USTR independently of the coalition reflected an increasing tension among environmental organizations with different perspectives on growth. "Pro-growth" environmental organizations believed economic growth had potential benefits for environmental protection by stimulating expenditures on environmental custodianship. In contrast, "adversarial" organizations opposed an economic growth model and viewed nonrenewable resources as finite and therefore compromised by unfettered economic activity and growth.[60] Audley differentiates between national environmental organizations that oppose an economic growth model and those that support it (1997:35). Figure 4.2, taken from Audley, ranks national environmental organizations involved in the NAFTA debates on the growth issue.

Although coalitional diversity can be a strength, it can also be a weakness because decision-makers can exploit differences to divide coalitions and sabotage coordinated activity (see Haines 1988:2 for a discussion of what he calls the "radical flank effect"). The philosophical differences among key environmental organizations on economic growth gave the USTR a wedge to exploit in dividing the coalition of organizations potentially opposed to fast-track continuation using environmental concessions. Moreover, the affinity between labor and environmental concerns increased the influence of potential swing environmental organizations. In the case of environmentalists, pro-growth organizations[61] profited from their affinity with labor groups and the labor-environmental rights frame without actually participating in a coalition with them. The affinity between environmental and labor claims provided them with political leverage in the legislative field, making them free riders that benefited from the new labor-environmental rights frame and the influence of labor. At the same time, however, they attempted to differentiate themselves substantively from the discourse of job loss and wage levels, associating such arguments with rhetorically weak protectionist claims. Representatives of

Spectrum of National Environmental Organizations[1]

More opposed to growth model			More supportive of growth model
Greenpeace Public Citizen Friends of the Earth	Sierra Club	Defenders of Wildlife National Audubon Society Natural Resources Defense Council	The Nature Conservancy Environmental Defense Fund National Wildlife Federation
	More Adversarial		More Accommodating

[1] This table comes from Audley (1997:35).

FIGURE 4.2 Environmental Organizations and Positions on Growth

four pro-growth organizations actually included statements in their congressional testimony that contradicted arguments labor unions made by
suggesting that NAFTA would create new jobs and decrease poverty.

NWF's meeting with USTR Hills signaled an early shift in its position
and strategy. After receiving assurances from Hills that environmental
concerns about the agreement would be addressed, NWF leaders decided
the best way to influence the USTR and other trade policy officials was
to separate themselves from labor activists (see Audley 1997). They focused on using key allies in the legislative field to achieve their trade aims,
gambling that by decoupling environmental and labor issues the USTR
would be more receptive to environmental issues than to labor concerns.
In the month immediately after meeting with Hills, NWF withdrew from
its position as one of the principal groups involved with MODTLE, severing
its explicit ties to a labor agenda. Hair argued that the interests of MODTLE
and the interests of the organization were no longer consistent and began
to tout the potential benefits of trade liberalization. According to an internal EPA memo: "apparently NWF's position on NAFTA has changed."[62]

Given most unions opposed continuation of fast-track, the ability of
swing environmentalists to determine the outcome of the legislative contest gave them critical leverage. Labor activists' ability to defeat fast-track
was diminished by the breakaway environmental organizations providing
cover to Democrats who wanted to support the business position in favor
of fast-track. If labor and environmental organizations had been united
against the non-extension resolution it would have had a better chance
of passing. For NAFTA supporters, environmentalists needed to be split
off from a coalition with labor to achieve the best chance of passage.
Coalitional politics and the division of government therefore affected the
unfolding NAFTA struggle.

Labor activists were less susceptible to divide-and-conquer tactics
even though many criticized the AFL-CIO for not doing enough to fight
against fast-track. Labor activists remained united against fast-track while
pushing the federation to take a much more active role in the struggle.
Labor cohesion was evident when the ACTPN, the highest advisory tier
in the mandatory advisory system for the USTR, revealed its March 1st
recommendations on fast-track. The Committee "strongly" recommended
the extension of the fast-track procedures with the "sole dissent of its
labor representatives," which was unanimous. The report also stated: "Of
the seven other trade policy advisory committees, all except the [Labor
Advisory Committee] support that recommendation."[63]

Trade Policy Field Turnaround

On May 1, 1991, President Bush outlined the action plan for NAFTA negotiations moving forward. In it, an "adequately funded" worker adjustment program was linked to NAFTA-implementing legislation.[64] And in a huge turnaround, trade policy officials agreed to appoint environmental representatives to the USTR advisory committees. They selected representatives from six environmental organizations—WWF, Nature Conservancy, NRDC, Audubon Society, League of Conservation Voters, and NWF—and one state-level EPA director to advise the USTR during negotiations.[65] The plan stated:

> USTR will include a representative of the non-governmental environmental organizations on the Advisory Committee on Trade Policy and Negotiations (ACTPN). Environmental representatives will also be invited to participate in the following trade policy advisory committees: [Inter-Governmental Policy Advisory Committee, Services Policy Advisory Committee, Investment Policy Advisory Committee, Industry Policy Advisory Committee for Trade Matters, Agriculture Policy Advisory Committee] . . . EPA will consult closely with non-governmental organizations on environmental issues as they arise in the context of ongoing U.S.-Mexico environmental relations.[66]

The representatives were culled from pro-growth environmental organizations least likely to oppose negotiations. They joined a total team of 1,000 USTR advisors organized on seventeen different negotiating committees.

The administration also coordinated efforts with Mexico's president through a two-level strategy to assuage domestic environmental constituents. Under the plan, U.S. and Mexican officials would pursue a "parallel track" for increasing environmental cooperation and expanding environmental protection through an integrated border environmental plan. It also included a requirement that an environmental review of NAFTA be conducted.[67] Environmentalists had won substantive gains for environmental improvements along the U.S-Mexico border. And for the first time, environmentalists had a recognized role within the trade policy field itself. However, the gains would not be sufficient to satisfy labor activists or environmentalists who did not adhere to a pro-growth vision.

Implications of the Fast-Track Struggle

On May 23, 1991, the House voted to continue fast-track by a vote of 231 to 192.[68] The vote split House Democratic leaders from their colleagues; Democratic House Speaker Tom Foley and Rep. Gephardt voted to keep fast-track in place, while Democratic House members voted almost two to one to end fast-track. Twenty-one Republicans also voted to end fast-track.[69] The Senate also voted down the resolution introduced in that chamber by Democratic Sen. Fritz Hollings to terminate fast-track authority by a vote of 59 to 36.[70] The House also voted for the Gephardt-Rostenkowski resolution—that memorialized the administration's promises in its action plan concerning labor and environmental standards and protections—by a vote of 329–86.[71]

The passage of fast-track was a disappointment to labor and environmental activists who fought to defeat it. It would be much more difficult to directly influence the course of negotiations between the three countries with fast-track in place, as the process significantly limited Congress's leverage over the content of the eventual agreement. Despite the loss, however, the anti-NAFTA coalition had influenced the process. Activists injected new issues into the trade debate, developed nascent coalitions that spanned social movement sectors, and forced opposed trade policy officials to make concessions to satisfy labor and environmental demands. Moreover the fast-track fight enabled activists to mobilize early and to develop alliances with congressional decision-makers who brought labor and environmental issues to the center of the trade debate.

Environmentalists' influence on trade policy was quite unexpected and therefore particularly compelling. They foreground the importance of both alliance-building and rule-making strategies between the legislative and trade policy fields that enabled environmentalists in a short period of time and with few resources to win concessions from trade negotiators. In the early stages of negotiations, environmental organizations used the former to gain legitimacy and throw the fast-track vote into doubt, and as negotiations progressed they used the latter to gain concessions and representation in the trade policy field itself. The relatively close fast-track vote put the trade policy elite on notice that NAFTA could be at risk even under fast-track procedures if sufficient support from Democratic House members was not built. This opened the door for environmental organizations to demand their inclusion in the trade policy field. Environmentalists were quick to highlight the results of their mobilization, as the president of the NRDC declared: "For the first time in history, the environment has entered [the] trade debate. The challenge ahead is to shape international agreements that promote sustainable development worldwide."[72]

It is important to emphasize that activists' efforts to improve NAFTA by demanding that labor and environmental concerns be addressed were possible because the support of labor allowed them to threaten the outcome of the NAFTA vote. This led trade policy officials to seek to engage environmental activists and ultimately try to split them from their labor partners. Trade policy officials also had to comply with statutory transparency requirements. As required by law, the USTR provided labor unions on the advisory committees and their legislative allies information (though not complete) about what they intended to negotiate, and met with legislators, labor unions, and environmental organizations. President Bush released his action plan for public comment. The partisan divide between a Democratic Congress and a Republican president also helped Congress hold almost monthly public hearings on the agreement during which activists provided testimony. These open channels allowed activists to leverage framing, rule-making, and alliance-building strategies across the trade policy and legislative fields.

As the dust cleared after the fast-track battle it became apparent that trade policy had undergone a significant transformation. The trade policy debate in the legislative field had expanded to include environmental and labor rights issues and a diversity of constituencies. A reporter for the *New York Times* noted the significance of the changes:

> What began six months ago as a routine Congressional decision on whether to renew the Administration's negotiating authority evolved into a passionate debate on America's place in the world economy. Members of Congress on both sides of the issue, under conflicting pressures from labor unions, businesses, and environmental lobbies, described the Administration's authority to negotiate trade agreements as probably the most important and contentious vote on an economic issue facing Congress this year.[73]

And a *Washington Post* reporter observed: "In spite of the acrimony and partisan politics affecting the debate over fast track, observers on both sides acknowledge that it has succeeded in popularizing the trade issue."[74]

The inclusion of new trade constituencies ensured a contentious struggle over the content and structure of the final agreement. Even a fast-track supporter recognized that: "For the first time different social groups have been brought into the negotiations over a trade pact. That puts pressure on the administration to come up with a treaty that is acceptable to all sides. Trade has become a public issue."[75] According to the coordinator of the Mexican negotiating team, Mexican negotiators recognized "that an overwhelming majority in the House wanted NAFTA to be the greenest, most labor-friendly agreement yet negotiated."[76] The opposition labor and environmental activists faced after the fast-track struggle only intensified during the next stages of the NAFTA battle, requiring them to seek out new ways to leverage strategies across fields in order to increase their chances of success.

Mobilizing Public and Legislative Hostility against NAFTA

ONCE CONGRESS ALLOWED fast-track to remain in effect, labor leaders and pro-growth environmentalists had official, though marginal, advisory roles in the trade policy field. Both used these positions to advocate for environmental and labor protections with field officials. Activists' marginalized position within the trade policy field, however, provided them with little direct leverage to influence the NAFTA negotiations. The anti-NAFTA coalition's main focus was therefore on the legislative field, where activists had key resources to broker: votes, money, information, and organizational support. Labor and environmental activists' strategy was to increase public hostility to NAFTA and harness that antagonism to influence legislators who would eventually be called upon to ratify the agreement. By creating a significant threat to final congressional passage of the agreement, they hoped to indirectly influence negotiators through concerns about legislative passage or to actually sink the entire agreement.

This chapter examines activists' mobilization of a mass movement of NAFTA opponents during the fourteen months of NAFTA's substantive negotiations beginning in June 1991 until August 1992, when the USTR completed NAFTA negotiations and President Bush notified Congress of his intent to sign the agreement before his term expired. While the AFL-CIO and pro-growth environmentalists concentrated on insider strategies, labor unions and many environmental organizations (united with other consumer, farmer's and faith groups operating in Washington, DC, as the CTWC and in the field as the FTC) created a strong anti-NAFTA coalition in the broader grassroots politics field and mobilized; they held local protests and rallies, wrote press releases, held forums with community groups and local politicians, and appeared in media outlets in over one hundred cities. More than sixty groups participated in the coalition, with local active coalitions in twenty states.[1]

The sheer size of the movement was a valuable asset in the legislative field. In addition, resources were brokered within the anti-NAFTA coalition. Environmentalists (and consumer, family farm, and faith groups) piggybacked on labor's greater influence in Congress, and labor benefited from the breadth and diversity of the other grassroots organizations. Together they deployed a combined strategy of traditional advocacy and mass-movement protests, publicity stunts, and education campaigns oriented to the decision-makers in Washington. They targeted legislative power through congressional members' ratification role, focusing on House members who were positioned in leveraged roles in the process or who were undecided and vulnerable to pressure tactics. Grassroots efforts augmented the visibility of decision-makers' positions and provided increased pressure on them in Washington. Activists not only challenged the elite ideological commitment to trade liberalization represented by NAFTA, but also opposed the routine machinations of how trade policy is accomplished in Washington. Straddling the realms of insider and outsider grassroots strategies, they created an oppositional trade movement that was internationalist, focused on the grassroots, and diverse in participation and message.

The grassroots mobilization during substantive negotiations helped alter public opinion. During substantive negotiations public support for a North American free trade zone dropped to 21 percent from a high of 72 percent at the time of the initial fast-track authority request, according to Gallup polls. The coalition also successfully leveraged grassroots mobilization to impact support in the legislative field. In August 1992, the House unanimously passed a resolution warning the president that the trade agreement should not weaken labor, environmental, health, or safety laws. In December 1992, when Bush signed the NAFTA agreement, few expected Congress to ratify it.

Part I: Mobilizing Public Opposition against NAFTA

Once substantive negotiations began, environmental and labor activists had a limited opportunity to directly impact the direction of the negotiations themselves. Although environmental actors now had established roles within the trade policy field, their position, like labor, was marginalized. Moreover, the labor-environmental rights frame remained oppositional within the field, generating considerable pushback from trade liberalization proponents, primarily in the Republican Party. Environmentalists with USTR advisory positions worked to promote environmental protections and had some success advocating for a more environmentally-oriented agreement. But pro-growth environmentalists learned what labor leaders had before them; given the reigning ideology of trade liberalization within the trade policy field, efforts to inject broader social welfare objectives through the USTR advisory committees proved largely ineffective; trade negotiators resisted the incorporation of labor and environmental concerns into broader U.S. negotiating goals. Instead, they pursued a parallel track approach to appeasing domestic constituents' concerns. Given the constraints within the field it became clear that additional social movement mobilization outside of it was needed to maximize negotiating outcomes and press trade policy officials to include labor and environmental protections into the substance of negotiations themselves.

Intersection between the grassroots politics and trade policy fields was attenuated, however, leaving activists few direct leverage points on the latter; rule-making, framing, and resource brokerage strategies would therefore be of little use. Instead, activists focused on the need for a final congressional vote on NAFTA and the ability to broker resources across the legislative and grassroots politics fields that resulted from congressional members' dependence on key political resources: votes, money, and organizational support. Their strategy was to increase public hostility to NAFTA, harness that antagonism to influence legislators, then use their leverage to maximize concessions or undermine the entire agreement.

Activists therefore used a three-pronged strategy to influence legislators: (1) educate local interest group members to increase opposition, (2) increase general voter antagonism to the agreement to threaten legislators with loss of votes, and (3) mobilize pressure on legislators by convening lobbying efforts in home regions to threaten loss of votes and organizational support. Mark Ritchie of the IATP emphasized the strategic benefits of connecting mass mobilization in the grassroots politics field with legislative pressure:

> At the end of the day, the Washington's people's contribution to all of these things is the single-mindedness of vote-counting and delivering of votes. At the end of the day, you're held accountable

in Washington for how the vote goes. And outside of Washington, we don't. In fact, for us, you're able to throw up your hands and say, "oh those terrible politicians." . . . So in a way, we were very lucky that the trade campaign grew to the size that it did, so that it could involve as many people as it did, so it could in fact have a grassroots and a Washington that could then be kind of equal partners. . . . I would say a real genius aspect of the trade work—which was not easy nor always happy, but was really crucial to the success—was the ability to move it in and out of Washington . . . When there was a fast-track vote looming or something else looming or a NAFTA vote looming, all the money and all the resources—everything got concentrated in Washington . . . And when there wasn't that kind of focus, then people and energy and money got moved out for more of the grassroots stuff . . . I think this was really an innovation.[2]

Another key innovation is what Public Citizen's Lori Wallach called the "you can't run you can't hide" nature of the broad coalition. In order to avoid getting played off each other by members of Congress (which Wallach reported occurred often at the beginning of the struggle), activists from different sectors began to lobby together: "By uniting everyone in one trade lobbying meeting in D.C. and one grassroots advocacy meeting with the target member in his or her district, it became clear what the choice was: be with your entire base united on one position. Or, betray us all and make clear you're voting for the corporations and against your base."[3] Activists' confidence that local grassroots pressure would have a powerful impact on legislators was bolstered by public opinion data. Polling suggested Americans' opinions on trade were not strongly held and could be swayed with new information. Gallup survey data collected at the beginning of the NAFTA struggle showed that although there was widespread support for the principle of free trade, respondents also strongly supported tariffs when U.S. jobs were at stake. More than half (54 percent) of those surveyed favored the use of tariffs to protect some sectors of the economy from foreign competition, while only 25 percent favored the elimination of tariffs.[4]

A survey conducted by the Garin-Hart Strategic Research Group for the AFL-CIO in April 1991 showed that more than half (58 percent) of respondents had little or no familiarity with the specifics of the agreement. But the poll revealed another compelling finding: after hearing pro and con arguments for the agreement, a majority of respondents shifted to opposition, with 53 percent against and 42 percent in favor of a North American free trade agreement. Pollsters found that the most persuasive argument was an environmental one, with 58 percent of respondents stating that the movement of companies to Mexico to avoid environmental regulations in the United States would be a strong reason to oppose. Job loss and wage depression due to plant movement was a close second, with 57 percent responding that that would be a strong reason to oppose it.[5] Thus the polls suggested early on the potential efficacy of rallying public opposition to NAFTA that could then be leveraged in the November 1992 presidential and congressional elections.

One of the earliest grassroots efforts began in Fall 1991 in response to the EPA's release of a draft of the administration's integrated border environmental plan for public comment. The binational plan, coordinated jointly between the EPA and the Mexican Secretariat of Urban Development and Ecology (SEDUE), focused on resolving significant pollution problems such as wastewater and hazardous waste disposal in six sister cities along the U.S.-Mexico border.[6] State and local officials, community representatives, and environmental activists generally agreed that the plan was vague and did not address the crucial issue of funding. More important, there was widespread support among pro-growth *and* adversarial environmental organizations that the environmental consequences of trade needed to be addressed in the substantive negotiations of any successful trade agreement.[7]

In September 1991, the two agencies held joint public hearings on the plan in San Diego; Tijuana; Texas; Calexico; Mexicali; Nogales, Arizona; and Nogales, Sonora.[8] The FTC mobilized a community response that resulted in large attendance in both U.S. and Mexican border cities. At the EPA's San Diego hearings, an FTC activist put on plastic gloves, grabbed what he described as a jug of toxic liquid found in a Tijuana neighborhood, poured it into a glass, and placed it in front of EPA and SEDUE officials, proclaiming: "Look at what 20 years of experimentation in free trade have done to the border."[9] Protestors picketed the San Diego hearing with signs that read: "The Plan Stinks."[10]

Environmental activists reported that their efforts were bolstered by an August 1991 decision by the GATT dispute settlement panel in the transnational negotiating field. It ruled that a U.S. ban on tuna from any country that failed to meet U.S. standards for protecting dolphins violated GATT rules.[11] Mexico was among the nations that brought the case to the GATT tribunal. The ruling hit home to a number of national environmental groups from across the political spectrum that the trade policy and the transnational negotiating fields now overlapped in ways that made domestic environmental policy vulnerable because protections could be struck down by trade lawyers with little environmental knowledge or experience. The result set off a backlash by activists, who worried it would set a precedent against "extrajurisdictional" laws protecting the global commons. The opinion was so important for mobilizing environmentalists on trade matters that a representative for Defenders of Wildlife explained: "In fact, in many ways, even though that had nothing to do with [NAFTA] per se, it had everything to do with NAFTA, and it really was the beginning of the modern trade era."[12] In order to avoid further contention by NAFTA opponents, Mexico declined to press for further GATT intervention at that time, and instead announced that it would undertake a series of unilateral steps to bring its fishing industry more in line with the United States in order to reduce the accidental killing of dolphins. The issue was revisited later.

By late 1991, CTWC and the FTC took the lead in organizing in the grassroots politics field. While the former coordinated legislative activity, press, and lobbying, the FTC worked to expand the number of coalition partners outside DC and mobilize the public more broadly around the agreement. The FTC's architects believed that to influence negotiations they needed to create a clamor among legislators' constituents and key NGO supporters; without it, legislators would look to each other and succumb to pressure from corporate interests that funded their campaigns. The FTC created a grassroots infrastructure and developed a mass education and mobilization campaign with a miniscule budget sustained largely through foundation grants and donation of staff and materials from participating organizations. The grassroots component of the NAFTA campaign was widespread, robust, and diverse in its membership, as a labor activist described:

> One of the best features of the local coalition was the frequent meetings where a wide variety of organizations and activists shared strategies and perspectives on trade issues. Committee meetings in Massachusetts included union representatives from the Teamsters, ILGWU, UE, IUE, and Letter Carriers. On the community side, the most active participants were from the Massachusetts Toxics Campaign, the Student Environmental Action Coalition, Massachusetts Save James Bay, the Lawyers Guild, several Central

America solidarity groups, and the Immigrant Workers' Resource Center.[13]

During the NAFTA struggle hundreds of local environmental, labor, agricultural, consumer, human rights, and church groups across the country joined the anti-NAFTA coalition.

The lack of access to trade policy officials and the need for public exposure to their anti-NAFTA efforts led both the DC-based coalition and grassroots activists to highlight their objections to the agreement in creative ways that often involved political theater, as activists searched for ways to get their message across. After a last-minute demonstration at the second round of negotiations in Seattle in August 1991, activists realized that the negotiation venues were an excellent place to attract media attention and highlight the secrecy of the meetings. Taking advantage of journalists' need for news as they waited idly for any information on the negotiations, activists hosted a spontaneous press conference at the meeting site. At subsequent negotiations, the hosting groups planned similar "citizen's receptions" involving conversations with the press and other publicity stunts.[14]

At the meeting in Seattle, the Washington Coalition for Fair Trade inflated a giant "Fair Trade" balloon at a demonstration of three hundred activists. At a negotiators' meeting in Texas in September 1991, activists met negotiators with picket signs, placards, and banners. In June 1992 in Washington, DC, CTWC set up a "hospitality suite" in the same building where negotiators convened. There they distributed food and educational materials, and some activists dressed in tuxedos handed out fake menus explaining the pesticides that could contaminate food under proposed trade rules.[15] Anti-NAFTA activist caravans drove through Tennessee, California, and Texas to mobilize opposition. The vans showed films and slides of environmental degradation in Mexico.[16] FTC leaders made an appearance at the Farm Aid V concert.[17] And at a 1992 meeting of negotiators in Washington, DC, CTWC activists dressed up as Presidents Nixon and Bush and handed out plungers to negotiators and the press in front of the negotiating site at the Watergate Hotel. The plungers read "Where's a plumber when you need one? Stop the Secrecy!" and "I survived the NAFTA ministerial." The faux Bush and Nixon declared: "We heard there might be leaked texts here! Take these plungers and plug up any information leaks you find! You wouldn't want the American people knowing what you've done here!" They left an extra plunger with the Watergate concierge for USTR Carla Hills.[18]

By the summer of 1992, the CTWC included approximately sixty national environmental, labor and consumer, family farm, and religious groups.[19] The FTC had twelve staff members operating in eleven states as diverse as California, Idaho, Pennsylvania, Vermont, Georgia, and Texas. Additional volunteer organizers and advisors operated throughout the country, with active local coalitions in twenty states. The field staff came primarily out of other grassroots organizations, including Jobs with Justice, Citizen Action, and NTC. They focused on activating constituency group work on trade issues in over one hundred cities through public meetings, hearings and presentations, and educational sessions with local grassroots organizations. They also met with members of Congress in home districts to educate them about the issues.[20]

A Growing International Coalition

The period of substantive negotiations also marked the real beginning of a truly international effort on trade and economic integration by NGOs in the Americas. The NAFTA campaign was characterized by efforts to build lasting and more egalitarian relationships between labor and environmental activists in the three countries (Kay 2005; 2011a; 2011b). As with labor unions, some organizations extolled a moral position on the importance of internationalism, while others were less compelled by internationalist ideals than by a pragmatic desire to derail NAFTA. Although MODTLE did not play a major role in the congressional lobbying efforts spearheaded by CTWC, they were instrumental in establishing an international solidarity alliance, organizing public consortia, and developing a trinational document setting forth an alternative to the proposed free trade agreement. Given that Canadian counterparts already had organized a cross-sectoral coalitional campaign that almost derailed the 1988 CUSFTA, the FTC and CTWC worked closely on campaign strategy with them to try to expand upon what they learned and what strategies were effective.

Several of the primary organizations involved with MODTLE—ILRF, IPS, and the DGAP—had organizational mandates that were international in scope. ILRF and DGAP had worked with organizations throughout Central and South America on labor rights, small-scale economic development among women, and democratic elections. Many MODTLE activists were entrenched in social networks with Canadian and Mexican activists. U.S. environmentalists working along the Mexican border also had relationships with Mexican activists. Not only were all of these activists internationally-focused, but they were also involved in trade for reasons that were inherently internationalist in outlook.

Concerns about global warming, endangered species, transborder pollution, maritime contamination, and ecosystem destruction had long occupied the attention of U.S. environmental organizations. The ability of the United States to enforce international environmental treaties through trade restrictions was a cornerstone of their concern about NAFTA. These groups sought to orient the trade debate in ways that would extend the focus beyond national borders. And they saw their ultimate trade-related goals as dovetailing with environmental organizations in Canada and Mexico. The inclusion of environmental groups from the beginning of the struggle also helped foster a more international focus that had not previously existed. For example Greenpeace USA, which played a leading role in the opposition to NAFTA, was part of an international organization that included branches in Canada and Mexico. This international linkage helped forge a perspective on trade that looked beyond the limited interests of groups in the United States.

The development and strengthening of ties among organizations in the United States, Mexico, and Canada largely occurred around their mobilization at the sites of the trinational negotiations. The negotiations provided activists with a meeting point around which to develop more coordinated activity and a common message. The most important of these meetings occurred at the third ministerial meeting in Zacatecas, Mexico, in October 1991. There ACN, MODTLE, and RMALC presented negotiators with a sixteen-point plan to alter NAFTA in favor of a "continental development agreement"[21] that advocated broader social and economic integration similar to the European model rather than limited trade and investment liberalization.

The proposal called for the reduction of Mexican debt, harmonization of work conditions, mechanisms to ensure human rights standards, national sovereignty over natural resources and food security, the improvement of environmental regulations, protection of the rights of workers, an increase in the minimum wages of workers in Mexico, and a code of conduct for transnational companies, among others.[22] While working together on the draft, activists solidified their common goals and points of contention. As the director of ILRF proclaimed at the opening of the proceedings:

Who would have thought fourteen months ago that we'd be here today, a coalition of traditionally suspicious sectors, having awakened

Congress to the social issues around free trade, having forced labor and environmental acknowledgement, having found real colleagues in Canada and Mexico, having influenced Mexican legislation, and having put trade on the national agenda and in the election in such a way that the Bush administration is having to be very cautious in addressing the American public on trade related issues.[23]

The creation of stronger ties among activists in all three countries allowed for a more richly nuanced analysis of trade in relationship to labor and environmental issues, as activists deepened their understanding of NGO positions in other countries and struggled to flesh out their wish list for the content of a truly trinational trade agreement.

The AFL-CIO's Changing Role in the Anti-NAFTA Coalition

As the developing anti-NAFTA coalition began to strategize for a longer-term campaign against NAFTA, the role of the AFL-CIO began to change. Although campaigns/networks such as the FTC courted the AFL-CIO's active participation during the fight against fast-track and the early anti-NAFTA struggle, and the labor federation seemed a natural partner because its leaders recognized the potential linkages between labor and environmental issues and trade, the AFL-CIO resisted formally joining others' campaigns. A coalition organization itself, the AFL-CIO generally refrained from participating in coalitions unless it had the controlling authority.[24] AFL-CIO representatives were also protective of their position as the dominant organization among Democratic allies in the legislative field. And although the majority of coalition organizations lacked official access to the trade policy field, unions were active members of the field, even if they were marginalized within it. AFL-CIO representatives were therefore well-positioned trade actors straddling both the legislative and trade policy fields. As an AFL-CIO official involved with the USTR Labor Advisory Committee explained: "At a certain level for us it was not a question of access. We had access whenever we wanted. There was a question of whether they would pay attention to what we were saying, by and large, which is quite a different matter. And that's not true, obviously, of the other elements of at least certainly the current trade coalition, where they did not have access . . . . But we did."[25]

Less progressive AFL-CIO leaders viewed the nascent anti-NAFTA coalition as too marginal, too grassroots oriented, and too powerless, and prevented the federation from officially joining it. In the field, and to some degree in D.C., more progressive AFL-CIO activists were receptive to their message and unofficially attended meetings and events. Campaign leaders also found other ways to create alliances with labor unions. As an FTC representative explained with respect to field strategy: "We kept the dialog and the communication link open. What we didn't tell them, but what we had already . . . we already had plan B for labor. And plan B was go around the AFL and start working with their affiliates and even deeper and further down the chain and start working with local unions and state federations and build a base at the grassroots."[26]

In D.C., key national labor unions most directly affected by trade such as the UAW, Amalgamated Clothing and Textile Workers' Union (ACTWU), International Ladies' Garments Workers' Union (ILGWU), International Union of Electronic, Electrical, Salaried, Machine and Furniture Workers (IUE), International Brotherhood of Teamsters (IBT), and International Brotherhood of Electrical Workers (IBEW) were actively involved in the broader anti-NAFTA coalition. And the coalition received a big boost in its legitimacy and visibility within the legislative field when powerful unions such as the UAW joined its efforts.[27] Citizens Trade Campaign's (CTC) founding board members included IBT, ILGWU, ACTWU, IUE, and UAW representatives.

Initially, AFL-CIO leaders pursued the issue of NAFTA negotiations through insider politics alone, using their position in the trade policy field and with key decision-makers in the legislative field to attempt to shape the substance of the agreement. This meant the language of trade-offs, accommodations, and operating within the realm of what was considered politically feasible. In contrast, anti-NAFTA coalition activists tried to change the parameters of what was politically attainable in terms of trade policy. Tom Donahue, the former president of the AFL-CIO, explained how the federation's initial emphasis was to try to achieve enough concessions to make NAFTA palatable to its membership:

> We did not start off saying no to NAFTA. There was always—I guess through the years of negotiations—there was always a "No NAFTA" effort by some people. But that wasn't the policy. The policy was to make it work for us. Indeed, we argued consistently—both [the head of the AFL-CIO Task Force on Trade] and I, and anyone that spoke for the federation—argued consistently that we understood perfectly that the fates of our countries were all linked, that

we argued for economic integration of the hemisphere, not free trade—which was a meaningless nothing.[28]

During the fast-track struggle the AFL-CIO was also limited from actively joining a truly international coalition against NAFTA by its ties to the CTM.[29] The lack of active AFL-CIO involvement in the coalition during the first two years of the NAFTA battle meant that coalition members did not have access to the full force of the organization's money or legislative influence. The vacuum of leadership left by the absence of the AFL-CIO, however, allowed activists on the boards of CTC, especially presidents and staff of its member-unions, and MODTLE, which had members from the faith and international solidarity and development sectors, to build campaigns that fit with their organizational strengths, philosophies, and preferred tactics. As a result, they focused more on mobilization in the grassroots politics field and prioritized internationalism and diversity in membership and message. Ultimately, the anti-NAFTA coalition had an effect on the AFL-CIO when it tried to broaden its coalitional reach and to embrace grassroots activism.

As substantive negotiations wore on, the AFL-CIO's position in the anti-NAFTA coalition began to change. Spurred by an unofficial severing of its exclusive relationship with the CTM—due to the CTM's support of NAFTA and unwillingness to promote better maquiladora wages and working conditions—the AFL-CIO began to establish stronger ties with independent Mexican unions and the anti-NAFTA coalition that was working with them. In summer 1992, Mark Anderson, the head of the AFL-CIO's Task Force on Trade, joined the FTC board of advisors. In a letter sent to all state labor federations and major central labor councils across the country, he outlined the work of the FTC and CTWC.[30]

The anti-NAFTA coalition's relentless efforts to kill NAFTA had had some impact on the average U.S. voter. Survey data suggest that the grassroots mobilization during substantive negotiations succeeded in altering public opinion. A Gallup poll conducted prior to the negotiations in March 1991 indicated that 72 percent of respondents were broadly supportive of a North American free trade zone.[31] Almost a year and a half later, in October 1992, that number had dropped to only 21 percent.[32] But perhaps even more significantly, activists had politicized trade, making it dinner table conversation—and a political issue with broad resonance across the country.

Part II: Harnessing Grassroots Antagonism to Influence Legislators and Throw NAFTA'S Passage into Doubt

Although activists' mobilization against NAFTA and the public opinion it helped shape provided a threat to legislators, the USTR still resisted the inclusion of labor and environmental protections in the agreement and the participation of environmental organizations not chosen by the Bush administration for USTR committees in the negotiating process. Environmental organizations excluded from the USTR panels registered their anger and frustration with the closed nature of the trade policy field. Public Citizen released a report in December 1991, for example, that criticized the exclusivity of the USTR advisory committees, urged the inclusion of consumer and environmental advocates on new panels, and demanded that the USTR convene public meetings. And they publicized extensive evidence of environmental misconduct by many of the companies represented on advisory committees.

By Fall 1991, members of Congress and pro-growth environmentalists who had supported the "trust but verify" approach were growing increasingly wary of the direction of USTR negotiating priorities. Not only had President Bush refused to create a separate and exclusively environmental working group in the negotiations, but also the USTR focused on traditional trade concerns without integrating environmental issues directly into the negotiations. In mid-September 1991 key House Democrats met with environmental groups to discuss their concerns. As a reporter for *Inside U.S. Trade* observed: "The meeting is significant in that members from two different environmental camps—one that did not outright oppose the provision of fast track negotiating authority and the other that did—will be in attendance. Part of the reason the meeting is possible at this junction, said an informed congressional source, is that the Administration's focus on traditional trade issues to the exclusion of a detailed integration of environmental issues into the NAFTA talks has heightened the skepticism of both moderate members of Congress and the environmental community."[33] In June 1991 Rep. Kaptur, one of the House members who had spearheaded the legislative fight against fast-track, helped organize a fair trade caucus to maintain indirect pressure on trade policy officials during negotiations.[34] Dubbed the Congressional Fair Trade Campaign, it consisted of forty-nine members (mainly Democrats, but also Republicans including Rep. Duncan L. Hunter), who voted against the continuation of fast-track. At its first organizational meeting in September, members decided to urge heads of relevant committees to hold hearings related to NAFTA.[35]

Even Senator Baucus, who had direct responsibility for the environmental portions of the trade agreement as chair of the Finance Committee's trade subcommittee and chair of the Committee on Environment and Public Works, recognized trade policy officials' intransigence on the environment. Baucus, a NAFTA supporter, registered his frustration with the administration at the end of September, stating: "The administration has been at best reluctant and at worst hostile to the idea of considering environmental issues in trade negotiations."[36]

USTR Hills further infuriated activists and their legislative allies when she refused to have the environmental review—part of President Bush's May 1 commitment to Congress—carried out by an independent and unbiased agency. Instead her office took direct responsibility for developing and conducting the environmental review with some assistance from the EPA. When it was released on October 17, 1991, environmentalists were outraged. The review explicitly rejected the linkage between trade liberalization and environmental issues. The official report rebuffed environmental arguments that the trade agreement would inevitably have negative environmental consequences. Rather, it argued that NAFTA would improve environmental quality because it would improve Mexico's economy, thereby increasing financial resources available for environmental protection.

In response to the environmental review, environmental organizations stepped up their pressure on negotiators. Public Citizen sued the USTR in federal court on behalf of itself, Sierra Club and Friends of the Earth. They charged the USTR of violating section 102(2)(c) of the National Environmental Policy Act (NEPA) for NAFTA by failing to conduct a broader environmental impact statement.[37] Although the NRDC and EDF did not join the lawsuit, they warned USTR representatives that they needed to comply with NEPA for NAFTA.[38] In addition, NWF released a list of the key environmental promises those officials made in exchange for fast-track continuation.[39]

Rep. Gephardt and his staffers also met collectively with environmentalists, including groups from both sides of the fast-track fight, to develop collective strategies. Rep. Wyden penned a letter to President Bush signed by seventy-three House Democrats in November requesting that he submit a separate environmental accord before presenting the completed NAFTA agreement for congressional approval. Forty representatives who had voted for fast-track reauthorization signed the letter, signaling the vulnerability of NAFTA's passage without an environmental accord.[40]

CTWC also mobilized in the legislative field to support efforts to exert increased congressional control over the labor and environmental aspects of trade negotiations. Its leaders worked with Reps. Waxman and Gephardt who co-sponsored congressional resolution 246, expressing the sense of the House that no trade agreement that undermined health, environmental, or labor standards would be approved.[41] They also worked with Senator Riegle who introduced congressional resolution 109 to alter the extension of fast-track to allow amendments in five substantive areas: labor standards, environmental standards, rules of origin, dispute settlement, and worker adjustment assistance.[42]

Due in part to CTWC's efforts, thirty co-sponsors signed onto congressional resolution 109.[43] The FTC also used the Riegle resolution to mobilize grassroots support.[44] Rep. George Brown—in consultation with labor and environmental activists from all three countries—called for co-sponsors for two bills making violations of labor and environmental laws unfair trade practices.[45] All of the proposed congressional resolutions had two purposes: to change the rules of the trade policy field short of a repeal of fast-track, and to signal to field members that labor and environmental concerns were crucial components of the win-set for ultimate ratification.

Even key legislators who supported NAFTA recognized the threat to its passage without stronger environmental commitments and stepped up the pressure on the administration. NWF, EDF, and WWF worked directly with Rep. Wyden and Sen. Baucus. Thirty-seven additional representatives, the majority from border states who had supported fast-track continuation, crafted a letter urging the president to pledge support for the border environmental plan with a specific inclusion in the 1993 budget.[46] On February 25, 1992, President Bush released the final version of his integrated border environmental plan. The plan called for $1 billion over three years for border environmental cleanup and infrastructure with funds from the federal government, border states, and private industry.[47]

In March 1992, NRDC began to organize various organizations' environmental demands into policy recommendations for negotiators. NRDC primarily worked with other pro-growth organizations. The Sierra Club was the only adversarial environmental organization invited to participate from the beginning of the process, although the others were included toward the end (Audley 1997:87). In June, NRDC completed the paper and all of the major national and border environmental organizations signed it with the exception of the NWF, which released its own document. The two position papers set the same general policy recommendations, including: (1) direct inclusion of policy recommendations in NAFTA; (2) the creation of a trilateral environmental commission; (3) protection of international environmental agreements; (4) protection of the right to set national standards for environmental, consumer health, and safety; (5) public participation in dispute proceedings and general implementation of NAFTA; and (6) funding for environmental assistance along the border.[48] Senator Baucus used his position in the trade policy field (as chair of the Finance Committee's trade subcommittee) to facilitate a direct meeting between the USTR and pro-growth environmental organizations. Although they had access to negotiators, however, environmentalists could not elicit satisfactory concessions. In July the NRDC president wrote a letter to President Bush explaining that the NRDC could not support the agreement as written.

Labor activists also began to solidify their demands in response to a leaked draft of NAFTA that the ACN obtained in March 1992. The confidential draft, dated February 21, included bracketed sections of text where consensus had not yet been reached. In response, ACN, the Canadian Center for Policy Alternatives, and Canada's Common Frontiers wrote "North American Free Trade Agreement Draft Text: Preliminary Briefing Notes." MODTLE and CTWC also prepared an analysis of the text in April titled "Too High a Price for Free Trade."[49] In May, trade policy field officials consulted with union members on the Labor Advisory Committee to determine the appropriate worker-training package for NAFTA. At a press conference held in Mexico City on July 26, members of ACN, RMALC, and MODTLE vowed to fight passage of the agreement if there were no changes in how labor and environmental issues were addressed.[50]

By July 1992, negotiators were quite concerned that NAFTA would not pass, and the USTR initiated a strategy to convince lawmakers committed to worker retraining and environmental protection to support the agreement. USTR Hills met with the chairpeople and ranking members of almost all House committees and convened with every member of the Ways and Means Committee. Environmental activists complained to Hills in the July 30 meeting that environmental considerations were grossly insufficient. At the final hour, Hills capitulated a bit to environmental demands; she announced that she intended to negotiate the establishment of a North American Commission on the Environment (Audley 1997:69).

At the end of July, in the days leading up to the vote on Gephardt and Waxman's House Resolution 246, CTWC activists delivered phony deeds to the Brooklyn Bridge to every House representative. The deed listed Bush's broken promises on trade, and was attached to a leaflet that read: "If you believe President Bush's promises on jobs, trade, and the environment . . . he's got a bridge he'd like to sell you."[51] The House voted unanimously 362-0 on August 6 to pass the resolution warning the president that the trade agreement should not weaken health, safety, labor, or environmental laws.[52] Gephardt highlighted the efficacy of activists' resource brokerage strategies between the grassroots politics and legislative fields when he singled out the work of the CTWC and FTC "for their tireless effort at getting this legislation before us today."[53]

Small Gains, but NAFTA Appears Doomed

On August 12, 1992, the USTR completed NAFTA negotiations and President Bush notified Congress of his intent to sign the agreement before his term expired. Whoever was elected the next president on November 3rd, however, would be responsible for shepherding the deal through Congress. During the almost year and a half of substantive negotiations, activists' ability to significantly improve Bush's agreement was minimal. Environmentalists involved in USTR advisory committees had successfully pushed for the inclusion of a preamble that acknowledged the linkage between trade and environmental issues and recognized the need for sustainable development. And labor had forced the administration to include a package of programs for U.S. workers displaced by NAFTA. But despite legislators' threats, negotiators were reluctant to address more substantial environmental demands. USTR Hills rejected proposals for a "green tax" and trade sanctions to protect the environment and workers' rights.[54]

Labor and environmentalists' most noteworthy accomplishment, however, was to politicize trade policy and mobilize strong opposition to NAFTA among the public and key legislators. Despite fierce opposition from most Republicans, and Democratic trade committee leaders such as Ways and Means Chair Rostenkowski, the House passed a resolution demanding that the trade agreement not weaken labor, environmental, health, or safety laws. Through their vote even legislators who had supported fast-track continuation fired a warning shot to the president signaling their willingness to kill NAFTA if it did not meet certain standards.

By this time, public approval of NAFTA had fallen considerably. According to a July 8, 1992, Time/CNN poll, 39 percent opposed it, while only 45 percent of Americans favored the agreement.[55] Legislators who supported NAFTA expressed concern that the public in general and constituents in particular did not support it. Indeed at the time of signing, it was believed that NAFTA did not have sufficient support for passage given the agreement's weaknesses on labor and environmental issues. In a July 24, 1992 letter to President Bush, Sen. Baucus wrote that despite his support for fast-track and the concept of a North American Free Trade Agreement, "If an agreement is submitted to Congress that does not adequately address the environmental issues, I will have no choice but to call for its renegotiation or rejections."[56]

Although activists rightly criticized the negotiations' lack of transparency, they took advantage of the limited access and information they did have to develop and gauge the impact of their own positions and mobilization in relation to the state. During substantive negotiations their combination of insider and outsider strategies mutually reinforced each other; they mobilized grassroots opposition to NAFTA and then harnessed that antagonism to influence legislators who, by threatening final passage, indirectly influenced the position of negotiators. Thus by utilizing a combination of insider and outsider strategies, and effectively brokering resources between the grassroots politics and legislative fields, activists set the stage for a contentious presidential election that would center in large part around NAFTA, and a subsequent dramatic fight in Congress over the passage of the agreement.

6

Using Institutional Leverage to Influence the Side Agreements

THE TIMING OF the final substantive negotiations catapulted the issue of free trade into the November 3, 1992, presidential election campaign and presented a problem for candidate Bill Clinton. Whoever won the election could renegotiate the agreement, or would have the arduous task of garnering congressional support for it. But Clinton knew that labor and environmental activists would vigorously resist the agreement as negotiated by his predecessor and that without changing the political dynamic, perhaps by adding labor and environmental protections, Congress probably would not ratify it. In an effort to distance himself from President Bush while eschewing protectionism, Clinton embraced a limited version of the labor-environmental rights frame to alter the political map on NAFTA. Under intense pressure from labor and environmental activists, Clinton announced on the eve of the election his support for supplemental labor and environmental agreements.

U.S. legislators' ultimate rule-making ability to determine NAFTA's fate meant that leverage points between the legislative and transnational negotiating fields proved critical for activists during supplemental negotiations.[1] Although negotiators determined the rules, or terms of the trade agreement, legislators influenced those rules and had the ultimate authority to institutionalize them or not through their NAFTA vote. The British Columbia trade minister underlined the significance of congressional rule-making leverage when he quipped after the completion of substantive negotiations: "now that the NAFTA has been initialed, only special interests in the U.S. stand a chance of changing the text by lobbying Congress. Canadians have no such opportunity."[2]

Thus during the period from March to August 1993 when the side agreements were negotiated, state institutions were invaluable to activists who leveraged rule-making strategies across them. Their efforts influenced the state by forcing negotiators to ratchet up the side agreement provisions in order to have any chance of NAFTA's passage. When supplemental negotiations began in March, negotiators in all three countries vowed that the side agreements would neither include trade sanctions (that is, enforcement mechanisms with teeth) nor be based on international standards. But activists continued to rally public opposition, and then harnessed that antagonism to influence legislators who then pressured negotiators by threatening final passage.

In this chapter, we reveal the cat-and-mouse game activists and their legislative allies played with negotiators, and show how the latter succumbed to pressure by strengthening environmental and labor protections at multiple points during negotiations. We also analyze the unexpected ability of environmentalists to push for and obtain stronger protections in the environmental side agreement than labor activists achieved in the labor side agreement. This is particularly surprising because unions were stronger and had substantially more political and financial resources to draw upon than did environmentalists.

The ability of both environmental and labor activists to ratchet up the side agreements was possible, in large part, because cleared labor and environmental advisors had access to draft negotiating texts. In fact, once elected, President Clinton vowed greater transparency and participation for activists in the negotiation process. And his administration delivered on that promise by providing access to key draft negotiating documents and trade policy officials who solicited their input (primarily to gauge minimal conditions necessary for passage). One AFL-CIO official revealed his ability to access draft documents: "I personally read every iteration of negotiations in the side agreement for a whole year and went through detail by detail . . . ."[3] Thus under Clinton activists offered critiques, as they had under the Bush administration. But the Clinton administration faced a deal dead in the water in Congress if they did not figure out how to address labor and environmental concerns.

Activists Push Clinton to Support Supplemental Negotiations

With the conclusion of substantive negotiations, labor and environmental activists anxiously awaited Governor Clinton's stance on NAFTA. For two months, President Bush attempted to press him to take a stand but he refused to take a public position.[4] Clinton's campaign staff reached out to labor and environmental leaders to help determine what position he should take. His staff debated two broad options—the "yes but" strategy and the "yes and" strategy. The "yes but" strategy encapsulated a general support for trade liberalization with a rejection of the specifics of the agreement. The "yes and" strategy combined general support for trade liberalization with a call for additional safeguards in the agreement. The AFL-CIO, Sierra Club, Public Citizen, and FOE all supported the "yes but" option and argued for renegotiation of the agreement, whereas pro-growth organizations such as NWF and WWF argued for support of the existing agreement, a "yes and" position (Audley 1997:69). To resolve this problem, the Clinton campaign political advisor "selected representatives from NWF and WWF to work with him and staff from the House Ways and Means Committee and the Senate Finance Committee to develop a position on NAFTA" (Audley 1997:69–70).

While waiting for Clinton to announce his position, AFL-CIO leaders decided to gear up for an anti-NAFTA legislative battle that required grassroots pressure. And their members were pushing for increased action and grassroots mobilization; labor union members were participating in FTC events and AFL-CIO affiliates were on the board of the CTWC—and actively questioning the AFL-CIO leadership on the issue. AFL-CIO representatives Ed Feigen and Mark Anderson began an unprecedented "grass roots anti-NAFTA action plan" in August 1992.[5] In a letter to Anderson, Feigen stated: "The Department of Organization and Field Services has received many inquiries on the Federation's NAFTA program and there is clearly a strong interest in the field for broad grassroots action."[6] The campaign kicked off with anti-NAFTA billboards placed strategically around the country. The AFL-led "Just Say No" campaign began just before the end of September 1992.[7]

Also in September, organizations that favored renegotiation or rejection—including the AFL-CIO, FOE, Sierra Club, National Farmers Union, Public Citizen, and others—united to sponsor a conference dubbed the Trade Conference for the 21st Century to influence the positions of Clinton and the other presidential candidates.[8] More than fifty organizations called for fundamental changes to, or rejection of, the agreement, and the conference was the first major event the AFL-CIO co-sponsored with other anti-NAFTA activists. Congressional allies also attempted to influence Clinton's stand. Representatives Kaptur and Bonior organized a letter to Clinton signed by ninety-six House Democrats calling on him to reject NAFTA and renegotiate the agreement. They pushed the labor-environmental rights frame, demanding worker rights, environmental protection, and health and safety standards, and emphasized that 500,000 jobs would be lost.[9]

The Clinton campaign ultimately decided to support the "yes and" option advocated by pro-growth environmentalists in an effort to shift the political dynamics enough to pass the pact, while avoiding the tag of protectionism. Clinton provisionally supported the agreement with the negotiation of additional safeguards on labor, environment, and import surges. Pro-growth environmentalists, who had pushed President Bush to create an environmental commission, however, continued their pressure on Clinton. As a result, he agreed to build on USTR efforts to establish an environmental commission. The other major adversarial environmental organizations signaled their regret that Clinton did not call for renegotiation, and criticized the agreement for a lack of assurance of sustainable development, a specific funding mechanism, and enforcement of environmental standards.[10] To placate unions, Clinton also agreed to establish a labor commission. This did not allay labor leaders' concerns either. Indeed, the AFL-CIO officially expressed "disappointment" with Clinton's conditional support of NAFTA.[11] They signaled that a labor commission would not be strong enough to garner their support.

The transparency of the U.S. ratification process and the uncertainty of passage in the United States helped bolster Clinton's claims that his hands were tied; the leaders of all three nations understood that without intervention of some kind, NAFTA would most likely not be ratified by the U.S. Congress. Although Canadian and Mexican negotiators were hostile to the idea of supplemental negotiations, Clinton's claims that the best way to assure passage was to placate labor and environmental constituencies was plausible on its face, and they ultimately (albeit grudgingly) agreed to labor and environmental side agreements.

After Clinton won the presidential election in November 1992, activists continued to apply pressure by fomenting public opposition to the agreement. In late 1992 the CTWC and the FTC united under the CTC, which incorporated as a non-profit advocacy organization that also had a research wing, with a mandate to "engage in charitable, social welfare, educational activities related to protecting the environment and the rights and well-being of citizens with regard to international trade policy."[12] CTC labeled itself the "most diverse coalition ever united" with sixty national organizations and three thousand participating grassroots organizations representing 25 million people.[13] After bringing in as executive director Jim Jontz, a former Indiana congressman, CTC launched the first wave of its campaign in December 1992 in preparation for the entry of the new administration.[14] The CTC directed activities from D.C., and the FTC acted as a grassroots partner. At around the same time, in November 1992 MODTLE changed its name to the Alliance for Responsible Trade (ART).

Together with ART, CTC leaders sent Clinton a letter on December 15 signed by fifty-two organizations arguing that the flaws in the agreement were sufficiently serious and therefore could not be resolved with supplemental agreements alone.[15] In contrast, DOW informed Clinton that the environmental side agreement could bring the support of most of the environmental community. The organization laid out five conditions that needed to be met: (1) open dispute resolution to the public, (2) a secure funding source for infrastructure and cleanup, (3) standards for production processes, (4) an effective deterrent to U.S. industries moving to Mexico to take advantage of weaker environmental laws and regulations, and (5) stronger environmental protections in international environmental agreements.[16]

Although these divergent strategies did reflect real differences in tactics and goals, the diversity among environmental organizations was not inherently counterproductive at this stage. As a CTC internal memorandum explained:

> It seems as some groups in the national coalition are promoting the "fix-it" message, state coalitions are taking a harder line with a no NAFTA campaign theme. Both of these messages are fine and will only help the national campaign as a whole address and spread awareness of its overriding concerns with the agreement. For some CTC member groups, being willing to discuss side agreements is a tactic that they find necessary in Washington in order to be at the table and be a credible part of the political debate over the NAFTA. In talking to the administration now, these groups are laying markers by which the finished agreement can later be judged. . . . In fact, it was generally understood that the national coalition depends on the state coalitions [sic] to take a harder line.[17]

Some organizations' pursuit of legislative opposition and others' efforts to amend the agreement reinforced each other to the extent there was unity on the bottom line commitment to fight to stop a final package that did not measure up. In contrast, pro-growth environmentalists used the coalition's opposition and campaigning to further their "yes and" position given the campaign created a real risk of nullification if the agreement were not fixed. On some level efforts to find acceptable terms provided adversarial environmentalists with a means to resist the protectionist label.

On December 17, 1992, when President Bush signed the agreement, labor and environmental organizations in each country protested the official signing ceremonies. Grassroots activity coordinated in opposition to the agreement also increased. The Massachusetts coalition, for example, launched a grassroots petition drive to oppose NAFTA. Thirty-five community and labor groups endorsed the drive and participated. The signature campaign began with press conferences throughout the state. As one activist explained: "The press coverage—and the extent of local participation—surprised many skeptics who didn't believe that such a seemingly abstruse issue could engage activists or local media at the grassroots level. Eventually, tens of thousands of signatures were gathered and turned in to members of the Massachusetts Congressional delegation."[18] Activists continued to apply pressure leading up to the beginning of supplemental negotiations. In February 1993, the AFL-CIO Executive Council issued its official position on NAFTA. It called for Clinton to renegotiate the agreement to promote "worker rights, strong labor standards, consumer health and safety, and environmental protection."[19]

Activists Apply Indirect Pressure on Negotiators

President Clinton's new USTR, Mickey Kantor, met with representatives of ART and the CTC during his first days in office. He expressed his willingness to solicit input from these organizations during the supplemental agreement negotiations and planned to use the supplemental negotiations to address an expanded role for public participation, among other issues.[20]

On February 3, 1993, President Clinton established an initial interagency task force on trade with representatives from the Labor Department, the EPA, and the Departments of Commerce and Treasury.[21] Labor Secretary Robert Reich made it clear that the purpose of the supplemental negotiations was to ensure the passage of NAFTA; the accords had to be sufficiently strong to sway labor and environmental activists in order to allow Democrats to vote for the agreement, without being so strong as to alienate trade liberalization supporters among Republicans. USTR negotiators acted with that mandate in mind. The two agreements were expected to be functionally similar, with the establishment of trilateral commissions with a minimal enforcement mechanism.[22]

Negotiators Respond to Activist Pressure

A key strategy activists used to strengthen the side agreements was to purposely maintain uncertainty about their win-set in order to press for the largest number of concessions.[23] *Inside U.S. Trade* reported that it was difficult for negotiators and members of the Clinton administration to determine the "bottom line" of labor and environmental groups and their congressional allies because they wanted to maximize their rule-making leverage on trade policy field negotiators by not stating minimums necessary for their support.[24]

This strategy of leveraging uncertainty between fields helped legislators ratchet up the environmental side agreement by bringing sanctions into play. Indeed, negotiators responded to the uncertainty by *changing their strategies* to incorporate trade fines and sanctions as a way to gain votes in the legislative field. Negotiators looked to House members' positions to determine the minimum concessions needed for passage. Rep. Gephardt's signals in particular made trade sanctions appear crucial to developing additional support for the agreement. As a U.S. negotiator explained:

> It was really tough to figure out what would be good enough. . . . The Mexicans made it absolutely clear that [industrial relations protections were] make-or-break—that they would ditch NAFTA rather than have sanctions attached to anything involving unions. . . . Initially, the U.S. wasn't clear on whether it was going to favor sanctions or not. Lloyd Bentsen was adamantly against sanctions for anything. But as Gephardt and others sort of came into play, and as there got more heat on the labor issue, Treasury switched, and the president came down in favor of sort of trying to get some sanctions. So the negotiating position actually changed. Very early on, there was a view that there would be no sanctions in the process.[25]

In an attempt to maximize the power of Democrats, House Democrat Sander Levin even urged colleagues to avoid stating their position until the side deals were negotiated.

Thus during each of six rounds of official negotiating meetings, negotiators responded to the pressure from activists and their congressional allies by significantly strengthening *both* side agreements. Initially, labor negotiators, led by Labor Secretary Reich, were much more insistent on the importance of enforcement mechanisms than EPA officials.[26] Canadian and Mexican negotiators unequivocally opposed all sanctions. Environmental NGOs and their congressional allies, however, applied pressure for sanctions, which enabled EPA officials, concerned that the environmental side agreement would be weaker than the labor agreement, to demand similar enforcement mechanisms to the labor side agreement. Thus quite unexpectedly, environmentalists ultimately strengthened two key provisions of the environmental side agreement that were initially weaker than the labor agreement: enforcement mechanisms and international standards.

U.S. negotiators argued from the beginning that the side agreements would need a minimal enforcement mechanism, but they did not initially include the ability to issue subpoenas or enforce sanctions. During the first round of negotiations that began on March 17, 1993, in Washington, DC, U.S. labor negotiators outlined three possible paths to handle labor issues. The first option included an "unobtrusive" labor commission that would only use "weak moral suasion" (Cameron and Tomlin 2000:183). The commission "would promote minimum standards for a narrow range of labor rights, requiring only a small staff," and would focus on "nonpolitical and easily defined worker rights, such as child labor, work hours, and health and safety" (Cameron and Tomlin 2000:183). Enforcement mechanisms would be minimal.

The second option involved a labor "commission with more independence, a larger staff, and a mandate to examine issues such as worker rights and participation, the link between wages and productivity, protection against downward harmonization of social security, and efforts to reduce inequality" (Cameron and Tomlin 2000:183–4). Language would be derived from "the Mexican constitution, the social provisions of the Canadian Charlottetown constitutional accord, and the European Social Charter" (Cameron and Tomlin 2000:184). The third option would incorporate the more inclusive second option and "add trade sanctions or similar border measures as a means of enforcement" (Cameron and Tomlin 2000:184).[27] The commission would serve as a watchdog and would respond to private groups' appeals, but its findings would be nonbinding.

Canadian negotiators opposed sanctions and rejected the idea of an independent labor commission. Their proposal mentioned the possible future negotiation of continent-wide labor standards. Mexican negotiators hoped for the weakest possible side agreements (Cameron and Tomlin 2000:185). They were wary of even limited intervention on these issues and rejected commissions that would supersede Mexico's domestic laws. In the first outline for the labor side agreement, trade sanctions for violations were conspicuously absent. Mexican president Salinas and his economic cabinet established three guidelines: the final agreements had to respect Mexico's sovereignty, could not introduce environmental or labor standards as "disguised protectionism" or renegotiate NAFTA more generally, and could not include traditional commercial transactions (i.e., no trade sanctions). Mexico's labor secretary was especially concerned about maintaining Mexico's corporatist system of labor relations, and the CTM supported this negotiating position (Cameron and Tomlin 2000:185).

Between the first and second round of negotiations activists rallied the public in the grassroots politics field and their allies in the legislative field. In March, the FTC hosted a series of events designed to inform the public, Congress, and the media about NAFTA. Coalitions of labor, environmental, farm, church, consumer, and citizen organizations in over thirty-five states participated. ART and CTC hosted a briefing on NAFTA for new members of Congress on March 25th.[28] And in April during the congressional recess, coalition organizations met with their senators and representatives at home and held community meetings.

When negotiators met in Mexico City in April 1993 for the second round of talks, U.S. labor negotiators pressed for the use of dispute resolution, whereas U.S. environmental negotiators did not. Thus proposals on the table for the labor side agreement were *still stronger* than for the environmental agreement. U.S. labor negotiators went beyond environmental proposals by calling for commitments to enforce North American labor standards based on internationally-recognized standards including freedom of association, freedom to organize and bargain collectively, prohibition against forced labor, minimum work age, wages and health and safety conditions, and against employee discrimination. In contrast, the environmental commission would only promote the strengthening and compatibility of environmental laws by assessment procedures, helping monitor committees.[29] The U.S. labor negotiating position also gave wider latitude and greater powers to a labor secretariat.

Pressure from U.S. negotiators ultimately had an impact on the transnational negotiating field, however. Mexican chief of staff José Cordoba Montoya ultimately agreed to include panels for disputes and sanctions for the violation of environmental laws in the environmental side accord. Pro-growth environmental organizations took advantage of the opening.[30] Led by Ken Berlin of WWF, organizations including NWF, NRDC, EDF, and the National Audubon Society attended secret meetings to create a politically feasible position for a supplemental environmental agreement. Senator Baucus, the chair of the Senate Finance Trade Subcommittee and Senate Environmental and Public Works Committee, backed their efforts. He coordinated with NWF and NRDC to make trade sanctions the bottom line for support among environmentally focused House members. The pro-growth environmentalists wrote a draft letter to the USTR organized around seven policy areas: "organization and structure of the North American Commission; enforcement of environmental regulation; clarification of environmental standards; funding for border and conservation projects; dispute settlement procedures; public participation; and international environmental agreements" (Audley 1997:89). They declared they could support NAFTA even if the environmental commission was not given the power to directly sanction polluters or issue subpoenas as part of its investigations.

The pro-growth contingent did insist, however, on a strong independent role for the commission and clarification of standards language in the text. The draft circulated among the organizations, which made minor modifications. Ultimately representatives from all five organizations with USTR advisory roles as well as EDF and DOW signed the letter (Audley 1997). On May 4, 1993, the signatory groups sent the letter, which outlined the provisions that they would need to support NAFTA, to USTR Kantor.[31] The letter marked a substantial scaling-back from previous demands, especially on the issues of trade sanctions and subpoena powers.

Environmental organizations involved in the anti-NAFTA coalition—including FOE, Sierra Club, Greenpeace, Humane Society, NTC, Clean Water Action, Earth Island Institute, and Rain Forest Action—were outraged by the position of the signatory organizations, which they viewed as a capitulation—and they refused to sign. The wedge between the two environmental factions thereby intensified. A leader of the FTC explained: "That rift and division within the environmental community had existed in Washington for a long time, everybody knew about it—but this issue really drove a cleaver into these groups, and the tension became enormous."[32]

One representative from a non-signatory organization argued that the letter should have insisted on the ability of the commission to seek access to industry information through courts, included the polluter pays principle for funding sources, and required a moratorium on challenges to laws that penalize all production process methods beyond their borders.[33] Adversarial environmental groups continued to press for additional demands. They received significant support from Rep. Gephardt, with whom they met on May 4. He agreed with their concerns and indicated that the position taken by environmentalists operating in the trade policy field was insufficiently tough to gain congressional approval.[34] Gephardt announced on May 11, 1993, that he intended to introduce legislation to allow the United States to launch cases against countries demonstrating a persistent pattern of labor or environmental law violations. But he also signaled that he would support NAFTA with the *right* supplemental accords, which forced negotiators to continue to try to acquire concessions to obtain his support.[35]

U.S. negotiators on the environmental side—under pressure from activists and their congressional allies—changed their position to endorse sanctions during the third round of negotiations in Ottawa in May 1993. U.S. negotiators pushed for trade sanctions to penalize the non-enforcement of domestic environmental laws, although they insisted they should be difficult to reach. They also called for an independent environmental secretariat with the ability to investigate claims and the right of NGOs to directly petition it.[36] Mexico and Canada opposed such autonomy and NGO participation.[37] They also rejected proposals for the labor side agreement to include trade sanctions and an independent secretariat with the right of NGOs to directly petition. Mexico rejected the idea of an independent regional secretariat altogether and suggested that the ILO prepare reports on regional labor conditions instead.[38]

Activists Make Final Push in the Grassroots Politics Field and Supplemental Negotiations Falter

After the third round of talks in Ottawa activists intensified their efforts in the legislative and trade policy fields. Twenty-eight environmental and conservation groups responded on June 8, 1993, by signing onto a paper analyzing the faults of the agreement. The paper, developed by adversarial organizations Sierra Club, Greenpeace, FOE, and the Humane Society, argued that trade sanctions should apply to non-enforcement of laws that affect global commons, transboundary issues, and trade and investment.[39]

Activists also continued their efforts across the country in the grassroots politics field. California Fair Trade Campaign activists contacted one thousand delegates prior to the April 1993 California State Democratic Party convention, and volunteers worked the convention floor. Their efforts bore fruit when the party adopted a "fair trade" resolution with broad support from the Latino, environmental, and rural caucuses, among many others. Outside the convention, Latino activists involved in Americans for Democracy in Mexico protested over human rights abuses in Mexico.

In May, CTC held a "National Week of Action" with events that spanned "a march in New York City to a tractorcade in Colorado."[40] In Northfield, Minnesota, activists created a car caravan to a company to protest its announcement that it would move 104 jobs to Mexico.[41] Rallies were held in St. Louis, Vermont, Portland, and Grand Forks, North Dakota.[42] A New York City march attracted 1,100 people, with activists from electrical and garment/textile unions, Greenpeace, the Bronx Clean Air campaign, Teamsters, and the UAW. The vice president of a local Teamsters union said that it was the first time in his forty years of labor activism he had seen so many different types of organizations mobilized.[43]

AFL-CIO affiliates—many of which were actively organizing in the grassroots politics field with the anti-NAFTA coalition—continued to pressure the federation's top officials to take a greater leadership role on the issue. The supplemental negotiations put the AFL-CIO in a difficult position; its leadership was caught between efforts to promote its influence among new administration officials and the demands of an increasingly agitated and mobilized segment of its membership base. The federation was under extreme pressure to back the Democratic president they helped elect. Administration officials met privately with labor leaders in an effort to persuade them not to publicly oppose supplemental negotiations, signaling that they would be active participants in the process. Moreover Clinton stirred unions' hopes that the labor side agreement would have teeth, proclaiming in a 1992 speech that a commission "should be established for worker standards and safety. It too should have extensive powers to educate, train, develop minimum standards and have similar dispute resolution powers and remedies. We have got to do this. This is a big deal."[44]

The AFL-CIO complied with the administration's request to hold judgment because its leaders did not want to antagonize potential allies in other policy battles and because the administration led them to believe their participation could influence the outcome. AFL-CIO officials therefore worked with the USTR to attempt to improve the labor side agreement while trying to publicly minimize opposition to the president. As the AFL-CIO's Mark Anderson explained:

> We opposed the Bush NAFTA because it had . . . nothing. . . [T]hen Clinton comes in with our support and says "I'm going to negotiate some other stuff, give me a chance, hold off." That's when we started the "Not this NAFTA." Before it was no, the Bush NAFTA sucks. So it was only after Clinton came in and we worked with the administration from January until August of that year trying to see if we could fashion a labor side agreement that we could then talk to the affiliates to see whether or not this is good enough for them to swallow.[45]

Despite their adoption of a "wait and see" position, the AFL-CIO demanded strong labor protections from the administration: a North American set of worker rights and minimum labor standards based on ILO standards, and unions' ability to file complaints of labor violations against governments *and* corporations in any North American country. These demands were consistent with those made by many other labor unions and organizations in the anti-NAFTA coalition, which consistently argued that the labor side agreement should provide significant enforcement mechanisms for key labor rights, including freedom of association and the right to strike and bargain collectively.

The work of labor and environmental activists in the grassroots politics field boosted congressional opposition to NAFTA by increasing the public's awareness and concern for its contents, and mobilizing local organizations and constituents to pressure their local representatives to oppose it. Combined with active lobbying efforts and the help of allies such as the Congressional Fair Trade Caucus, activists' efforts paid off—by early June the supplemental negotiations were in trouble and NAFTA appeared unlikely to pass. President Clinton acknowledged in remarks to the Business Roundtable on June 9, 1993, that NAFTA would not pass the House at the time: "A lot of members [of Congress] are rebelling against NAFTA because they see it as the first trade agreement we've ever made where we're making investment easier in another country for the purpose of setting up production to sell in our market, not theirs."[46]

U.S. negotiators warned that without labor and environmental secretariats the agreement would likely have little chance of passage in the House. The next three rounds of talks (in Washington, DC, in early June, Cocoyoc, Mexico in early July, and Ottawa in late July) therefore significantly ratcheted up the two side agreements. U.S. negotiators met outside DC in early June but failed to overcome differences related to the use of trade sanctions and the powers of the regional secretariats. To compound problems for negotiators and the administration, a federal judge deciding the Public Citizen NEPA case ruled that an environmental impact statement was necessary for NAFTA to be valid, and the U.S. district court ruled that the United States had to conduct one "with all deliberate speed."[47] The administration appealed the ruling.[48]

Activists responded by stepping up their pressure. Representatives from RMALC, ACN, ART, and the CTC delivered a joint statement calling for a halt to negotiations while the environmental impact statement was implemented.[49] In July 1993, the president of the National Audubon Society wrote a letter to USTR Kantor stating that the administration was at risk of losing the support of five of the seven environmental groups that might support its passage. He argued that the U.S. negotiating position had failed to incorporate clarifying language that would, among other things, spell out new rules on standards and adequately deal with dispute resolution, particularly on the issue of public participation. He added that the proposed threshold for triggering the dispute process was too high, and that the environmental commission needed to be adequately funded.[50]

In July, CTC's legislative task force scheduled meetings with one hundred legislators to discuss the problems with the side agreements.[51] Members of Congress working with unions and environmental organizations delivered one-minute speeches on the House floor every day the House was in session throughout the month.[52] Their congressional allies focused on four major themes: jobs, family farmers, environment, and human rights.

Activists' and legislators' pressure had an impact—by July all three countries agreed to form labor and environmental secretariats. That month labor negotiators approved the "Cocoyoc Compromise" language initially set forth by Mexico and the United States in negotiations. They agreed to four bodies with distinct roles to administer the labor accord: a commission, a ministerial council, national administrative offices, and an international coordinating secretariat. The sixth round of negotiations in Ottawa involved the most difficult and contentious phase of supplemental bargaining. The United States pushed for the agreement to create a higher standard, while the other two countries wanted the agreement to be based on each nation's existing laws. Canada was faced with the problem that most of its environmental laws were under provincial jurisdiction, whereas Mexico did not want to alter its system of corporatist bargaining. Finally the parties compromised on using "mutually recognized" laws rather than international standards.[53] They agreed on eight labor principles, including freedom of association, the right to bargain collectively, the right to strike, prohibition against forced labor, and a ban on child labor. But these standards would be objectives rather than actionable obligations.[54]

At a July 30, 1993, press conference, it appeared that the United States and Canada were still sharply divided on the issue of trade sanctions. Mexico had previously proposed health and safety standards as areas that could be scrutinized. Informed sources said that Mexico would probably accept adding minimum wage laws and child labor laws to that list. USTR Kantor informed members of Congress at an August 3 hearing that Mexico had agreed to provide better access to its court system for the enforcement of national labor laws, using the intellectual property provisions as a model. But the stymied negotiations threatened NAFTA's passage. House Whip Bonior, who was leading the opposition in rounding up votes, said during a July 27 press conference that if the agreement came up for a vote at the time, opponents would defeat the accord "handsomely."[55]

The Democratic whip count at the end of July showed more than three times as many Democrats leaning against the trade pact as leaning in favor. House Speaker Tom Foley confided to a diplomat in July that he thought NAFTA was dead and that there was not anything Clinton "or anyone on the planet" could do about it.[56] Senator Bill Bradley's aide also warned the National Association of Manufacturers on July 14 that the Senate passage of NAFTA was no sure thing, as reported in *Inside U.S. Trade*:

Senators are very nervous about casting a pro-NAFTA vote, because "there is a level of passion on this issue among unions and environmentalists and the populace as a whole that is striking," he said. Unlike previous trade agreements, he said, NAFTA "is not an inside game" but has become a grassroots "lightning rod" for expressing dissatisfaction with the economy and anxiety about the future.[57]

Indeed as the NAFTA vote loomed it appeared that the combination of insider and outsider strategies activists deployed had succeeded in throwing the agreement's passage into doubt.

Labor's Critical Strategic Blunder

Although the strategies of the environmental and labor movements reinforced each other during the first stages of the NAFTA struggle, the efforts of environmentalists worked against labor's strategy during supplemental negotiations. AFL-CIO officials initially worked with the USTR to try to improve the labor side agreement. Environmentalists, in contrast, actively organized at the grassroots level along with some AFL-CIO affiliated unions that tried to prod the federation into assuming a more active role in the struggle.[58]

By summer 1993, however, AFL-CIO leaders determined that the labor side agreement would be too weak to warrant their support. AFL-CIO secretary-treasurer Tom Donahue made the federation's position clear in a letter to USTR Mickey Kantor: "The administration's proposal fails to identify even minimal labor rights and standards to be enforced, establishes an oversight process so vague, discretionary, and protracted that a timely resolution of a dispute would be virtually impossible, makes individual violations of even national law non-actionable, and provides at the end of the process no effective remedies."[59] He argued that the proposed changes represented a weakening of remedies under U.S. law, as NAFTA would supplant GSP regulations on international labor rights.[60]

The AFL-CIO leadership decided their best strategy was to kill the entire deal. They therefore launched a grassroots campaign to bring resource leverage to bear in the legislative field.[61] In addition to holding press conferences, town hall meetings, and plant gate demonstrations and lobbying local government representatives, the federation's Task Force on Trade organized mail-in campaigns and displayed billboards across the country. The AFL-CIO also became a more active participant in the anti-NAFTA coalition by coordinating with member organizations and contributing money to its efforts. Thus the AFL-CIO turned its focus away from the trade policy and transnational negotiating fields to the anti-NAFTA campaign in the grassroots politics field, and to garnering support for votes against NAFTA in the legislative field.[62] As Mark Anderson, who led the AFL-CIO Task Force on Trade suggested, the shift in the AFL-CIO's strategy likely came too late:

> And when they finally came out with these agreements and it was in August 1993 that's when we said these agreements these suck, no, we're going to try to take it down. Now that may have been a tactical mistake on our part . . . Because that gave us a very short window to try to mobilize and get stuff up, it was mid-to-end of August. And so then the vote was when, in November? So at most you're talking about a three month window.[63]

The decision proved to be significant for the outcomes of both side agreements. Without AFL-CIO pressure in the trade policy field, pro-labor U.S. negotiators had little additional ability to threaten their Canadian and Mexican counterparts with legislative rule-making leverage by stating bottom-line labor demands to ensure passage. As U.S. labor negotiator Steve Herzenberg explained:

> The U.S. labor movement was pretty ineffectual. All they [the AFL-CIO Task Force on Trade] would tell the U.S. negotiators is that we would never support this thing, and if you strengthen it, it will be a little less of a [war] by the U.S. labor movement. So there was nobody on the outside putting any pressure on the U.S. negotiators which would lead them to make a pragmatic calculation to make the agreement stronger . . . I think the U.S. labor movement could have put pressure and that could have led to a different agreement.[64]

Rule-making strategies among the legislative, trade policy, and transnational negotiating fields proved decisive in the final unexpected outcome of supplemental negotiations; environmentalists used these strategies to maintain pressure on legislators and negotiators, *and* Mexican negotiators used them to press for their own preferences in the absence of sufficient pushback from labor. Rep. Gephardt and Senator Baucus informed USTR Kantor at the beginning of August that the threat of trade sanctions was crucial to ensure that national laws were enforced.[65]

When agreement could not be reached on international standards and sanctions, the lead Mexican negotiator met with Rep. Gephardt, who emphasized that sanctions were essential for U.S. legislative passage. As a result, Mexican negotiators agreed to accept sanctions for both agreements in exchange for a narrower labor scope that excluded trade sanctions for violations of core labor rights such as freedom of association, collective bargaining, and striking.[66] Environmental law remained broadly defined.

Although it could be argued that the stronger environmental side agreement had less to do with activists' pressure than with business opposition in the United States to strong labor rights protections, the data reveal that many business representatives did not push for stronger environmental over labor sanctions; they were on record as similarly opposed to both. Business organizations publicly and privately expressed their concern with and opposition to a strong environmental side agreement. Representatives of the Chamber of Commerce criticized both side deals, saying they had not been adequately consulted. An April 1993 letter from the International Vice President of the U.S. Chamber of Commerce to USTR Kantor, however, focused almost exclusively on concerns with the environmental side agreement: "I must frankly tell you that there is considerable concern in the business community about the direction U.S. proposals in the environmental side agreement negotiations appear to be taking and that this could jeopardize our members' continued support for the NAFTA. Their concerns relate both to the structure and powers of a prospective North American Commission on the Environment and to proposed provisions for the use of trade sanctions under some circumstances."[67] USA*NAFTA, a coalition of 2,300 companies and corporate lobbying organizations dominated by CEOs from the largest U.S. companies, released a press statement on June 30, 1993, criticizing a U.S. District Court decision to require an environmental impact statement for NAFTA in the case filed by environmental NGOs.[68]

Like USA*NAFTA, influential business interests such as the U.S. Chamber of Commerce, the National Association of Manufacturers, the Business Roundtable, and the U.S. Council for International Business criticized the side deals and opposed trade sanctions.[69] Despite their money and access which allowed them to influence the content of the agreement, however, business advocacy as it related to the legislative battle was relatively ineffective, according to key NAFTA supporters.[70] White House and congressional officials did not credit the business coalition with making a difference in the legislative fight. President Clinton complained in September 1993 that businesses were not doing enough to help support passage of the agreement.[71] At the end of October 1993, House Minority Whip Newt Gingrich called the business effort "pathetic" and ineffective.[72] The business mobilization was declared "a joke" and "a failure." As a White House official explained: "Corporations and trade associations are very bad at grass roots. They can do very well at tax cuts, and against tax increases, but on major policy issues, they're not good at all at getting their employees to contact Congress. The employees just don't care enough."[73]

White House NAFTA advisor Bill Frenzel acknowledged that local business efforts at the end of October 1993 had not yet produced results. He said that "he has talked to 'literally hundreds' of members of Congress and has found only one who got one-third of its mail in support of NAFTA. The rest of members report a ratio of 100 to one on mail against the agreement, and almost none have received calls in favor of NAFTA."[74] USA*NAFTA state captains complained to Washington headquarters that NAFTA was not a salient issue among businesses generally, and that it was difficult to get small and medium-sized businesses to join the coalition.[75] Although business support for NAFTA certainly influenced its passage, corporate interests' advocacy does not fully explain how activists were able to influence the outcome, and why environmentalists had more success in ratcheting up the environmental side accord than their labor counterparts.[76]

Because supplemental negotiations were not inevitably a zero-sum game, a stronger environmental side agreement *did not* have to come at the expense of a weaker labor agreement. The AFL-CIO could have pushed harder for stronger protections or worked more closely with environmentalists to create a common bottom line for both agreements. The AFL-CIO strategy to kill the agreement in the legislative field through pressure from the grassroots politics field would likely have been successful if environmental concessions had not blunted legislative opposition. Environmentalists were able to utilize strategies to leverage across state fields at all stages of negotiations to successfully ratchet up the environmental side agreement. Indeed, had environmentalists not been waiting and banging at the door, they would likely have achieved nothing. But their decision to focus their pressure between the legislative and transnational negotiating fields in the final months before the agreements were finalized proved to be judicious, because it was here that the final horse-trading occurred, and it tipped the final balance to achieve an unlikely and unpredicted outcome.

Although the AFL-CIO maintained a higher position in the influence hierarchies of the trade policy and legislative fields than environmentalists, the structural differences between their concerns were laid bare. Labor concerns touched the heart of Mexico's economic relationship with the United States and its means of attaining its capital needs. The intensity of Mexican negotiators' preferences for a weak labor agreement far outweighed their preferences for a weak environmental agreement. And it was not countered by an equally strong preference by President Clinton for a strong labor agreement.

In this final battle over continental economic integration, the split between pro-growth and adversarial environmental organizations and the former's ability to find a middle ground in the supplemental agreements enabled Clinton to claim a victory for fair trade goals while failing to meet labor's key demands. Ironically, the labor movement's ability to remain united in their opposition to NAFTA prevented negotiators from dividing it; there were no conciliatory unions to offer concessions to. Union's collective refusal to settle for a weak labor side agreement ironically provided an incentive for key decision-makers to garner votes for passage rather than improve the agreement for unions willing to negotiate.

The Outcome: Comparing the Side Agreements

USTR Kantor announced August 13 that the labor and environmental side agreements were complete, as was a separate import surge accord. Both agreements included the trade sanctions considered crucial by U.S. negotiators for securing congressional support.[77] The NAFTA package included funding for environmental infrastructure projects along the border and a comprehensive worker adjustment program.[78] As negotiations ended, the lopsided nature of the supplemental agreements was fully revealed. Labor activists had not achieved the basic labor rights protections at the heart of their demands, whereas pro-growth environmentalists gained even more than they asked for.

Although both side agreements emphasized the enforcement of domestic law and created multilateral organizations, the agreements were clearly unequal in scope and potency. There are broad similarities in the labor and environmental supplemental agreements and the institutions they created, and in the description that follows we discuss them as they were originally written and intended to function in 1993. The North American Agreement on Environmental Cooperation (NAAEC) and the North American Agreement on Labor Cooperation (NAALC) focus on the enforcement of domestic law to address concerns about the effects of NAFTA. To accomplish this goal, both agreements established a commission with a ministerial council and a secretariat to adjudicate relevant disputes in international trade matters related to domestic law. The councils, which are comprised respectively of the equivalent of the environmental and labor ministers from each country, promote cross-border cooperation and resolve disputes emerging from the trade agreement. If it is found that a country has persistently failed to enforce a relevant law, fines and ultimately trade sanctions may be enforced.[79] The secretariats provide operational, research, and technical support for the councils.[80]

However, the environmental side agreement is much stronger than the labor side agreement in scope, enforcement powers, and public participation. Although the Commission for Environmental Cooperation (CEC) can rule on the enforcement of any domestic environmental law, the Commission for Labor Cooperation (CLC) is quite circumscribed in what labor laws it may address. CLC evaluations are restricted to mutually recognized labor law, preventing the use of dispute resolution for innovative, far-reaching, or more protective domestic labor law. Further, the CLC may only level trade sanctions in disputes that involve occupational safety and health, child labor, or minimum wages. Mexico's minimum wage levels fall far below the poverty line, making the minimum wage component of limited usefulness. Violations of laws protecting the right to organize, strike, and bargain collectively may only be subject to ministerial consultations and are conspicuously absent from the covered trade sanction list. The CLC prevents action on exactly those worker rights deemed essential for independent union activity and a meaningful protection of workers' rights (see Kay 2005; 2011a; 2011b).

In addition, the CEC includes the institutionalized participation of nonprofit and nongovernmental representatives. The NAAEC established a Joint Public Advisory Council (JPAC), comprised of five members from each country, to advise the Council. As described on the CEC website:

During negotiations for the North American Free Trade Agreement (NAFTA), citizens, public interest groups, and environmental organizations brought the issue of the environmental effects of liberalized trade into the free trade debate, a debate that eventually led to the negotiation of the side agreement NAAEC and the creation of CEC. The mandate of JPAC is to provide advice to the Council on any matter within the scope of the North American Agreement on Environmental Cooperation (NAAEC). JPAC ensures that the views of the North American public are taken into account when formulating its advice to the Council. This commitment to public participation makes the CEC unique and provides a model for other international organizations.[81]

The NAALC does not have a comparable JPAC. The NAALC has the ability to convene an Evaluation Committee of Experts (ECE) to resolve some public submissions, but it is not comparable to a JPAC. If ministerial consultations do not resolve a submission, any country may request the establishment of an ECE. The ECE presents a final report to the Council. ECEs may only be convened to examine trade-related matters, those covered by mutually recognized labor laws, and those related to child labor, minimum wage, or occupational health and safety.[82]

The CEC enables NGOs and members of the public to submit claims of enforcement failure directly to its transnational "Citizen Submissions on Enforcement Matters" mechanism. While NGOs, labor unions, and individuals may file public submissions with the NAALC, they must do so via National Administrative Offices (NAOs), that are housed within each government's labor department.[83] Submitters must follow the rules created by their own country's NAO. If the submission is accepted for review the NAO evaluates it, and can subsequently recommend ministerial consultations, which involve a transnational review. The NAALC procedure therefore creates an extra step before a submission can be considered for transnational review.[84] The different structural and procedural components of the commissions mean that the CEC has a much broader jurisdiction, a far greater role for public participation, and greater enforcement power than the CLC, which lacks the ability to take action on precisely those worker rights deemed essential for independent union activity and a true protection of workers.

Activists Dissatisfied with the Side Agreements

When the side agreements were unveiled on August 13, 1993, activists in the anti-NAFTA coalition expressed their unanimous disdain and vowed to collectively fight NAFTA's passage. Coalition members from all three countries met at the end of September to discuss short-term and medium-term strategies and goals. All agreed that the priority was to defeat the agreement in the United States, the country with the best opportunity for leverage, and to increase public debate on the issue in Mexico and Canada. They launched an unprecedented mobilization in the grassroots politics field designed to inform the public and to pressure members of Congress about NAFTA. By the fall of 1993, activists maintained state-wide coalition participants in forty-three states. They held news conferences, arranged local meetings with their elected representatives, conducted border trips, canvassed door to door, initiated postcard drives, and held public protests.

Leverage between the grassroots politics and legislative fields once again significantly diminished the chances of the agreement's passage. The uncertainty surrounding domestic win-sets even for the president was evident at the end stages of the NAFTA struggle. Pro-NAFTA lobbyist Ken Cole proclaimed: "NAFTA is very unusual. People are coming out in ones and twos . . . for or against, and they're actually holding press conferences, announcing where they stand. It's unprecedented—I mean, you just don't do that."[85] He added, "We basically have all the Republicans we're going to get. Now we're at hand-to-hand combat for Democrats."[86] Pro-NAFTA leaders expressed skepticism that the supplemental negotiations would overcome legislative divisions. The private view of most senior officials in the administration was that the president should jettison the accord and "cover his tracks."[87] Pro-trade Republican Representative Fred Upton of Michigan acknowledged: "Being for NAFTA right now is like being for a congressional pay raise. The sentiment is all against it."[88]

Despite these prognostications, however, President Clinton stitched together enough votes to ensure NAFTA's passage in Fall 1993. Clinton turned to individual trade and nontrade side payments to unaligned members of Congress in a last-ditch effort to secure sufficient votes for passage of the agreement. Quipped columnist George Will: "votes are for sale and the President is buying."[89] The agreement on a North American Development Bank (NADBank), at a cost of at least $250 million to the United States, was among the most expensive deals and was oriented toward eight Latino legislators.[90] Estimates of the costs of the deals ranged from $300 million to $4.4 billion.[91] An anonymous businessman added: "I don't think I've ever seen as much retail politics in a trade agreement. The

Mexican Government is truly amazed at the bazaar—that's b-a-z-a-a-r—nature of this."[92]

Ultimately, NAFTA hinged on a narrow voting margin in the House. On November 17, 1993, the House voted 234 to 200 for the agreement.[93] The margin was due in large part to an unexpectedly large turnout of Republicans; 102 Democrats also voted in favor.[94] Bonior, who led the anti-NAFTA effort, said that most of the slippage had occurred from less Republican opposition than expected.[95] Secretary-Treasurer Donahue of the AFL-CIO blamed the result entirely on the president's ability in such a close vote to bestow side payments to members of Congress: "The vote was not indicative of the tightness of the campaign by the time the vote came. We got rolled by the Republicans. But we pulled an awful lot of Democrats on that vote. And we only got beat because Clinton and the Republicans were making book."[96] On November 20, the Senate voted to approve NAFTA 61–38.

The Significance of Supplemental Negotiations and Open State Channels

Although labor and environmental activists almost universally viewed NAFTA's passage as a crushing defeat, they had influenced the state's bargaining position and strategy by using insider and outsider strategies at key moments to threaten NAFTA's passage. They helped to ensure that the concept of connecting labor rights and environmental protections to trade agreements was newly established. The NAALC and NAAEC—unprecedented for linking trade and labor and environmental rights for the first time in a free trade agreement—would not have existed at all were it not for the activists' constant pressure that threatened NAFTA's passage. They had indeed achieved the only institutionalization of fair trade concerns through the establishment of the labor and environmental commissions, as well as through the inclusion of environmentalists in USTR advisory committees. They educated members of Congress on fair trade issues and established important alliances with key members. Their linkage of environmental and labor issues and trade was legitimized in the trade policy and legislative fields. They changed the parameters of the trade debate.

In addition, activists established a broad and diverse coalition with grassroots support that created important alliances between previously wary organizations. They expanded advocacy networks and developed an organizational infrastructure that extended beyond the anti-NAFTA campaign itself. Finally, they established a floor for trade battles to come, in Latin America and beyond. Fair trade advocacy would not end with NAFTA.

7

Pushing Back against the State

TRADE BATTLES AFTER NAFTA

THE INK HAD barely dried on NAFTA when the next round of trade battles began. President Clinton sought fast-track renewal in 1997 and 1998. Labor unions, environmental organizations, and their congressional allies successfully pushed back, punishing him for NAFTA by denying him a new delegation of fast-track authority and putting Clinton in a difficult position to continue to promote free trade agreements. The impact on Clinton's trade agenda was powerful. Without fast-track authority, Clinton was not able to pass any other free trade agreement during the rest of his two terms in office, making his push to admit China to the WTO his only other major trade achievement.[1] Of the fast-track defeat, Destler writes:

> Still, social issues had suddenly become the "800-pound gorilla" of trade policy. The main players and institutions were ill-equipped to deal with them. Their pre-1990 exclusion from the central trade debate had helped facilitate bipartisan consensus. But now they had forced their way to the trade policy table, presumably to stay. (1995:269)

Fair trade activists were at the trade policy table to stay. NAFTA indelibly changed labor and environmental activists' understanding of, and engagement in, trade policy. It was a watershed agreement that laid the foundation for all future trade policy debates and political struggles around trade not just in North America, but around the globe. NAFTA was primarily and fundamentally about changing the rules of the global economy; activists realized that trade policy linked domestic and international issues in critical new ways, and that the stakes of trade policy were therefore incredibly high. They were committed to future trade battles. And this required them to be prepared and proactive on trade policy advocacy. In NAFTA's wake, unions re-evaluated key domestic policies and made significant changes to their internal departments to deal with the restructuring of the regional economy. The AFL-CIO, for example, strengthened its Task Force on Trade, restructured its international and public policy departments, and hired more economists and lawyers to focus on trade issues.

Activists' commitment was met with new resolve from President Clinton and his successors who responded to activists' pushback on trade by trying to marginalize them and their arguments, and by trying to maintain divisions between pro-growth and adversarial environmental organizations. The strategy of maintaining exclusion, division and secrecy, which began with Clinton, reached its zenith during the Obama administration. Ironically, that the Obama administration began to formally classify draft trade agreements and threaten people who shared information with those outside the official advisory system using national security laws, was a testament to the impact of activists' mobilization against NAFTA. The opposition to neoliberal trade policy and policymaking was so effective that the state responded by undermining democratic practices around trade.

In this chapter we examine how the state and activists continued their cat-and-mouse game in relationship to trade policy after NAFTA's passage. We show how activists shifted their strategies in response to limited institutional opportunities and access by foregrounding issues of democracy rather than labor and environmental rights. As they did during the NAFTA struggle, activists continued to push back against the state in their effort to influence trade policy in subsequent trade battles.

Clinton's Stymied Post-NAFTA Trade Agenda

The Clinton administration adjusted to the new politicization of trade policy by trying to delegitimize, divide, and thwart opposition. Although he was emboldened by his NAFTA win, the vote was narrow, and the Democrats had lost control of the House of Representatives in the 1994 elections. Clinton decided to double down on trade. Less than a year after NAFTA went into force, Clinton and his key counterparts across the Americas introduced the FTAA in December 1994 at the Summit of the

Americas in Miami. FTAA, which would include thirty-four nations and extend free trade across the Americas, was touted as "NAFTA on steroids" (Roberts and Thanos 2003). During his presidency, Clinton did not make any FTAA negotiating texts available to the public. Between 1995 and 1997, the Clinton administration also conducted secret negotiations of the MAI. In 1998, an OECD insider leaked a draft copy to a Canadian NGO that revealed that it would create ISDS mechanisms similar to NAFTA's chapter 11—international investment rules that would supersede national laws and "gave corporations a right to sue governments if national health, labor or environment legislation threatened their interests."[2] Soon after, the negotiations over the MAI failed. Pressure from labor, environmental, and other civil society organizations, particularly those in France and Canada, were instrumental in bringing about MAI's collapse.

Labor, environmental, and other anti-free-trade activists were outraged by the Clinton administration's efforts to stymie public participation in trade negotiations. In 1997, activists, including the CTC and ART joined with Latin American activists to create the Hemispheric Social Alliance to oppose the FTAA. In April 2001, just months before 9/11 at the fifth FTAA Summit of the Americas meeting in Quebec City, over sixty thousand protesters—an unprecedented number—clashed with police and kept a rapt international public glued to the news. Protesters converged again two years later at the 2003 Summit in Miami. By 2005, after years of ceaseless pressure from large labor federations and environmental organizations, and with opposition from nations such as Brazil, Argentina and Venezuela that rejected key provisions, FTAA negotiations stalled indefinitely, effectively killing the agreement. The FTAA died in Mar del Plata, Argentina, after over a decade of negotiations.

After NAFTA, all subsequent U.S. trade agreements have included labor and environmental components, and the frameworks, in general, have been strengthened over time. Most important, the twinning of labor and environmental rights as a key encapsulation of fair trade principles has been cemented since NAFTA's passage. Soon after the 1999 "battle of Seattle" when activists flocked to protest the WTO talks and violent confrontations with police ensued, President Clinton issued Executive Order 13141, which committed to "factor environmental considerations into the development of its trade negotiating objectives." Some observers linked the two events, as a report prepared for Congress suggested: "Some view this Executive Order as the Clinton Administration's response to criticisms of the environmental effects of United States trade policy expressed before and during the. . . . (WTO) talks."[3]

Under pressure from labor and environmental activists after NAFTA's passage, the Clinton administration did seek their feedback and provide some transparency on a low-stakes Jordanian free trade agreement that would have minimal economic impact on the United States. In September 2000 the USTR released an economic impact study and a draft environmental review of the impact of the agreement, and solicited public comments from labor and environmental organizations. The AFL-CIO, Sierra Club, and other key environmental groups responded by demanding that labor and environmental standards be incorporated into the text of the agreement, rather than through side agreements, as they were in NAFTA.

The USTR ultimately responded to the pressure from activists and their legislative allies by incorporating labor and environmental issues into the main text of the agreement for the first time, rather than through side agreements. Unlike NAFTA, which focuses on the enforcement of domestic laws, the Jordanian agreement explicitly subjects the rights to organize and bargain collectively to the dispute mechanism process, treating them like other trade distortions. Although the USTR finished negotiating the Jordanian agreement in 2000, Congress did not pass it until 2001 under the Bush administration. With the exception of China's permanent normal trade relations status (which led the way for the country to join the WTO), during the two terms President Clinton was in office, the only trade agreement he managed to negotiate and get through Congress was NAFTA.

George W. Bush: Cementing the NAFTA Model with Low-Stakes Regional and Bilateral Agreements

The fast-track mechanism continued to be controversial in Congress during the George W. Bush administration. In late 2002, after a two year battle that began shortly after Bush entered office, Congress renewed fast-track (newly renamed trade promotion authority, or TPA) by only two votes after holding a late-night vote. Once he secured TPA, President Bush set an ambitious trade agenda that included a new round of multilateral negotiations through the WTO (the Doha Development Round).

When multilateral negotiations reached an impasse after talks stalled in Cancun, Mexico in 2003, the administration turned to bilateral and regional agreements across the Middle East and Latin America following a "competitive liberalisation" strategy (Destler 2005), whereby agreements signed with "willing" countries would put pressure on recalcitrant ones to sign onto multilateral agreements in future negotiations (Chorev 2009).

When the FTAA died in Mar del Plata in 2005, the administration applied the coalition of the willing strategy to try to isolate Brazil, Argentina, the Caribbean, and other nations that had rejected the FTAA, which was modeled after NAFTA. That became the Dominican Republic-Central America Free Trade Agreement (CAFTA-DR) among the United States and five Central American countries (Costa Rica, El Salvador, Guatemala, Honduras, and Nicaragua) and the Dominican Republic. The administration also initiated bilateral negotiations with Peru, Panama, Colombia, Bolivia, and Ecuador, and resumed negotiations Clinton had begun with Chile. In addition, it sought to create a U.S.-Middle East Free Trade Area, and to that end initiated negotiations with Morocco, Bahrain, Oman, Egypt, Saudi Arabia, the United Arab Emirates, Kuwait, Qatar, and Yemen (an agreement with Israel was implemented in 1985). The USTR also initiated an agreement with Australia, took over an agreement that President Clinton began with Singapore, and worked on the agreement that Clinton had concluded with Jordan but had run out of time to pass.

During his time in office, President Bush's greatest impact on trade policy was cementing into place NAFTA as the model for free trade agreements by getting them passed with fourteen countries, and launching the WTO Doha Round. Despite his ambitions, few of these agreements, however, had major economic or political significance. During his first term, Bush was able to shepherd four bilateral agreements through Congress: Jordan, Chile, Australia, and Singapore. During his second term, Congress ratified CAFTA-DR, and bilateral agreements with Bahrain, Morocco, Oman and Peru. In general, these agreements had minimal economic benefits. Trade with Bahrain, for example, accounted for only three one hundredths of 1 percent, and Oman less than 0.5 percent of all U.S. trade in goods (Chorev 2009:137–140).

President Bush's ambitious trade agenda was stymied, in part, by legislators who were able to gain some leverage during his two terms in office (Chorev 2009). Bolstered by activists who rallied public opposition, legislators had a unique opportunity to pressure the administration for labor and environmental concessions—as they had during the NAFTA negotiations. In addition, facing trade agreements with small economic benefits—and therefore low political stakes—provided legislators with cover; unlike with NAFTA, the political fallout was likely to be low. As Chorev explains:

> ... the Bush administration launched a large number of negotiations and signed many agreements but struggled to win ratification in Congress, especially after the 2006 elections. This was not because Congress was uncharacteristically protectionist, or because Bush was exceptionally partisan. Rather, Bush's own strategy of preferring bilateralism to multilateralism gave Congress ample opportunities to play hard. Each bilateral or regional agreement provided a stage for critics and allowed Congress to confront the administration with demands for concessions. Somewhat ironically, therefore, a bilateral strategy provided greater leverage to domestic actors who seized the opportunity to slow down Bush's agenda. (2009:144)

The need to satisfy labor and environmental demands for congressional passage provided an additional incentive for Bush to maintain some transparency and public participation in trade policy. Unlike President Clinton, who released no public draft of the FTAA, the Bush administration released three draft documents of the FTAA. The first was made available in 2001—seven years after negotiations began and the year Bush took office—and the second and third drafts appeared in 2002 and 2003 respectively.

President Bush also shared draft negotiating texts and strategies with members of Congress. This transparency allowed activists and their legislative allies to press for concessions, however small. Indeed the debate in Congress over the passage of the Singapore agreement focused in large part on the impact of its labor and environmental provisions as a template for subsequent trade agreements.[4] The Singapore agreement includes an expanded section on labor relative to the trade agreement with Jordan and a two-page annex on the requirement for the Labor Cooperation mechanism. It affirmed the ILO Declaration of Fundamental Principles and Rights at Work and stated it is inappropriate to encourage trade by weakening protections. As with NAFTA, the focus is on enforcement of a country's own labor laws. Unlike NAFTA, the joint committee that oversees dispute settlements specifically includes labor. Damages, however, are limited to $15 million inflation-adjusted dollars, per violation, which has been widely criticized as insufficient.

CAFTA-DR proved to be particularly contentious for the Bush administration. In Costa Rica, where passage required a national referendum vote, unions, labor federations, and civil society organizations launched a massive campaign against it with support from the AFL-CIO, the Canadian Labour Congress, and the International Trade Union Confederation. Although they lost the struggle, activists pressured the Bush administration to include an environmental cooperation agreement implemented by the EPA through an action plan developed in partnership with the U.S. Agency for International Development, the U.S. Department of State, and the CAFTA-DR countries. After activists argued that lack of labor law enforcement was the primary problem in the region, Bush agreed to contribute millions of dollars to hire and train new labor inspectors in Central America as part of the deal. The USTR also included the labor rights section as a chapter of the agreement and not as a side agreement.

In the wake of the 2006 elections, the Bush administration reached an impasse with Democrats, who were essential for the ratification of various agreements that had already been negotiated and signed. Democrats used their leverage to push for stronger labor and environmental standards. The resulting "May 10th Compromise"—brokered by Democratic representatives Charlie Rangel and Sander Levin—forced President Bush (but not future administrations) to amend agreements that had already been signed, and to adopt a stronger international standard for them, as Chorev explains:

> new provisions would require the implementation and enforcement of multilateral environmental agreements and the adoption and maintenance of their own labour laws as well as the five core standards of the International Labour Organization. Those standards bar forced labour, child labour and discrimination in the workplace while protecting the rights of workers to organise unions and bargain collectively. The new guidelines applied to labour standards the same enforcement mechanism that governed other areas of dispute, potentially resulting in punitive tariffs rather than mere fines. (2009:141)

Once the May 10th compromise was in place, the Bush administration was forced to renegotiate trade agreements with Colombia, Peru, Panama, and South Korea to include its provisions in order to increase the like-lihood of passage. On the environmental side, for example, the 2007 agreement between the United States and Panama holds the Panamanian government to the same level of accountability for meeting environmental commitments as it holds the government for meeting all other commitments from market access to intellectual property protection. Moreover both countries agree to not weaken existing environmental laws or reduce environmental protections in any way that will give domestic producers an advantage over the other country's exporters. The agreement also created a public submissions process through an independent secretariat for environmental enforcement matters and an environmental affairs council to oversee implementation of the environment chapter, which mandates public participation.[5]

After eight years in office, President Bush was able to shepherd nine free trade agreements through Congress, however most were relatively insignificant, accounting for small percentages of all U.S. trade in goods. What began as an ambitious trade agenda amounted to little for his administration and the Republican Party if measured by economic impact alone. But in political terms, his achievements were significant: he locked in the NAFTA model, extending it to nine other trade agreements. Although activists and their congressional allies were able to thwart his agenda and force him to minimally strengthen labor and environmental protections, they were profoundly dissatisfied with the direction of U.S. trade policy. They soon looked to the incoming Democratic president to strengthen future trade deals.

Obama: Trade Negotiations as Classified Information

As a senator, Barack Obama had criticized trade deals that lacked strong labor and environmental protections, and voted against CAFTA-DR. As a presidential candidate, Obama articulated his support of free trade with enforceable labor and environmental protections. On multiple occasions during the Democratic primaries he even promised to renegotiate NAFTA if elected: "NAFTA's shortcomings were evident when signed and we must now amend the agreement to fix them."[6] In the 2008 presidential election Obama won by a landslide, carrying every state in the Midwest (which he repeated, with the exception of Indiana, in 2012). Activists were hopeful. As a trade specialist with the Sierra Club explained to a *New York Times* reporter in 2009: "We were obviously very encouraged by what Obama the candidate was saying on the campaign trail in terms of needing to recognize the deficiencies of NAFTA and to strengthen it. . . . We're eager to work with the administration in having that conversation."[7]

As his first term began, however, Obama faced the worst economic crisis since the Great Depression. He soon backpedaled on his promise to renegotiate NAFTA, and in August 2009 during his first official NAFTA summit with Mexican president Calderon and Canadian prime minister Stephen Harper, the renegotiation of the agreement was not on the table. As Obama explained: "At a time when the economy has been shrinking drastically and trade has been shrinking around the world . . . we probably want to make the economy more stabilized in the coming months before we have a long discussion around further trade negotiations."[8]

Despite his reluctance to renegotiate NAFTA, Obama immediately continued to push through trade deals initiated by President Bush with Colombia, South Korea, Panama, and among Pacific Rim countries to expand the Trans-Pacific Strategic Economic Partnership Agreement, which originally included Brunei, Chile, Singapore, and New Zealand. By 2008 eight other countries joined the negotiations of the renamed Trans-Pacific Partnership Agreement (TPP), including the United States, Mexico, Peru, Canada, Australia, Japan, Malaysia, and Vietnam (other countries expressed interest in eventually joining). During his 2013 State of the Union address, President Obama called for the negotiation of a free trade agreement with the European Union, and in February the first round of talks began on the Trans-Atlantic Free Trade Agreement (TAFTA), which was later renamed the Trans-Atlantic Trade and Investment Partnership (TTIP).

The Colombia agreement was particularly contentious because the country was notorious for its high rate of assassinations of labor activists and union leaders. Like his predecessor, Obama provided some transparency to labor activists on the terms of the low-stakes agreement with Colombia. U.S. and Colombian unions' collective and coordinated opposition to the U.S.–Colombia Free Trade Agreement delayed the vote for years. And ultimately, pushback from labor activists forced President Obama to negotiate a labor action plan with Colombian president Juan Manuel Santos prior to the congressional vote to address labor rights issues, including the high rate of assassinations of Colombian unionists.

Although unions derided the plan for not going far enough, they acknowledged that it did have "several meaningful provisions"[9] and that "limited progress has been made in some areas."[10]

During the TPP negotiations the Obama administration heightened the secrecy with a Freedom of Information Act national security exemption for negotiating documents that limited public access to information. The administration also required TPP countries to agree to a confidentiality agreement that keeps negotiating documents except the final text secret for five years after it is signed or negotiations fall apart. Finally, they began to treat texts of the agreement as classified information, and threatened that cleared advisors who revealed the texts to their colleagues and constituents could be prosecuted. Administration officials also prevented many members of Congress and their staff from accessing the text and commenting on it. As journalists noted: "The U.S. government treats trade negotiation texts as classified information."[11] According to activists, after several leaks occurred, USTR Michael Froman wanted to be able to penalize those who discussed cleared briefings, and marginalize opponents by claiming they were ignorant about the agreement. A 2015 *New York Times* op-ed by an Ohio State University law professor explained the administration's justification for the secrecy:

> The level of secrecy employed by the Office of the United States Trade Representative is not typical of how most international agreements are negotiated. It's not even how our negotiating partners say they want to operate. Yet it is the way that the Obama administration handles trade deals, from a failed anti-counterfeiting agreement more than two years ago to the TPP today. The trade representative's office keeps trade documents secret as national security information, claiming that negotiating documents— including work produced by United States officials—are "foreign government information." The justification for secrecy in trade is that negotiations are like a poker game: Negotiators don't want to reveal their hand too soon, or get pressured by concerned domestic constituencies. But the trade representative's office takes this logic too far. After being forced to turn over documents in a 2002 lawsuit, it began regularly classifying trade documents. Now the office uses classification to invoke the national security exemption to open government law.[12]

The lack of transparency and participation that characterized the Obama administration's negotiating strategy was embittering to many unions, environmental organizations, and other civil society organizations—and ironically even to conservative Republicans who generally supported free trade. As reported in the press:

> Democrats in the House and Senate have complained for years about the secrecy standards the Obama administration has applied to the TPP, forcing members to jump over hurdles to see negotiation texts, and blocking staffer involvement. In 2012, Sen. Ron Wyden (D-Ore.) complained that corporate lobbyists were given easy access while his office was being stymied . . .[13]

> On 15 May [2012], House Oversight Committee chairman Darrell Issa (R-Calif.) called for more transparency in the negotiation process and leaked the entire draft intellectual property chapter from the Trans-Pacific deal to the public on his website. Although the document previously was available over the Internet through legally ambiguous channels, Issa's move dramatically increased political pressure on the administration to share more information about the deal with the public.[14]

In a 2012 letter to President Obama, Senator Wyden addressed the administration's failure to adhere to the Trade Act of 2002 that requires the executive branch to share trade documents with all members of Congress:

> [Mr.] President, Congress passed legislation in 2002 to form the Congressional Oversight Group, or COG, to foster more USTR consultation with Congress. I was a senator in 2002. I voted for that law and I can tell you the intention of that law was to ensure that USTR consulted with more Members of Congress not less. In trying to get to the bottom of why my staff is being denied information, it seems that some in the Executive Branch may be interpreting the law that established the COG to mean that only the few Members of Congress who belong to the COG can be given access to trade negotiation information, while every other Member of Congress, and their staff, must be denied such access. So, this is not just a question of whether or not cleared staff should have access to information about the TPP talks, this is a question of whether or not

the administration believes that most Members of Congress can or should have a say in trade negotiations. Again, having voted for that law, I strongly disagree with such an interpretation and find it offensive that some would suggest that a law meant to foster more consultation with Congress is intended to limit it. . . . I—and the vast majority of my colleagues and their staff—continue to be denied a full understanding of what the USTR is seeking in the agreement. . . .[15]

Senator Wyden concluded the letter by informing the president that he intended to introduce legislation clarifying the intent of the COG statute that: " . . . gives all Members of Congress and staff with appropriate clearance access to the substance of trade negotiations."[16] While even the staff of the senior Democrat on the committee of jurisdiction was denied access to TPP documents, the press and public were left entirely in the dark. In 2013, Yale Law School's Media Freedom and Information Access Clinic filed a lawsuit against the USTR for failing to provide a journalist access to TPP-related documents under a Freedom of Information Act request filed in 2012. As reported in the *Washington Post*:

According to Wednesday's lawsuit, it took USTR nearly a year to respond to the request, and USTR refused to provide most of the documents [reporter William] New had requested. Instead, USTR responded that the "draft text of the TPP, circulated among TPP negotiating parties is classified per Executive Order 13,526." That executive order relates to national security information. "It seems puzzling to us that any of these documents should be classified," [Yale law student Joshua] Weinger argues, since the documents they're seeking relate to copyright and patent law, not normally regarded as national security issues. USTR also declined to provide information about correspondence between USTR and industry groups, arguing that the communications fell under the "deliberative process privilege," designed to protect the confidentiality of the executive branch's internal deliberations.[17]

Members of Congress and critics were quick to point out President Obama's divergence from his predecessors on transparency and public participation in trade negotiations. Among the key issues were that Congress members: 1) could only see TPP text at all after 2012; 2) could only see TPP text without staff (who were not allowed to see it at all); 3) could only see TPP text in a secure room in the capitol; 4) could only see a few chapters at a time; 5) had to surrender their cell phones before entering the room to read TPP text; 6) could not take notes while in the room, and; 7) could not talk about the TPP text. When asked by a journalist if Obama's level of secrecy around trade agreements is "really unprecedented," the AFL-CIO's director of policy and special counsel responded that those who: "have been personally involved in trade negotiations for the last 20 years or so are universally of the opinion that this is the most secretive process that they've ever experienced."[18] A trade policy analyst echoed these points and also highlighted the lack of access for even advisors with security clearance under the Obama administration:

> But the ability of TPP critics like me to point out the deal's many failings is limited by the government's surprising and unprecedented refusal to make revisions to the language in the TPP fully available to cleared advisors. Bill Clinton didn't operate like this. During the debate on NAFTA, as a cleared advisor for the Democratic leadership, I had a copy of the entire text in a safe next to my desk and regularly was briefed on the specifics of the negotiations, including counterproposals made by Mexico and Canada. During the TPP negotiations, the United States Trade Representative has never shared proposals being advanced by other TPP partners. Today's consultations are, in many ways, much more restrictive than those under past administrations. . . . despite clearances, and a statutory duty to provide advice, advisors do not have access to all the materials that a reasonable person would need to do the job. The negotiators provide us with "proposals" but those are merely initial proposals to trading partners. We are not allowed to see counterproposals from our trading partners.[19]

Critics also emphasized how a conservative Republican administration under George W. Bush was more forthcoming with trade documents than the Obama administration. As a journalist reported: "the actual text of the [TPP] agreement remains under lock and key. That represents a significant break from the Bush administration, which in 2001 published the text of a proposed multinational trade agreement with Latin American nations."[20]

Of course, the Bush administration's release of the draft text of the FTAA is what many advocates *and* opponents of free trade attribute to its downfall. A 2012 Reuters article quoted Ron Kirk, USTR during the Obama administration from 2009 to 2013, who blamed the release of the FTAA on the failure of the negotiations:

> "There's always that tension between when you release and not," Kirk said, noting that about a decade ago negotiators released the draft text of the proposed Free Trade Area of the Americas and were subsequently unable to reach a final agreement.[21]

AFL-CIO trade specialist Celeste Drake also referenced the Bush administration's release of trade documents, but came to a very different conclusion than USTR Kirk:

> Under the Bush administration when the former USTR Robert Zoellick said let's be totally transparent, let's publish the actual working text of the Free Trade Agreement of the Americas on-line. And people will see what we're doing and they won't be as afraid of it being behind closed doors. And then, subsequent to that negotiations fell apart. So maybe the wrong lesson was learned in that if you're public about what you're doing, you can't do trade. I think—you know, to some extent if you're public about what you're doing and what you're doing is not good for the public, that's the right answer.[22]

Senator Elizabeth Warren echoed this perspective on April 22, 2015, when she released a statement about the secrecy of the TPP negotiations during the height of the Senate battle over fast-track continuation:

> Have you seen what's in the new TPP trade deal? Most likely, you haven't—and don't bother trying to Google it. The government doesn't want you to read this massive new trade agreement. It's top secret. Why? Here's the real answer people have given me: "We can't make this deal public because if the American people saw what was in it, they would be opposed to it." **If the American people would be opposed to a trade agreement if they saw it, then that agreement should not become the law of the United States.**[23]

Outrage over the secrecy of the TPP and TTIP was not limited to the United States. An op-ed that appeared in New Zealand captured activists' discontent:

> Its ambition to reset global trade rules is without precedent, and its repercussions include the ability for transnational corporations to dictate changes to New Zealand laws. It represents one of the greatest ever threats to New Zealand sovereignty. Yet when you consider what is at stake, it is extraordinary that the Government, despite multiple requests from many sectors, has consistently refused to release any detail of what is being negotiated, even to expert panels or select committees. Furthermore, it is disturbing that although the negotiations are completely concealed from the New Zealand public, they are available to more than 600 US corporations, who appear to influence the negotiating process. These corporations are likely to set terms that further their interests, ahead of those of the New Zealand people, who can't even be sure which of their interests are threatened.[24]

The international ramifications of this secrecy were obvious—if the U.S. public was being kept in the dark about these negotiations, then so was the rest of the world.

Critics of the agreements in various countries pointed to the Obama administration—and particularly the required confidentiality agreements with its trade partners—as the source of the secrecy. In 2014 the European Ombudsman (EO), at the urging of NGOs and activists across Europe, launched an inquiry into the secrecy of the European Commission (EC) in negotiating the TTIP. In January 2015 the EO recommended that the EC proactively offer more public access to negotiating documents and provide more balanced and transparent public participation in the negotiating process. Although the recommendations were not binding, the EC released some of its negotiating documents. As the New Zealand op-ed noted:

> The secrecy surrounding the [TPP] is even more incomprehensible in view of the fact that the European Commission has decided to release a raft of its own negotiating documents from the parallel Trans-Atlantic Trade and Investment Partnership (TTIP) agreement. The European Union Ombudsman has stated, "It is vital that the commission inform the US of the importance of making,

in particular, common negotiating texts available to the European public before the TTIP agreement is finalised [to] allow for timely feedback to negotiators in relation to sections of the agreement that pose particular problems. . . . It is preferable to learn of such problems sooner rather than later".[25]

The German press highlighted how the draconian security measures implemented in Washington were replicated in Europe at the Obama administration's insistence:

The US position has softened somewhat. Until May, the consolidated texts weren't available in the EU member states at all. There was a reading room at the US mission in Brussels where cleared officials could view the draft documents. Under pressure from the member states, Brussels negotiated with Washington to make the documents more accessible. The two sides agreed to set up reading rooms in US embassies throughout the EU. The current arrangement is based on the practice in Washington, where select officials are given clearance to read draft trade documents in secured rooms. . . . Many believe the process is still too opaque. . . . those officials who have been cleared can only access the reading room two at time, twice a week, for two hours each session. And they can only use a pencil, pen and paper to take limited notes. . . .[26]

As demonstrations against TPP and TTIP raged across Europe, Australia, and New Zealand, a primary theme among protesters was the lack of transparency and participation in the negotiations. What they perceived as the eclipsing of democratic practices, in the service of corporate power, galvanized mobilization against the agreements and the governments determined to implement them.

Efforts to Improve Trade Policy

The Obama administration's secrecy on TPP arguably helped pave the path to the pact's demise. It created enormous suspicion and angered and alienated prospective congressional and civil society allies. Without the necessary information to engage the process meaningfully, coupled with an unbending rejection by trade policy officials of any modifications that would improve labor and environmental protections, activists' only option for influencing trade policy became a zero-sum game to try to kill the TPP and future agreements by either electing allied politicians or by trying to make business as usual impossible using different kinds of challenges to authorities. In trade battles after NAFTA, activists' efforts to improve trade agreements has been mixed. The pressure they applied with congressional allies forced President Bush to acquiesce to the May 10th compromise. Because the compromise only applied to the trade agreements Bush was negotiating, activists sought binding legislation with similar provisions for all future trade agreements.

After President Obama's election, unions and environmental organizations helped to craft the Trade Reform, Accountability, Development and Employment (TRADE) Act of 2010 (modeled after similar 2008 legislation), which was reintroduced in the 2009–2010 congressional session as a "progressive path to a new trade and globalization policy."[27] The proposed TRADE Act required the Government Accountability Office to review existing free trade agreements on a variety of economic, human rights, social, and environmental indicators. It established rules that must be included in the main text of all trade agreements, including: core labor standards, human rights, and environmental and consumer protection rights, and required that the gaps between new rules and existing agreements be remedied. Most significantly, activists demanded that the act require dispute resolution and enforcement mechanisms for labor and environmental terms to be at least as stringent as those that cover the commercial provisions of trade agreements. Activists hoped the legislation would "capture the reforms promised in the 2008 Democratic platform and the campaign commitments made by President Obama and the 71 House and Senate members elected in 2006 and 2008 who replaced those who had voted for NAFTA and the [WTO]."[28] With more than 160 cosponsors but insufficient votes for passage, the bill was never put to a vote. Over 350 unions and other civil society organizations, however, pushed for the legislation.

Because the interests supporting the trade agreement model established with NAFTA have fiercely defended their gains and held sway with Democratic and Republican presidents, activists' ability to shape and influence the content of individual trade agreements has been severely restricted. Thus, labor unions and environmental organizations have tried to make them more friendly to workers and the environment by electing and developing allies in Congress and the White House. In a radical shift from their NAFTA-era strategy of supporting pro-labor Democratic legislators regardless of their stance on individual trade agreements, the AFL-CIO decided to deploy the full force of its political and financial resources during the TPP and TTIP battles by pressuring legislators to vote against TPP, and punishing those who did not.

In the spring of 2015 prior to the vote on fast-track legislation that granted President Obama the ability to negotiate, sign, and enter into trade agreements before Congress approves them, AFL-CIO unions announced that they would freeze campaign contributions to all members of Congress until the fast-track vote. They also vowed to punish them with negative ads, phone blitzes, and protests. As reported in the *Wall Street Journal*:

> Unions have opposed the TPP through demonstrations, letters to lawmakers and political ads, but withholding political contributions is a more forceful way of flexing their muscle. In the 2014 midterm elections, unions—the lifeblood of the Democratic Party— contributed about $65 million from their political-action committee, or PACs, to candidates, nearly all Democrats. "Every single union in the AFL-CIO has agreed to join together to send Congress a message that if you mess with one of us you mess with all of us," Harold Schaitberger, president of the International Association of Fire Fighters, said Monday at the union's legislative conference in Washington. "We need to cut the spigot off.". . . . Many Democrats publicly oppose the fast-track legislation. Still, the unions plan to temporarily cut off contributions to all members of Congress. "The reasoning is that this will put pressure on some of the Democrats who support the position of labor to put pressure on those who don't," said Thomas Buffenbarger, president of the International Association of Machinists and Aerospace Workers union.[29]

Fast-track was defeated in the House in May 2015, and a month later, in early June, the AFL-CIO followed through on the threat by running ads against Rep. Kathleen Rice, who initially opposed and then registered her support for fast track. Activists in her pro-union Long Island, New York district protested, and the president of the New York AFL-CIO issued a scathing critique: "We thought Rep. Rice stood with us. Clearly she has now chosen corporate interests over workers and has decided to put American jobs at risk. . . . Her betrayal will not be forgotten. Sadly, constituents are now left to wonder which Kathleen Rice they voted for—the one who promised to fight for working families in Nassau County—or the one who ignores their needs as soon as she gets inside the beltway."[30] After Rep. Ami Bera, a Democratic congressman from California also flipped positions and wrote an op-ed supporting fast track, unions put $84,000 into negative ads directed against him.[31]

The White House responded quickly. President Obama announced his unwavering support for Democrats who backed the fast-track vote:

> As the White House pleads with House Democrats for votes on trade, President Barack Obama is sweetening the deal with an offer of presidential campaign support if Democrats come under fire for their votes from unions and liberals in 2016. Obama has given personal assurances to Democratic lawmakers that they'll have his strong support next year if they vote yes on granting him the authority he says he needs to negotiate the best trade deals with Europe and the Asia-Pacific region. At the same time, White House officials have sought to differentiate Obama's offer from the more heavy-handed tactics they say the unions are deploying to scare Democrats—like attack ads and public rallies outside their offices. (Lederman 2015)

On June 12th, House Democrats stopped the president again when they voted against trade adjustment assistance legislation that was tied to and necessary to move fast-track forward. Obama doubled down and made a deal with Republicans to gut the trade adjustment assistance legislation in order to get necessary Republican votes, and to create a stand-alone fast-track bill. Republican congressional leaders also agreed to bring the bill to a vote. Thus, on June 18th, with only twenty-eight House Democrats voting yes, fast-track was narrowly passed 218-208. That was followed by a June 24th Senate vote of 60-38 granting President Obama fast-track authority. On October 5, 2015, a final deal for TPP was reached among the signatory countries, and in early February 2016 Obama signed the agreement.

From the day TPP was signed the Obama administration prioritized its passage during the lame duck session but could not muster the necessary votes in the House and in district-by-district organizing. The divisive strategy Obama used to get the fast-track bill through Congress infuriated many and led to even more opposition to and mobilization against TPP. A congressional vote was not held during the last days of Obama's administration. Shortly after his inauguration, President Trump formally buried the U.S. TPP role by notifying the other countries that the United States would not further pursue approval.

A Shift in Framing: From Rights to Democracy

The efforts of presidential administrations after NAFTA to maintain secrecy and quash public pushback to trade negotiations also had an effect on labor and environmental activists' rhetorical strategies against TPP and TTIP. Although anti-NAFTA activists raised issues of public transparency and participation as part of their struggle, their primary focus in congressional hearings was on labor and environmental rights and protections. Our analysis of all 143 testimonies provided by labor and environmental organizations[32] during the twenty congressional hearings held between May 21, 1990 and May 24, 1991 reveals that less than half of the organizations mentioned issues of public and democratic participation. Among the labor organizations, only four of the twenty raised these issues. A search of all issues (over six hundred) of *Inside U.S. Trade* articles related to NAFTA negotiations reveals that the focus of political discussion on the Hill prioritized and foregrounded concerns related to labor and environmental protections, not transparency.

Like TPP and TTIP, NAFTA contains ISDS mechanisms in chapter 11 that allow foreign investors to sue governments through extrajudicial private tribunals if they believe a government law, regulation, or policy violates their right to "fair and equitable treatment" or lowers their expected profits. ISDS mechanisms irrefutably undermine democratic practices: the tribunals and their proceedings, findings, and decisions are secret and not subject to public disclosure. The public cannot participate even though the laws being challenged were created democratically. Moreover, they are final and binding, bypassing other domestic court systems such as the U.S. Supreme Court, and taxpayers bear the burden if the government being sued loses to an investor or corporation.

In practice, ISDS mechanisms are used to undermine domestic labor, environmental, health and safety, and consumer protections laws. Under NAFTA's ISDS mechanisms, for example, a corporation sued and won 15 million dollars from the Mexican federal government when a local government denied it a permit to operate a toxic waste dump. ISDS cases are proliferating across the globe: Germany's decision to phase out nuclear power resulted in a suit by a Swedish corporation, and a French company initiated a suit against Egypt when it increased its minimum wage. A brouhaha arose over ISDS mechanisms in North America when Canada's *Financial Post* and *The Globe and Mail* reported in March 2015 that a Canadian corporation was considering using NAFTA's ISDS mechanisms to sue the U.S. government for not approving the controversial Keystone XL pipeline.[33]

During NAFTA's negotiation, labor and environmental activists raised concerns about chapter 11, but did not make those concerns primary during the NAFTA battle. After NAFTA, however, activists began to focus much more attention on ISDS mechanisms, which began to proliferate as new trade agreements were passed and have been replicated in trade pacts between the United States and Colombia, Peru, Bahrain, Singapore, Morocco, Oman, South Korea, Panama, and in CAFTA-DR. Public Citizen, Friends of the Earth and the Sierra Club pushed the issue to the forefront.[34] It is important to emphasize that the privatization of governance mechanisms through trade agreements that undermine democratic procedures has spurred labor unions and environmental organizations to remain engaged in the trade policy arena and build new alliances with a broad array of civil society organizations to fight against ISDS mechanisms.

ISDS mechanisms incense activists not only because they threaten labor and environmental rights and protections, but also because they undermine democratic processes, as the AFL-CIO explains: "Are these the kind of cases we want European companies (in the case of TTIP) or Pacific Rim companies (in the case of TPP) to bring against U.S. laws and regulations? The American people should be deciding what our policies should be, rather than letting foreign companies and their investors hold us up for ransom every time they don't like our laws."[35] Unions have lobbied and worked with members of Congress, filed lawsuits, and engaged in grassroots organizing to try to eliminate these mechanisms from trade agreements.

Activists' post-NAFTA discourse has noticeably shifted to a greater focus on issues of democracy, which resonate across many civil society organizations. In an interesting twist, they cited the opposition of key economists such as Nobel laureates Paul Krugman and Joseph Stiglitz, who shifted from their previous support of free trade agreements—including NAFTA—to assail the TPP and TTIP. As Stiglitz explained in a *New York Times* op-ed in March 2014, one of his primary concerns was ISDS mechanisms:

> The secrecy might be enough to cause significant controversy for the TPP. What we know of its particulars only makes it more unpalatable. One of the worst is that it allows corporations to seek restitution in an international tribunal, not only for unjust expropriation, but also for alleged diminution of their potential profits as a result of regulation. This is not a theoretical problem. [A company] has already tried this tactic against Uruguay, claiming that its antismoking regulations, which have won accolades from the World Health Organization, unfairly hurt profits, violating a bilateral trade treaty between Switzerland and Uruguay.[36]

In 2011, Public Citizen, Oxfam, FOE, and the Institute for Policy Studies, with help from Central American solidarity groups, the Sierra Club, and the Teamsters International Department, organized a protest against a CAFTA-DR tribunal in Washington DC. The tribunal was adjudicating a CAFTA-DR ISDS case brought against the government of El Salvador by a Canadian gold mining company after the government enacted a ban on mining for domestic and foreign firms because of water contamination issues. The firm had a permit to operate a mine on a claim area they had explored before the ban. Activists broadcast the protest live via radio into the gold region in El Salvador where a local protest was held. They also presented a letter to the tribunal and the WTO signed by 240 labor unions and civil society organizations from the United States and Central America that demanded an "end to the trampling of democracy" and insisted that the case be thrown out.[37]

In 2013, over 160 U.S. and European labor, environmental, and other civil society organizations wrote a letter to the USTR and the European Union Commissioner for Trade, opposing ISDS provisions in TTIP and demanding their removal from the agreement. In July 2014, the AFL-CIO and the European Trade Union Confederation crafted a Declaration of Joint Principles on the TTIP that states: "We envision a people and planet-centered agreement that respects democracy, ensures state sovereignty, protects fundamental labor, economic, social and cultural rights, and addresses climate change and other environmental challenges."[38]

Labor and environmental activists' efforts to try to kill TPP and TTIP also included insurgent practices. On January 26, 2015, during a historic blizzard in New York City, hundreds of protesters gathered outside the Sheraton New York Times Square Hotel where negotiations over the TPP were taking place. The activists voiced their disagreement over the secrecy of the negotiations, as well as the deal itself. They shouted, sang, chanted, banged drums, and as the crowd swelled, police officers had to move protesters to the other side of the street. One man shouted, "If the [expletive] TPP is so great, let me see the [expletive] text."[39] Another protester, from Mexico, likened the TPP to NAFTA, reminding the crowd that "We fought for five years and we lost . . .We were right."[40] The next day, protesters interrupted a Senate hearing on TPP multiple times and were ultimately removed by Capitol police.

Protests have not been limited to the United States. Between 2012 and 2015 thousands of protesters mobilized and marched against the TPP in Mexico, Canada, New Zealand, Malaysia, Australia, and Japan. The struggle against TTIP galvanized transnational mobilization across Europe. On October 11, 2014, labor unions and other civil society organizations coordinated marches and protests to oppose TTIP in twenty-one European countries, and the Stop TAFTA coalition organized a global day of action against free trade on April 18, 2015. Donald's Trump's victory means TTIP's future is uncertain, as EU Commissioner for Trade Cecilia Malmström noted in a speech she delivered in Brussels in January 2017: "The election of Donald Trump seems likely to put our EU-U.S. negotiations firmly in the freezer at least for a while."[41]

President Trump has signaled his preference for bilateral, rather than multilateral agreements. His confidence that he can get better trade deals with individual countries may not be unwarranted. However, this is not simply because bilateral negotiations allow him to exert asymmetrical power to extract more concessions; they also provide fewer opportunities for international opposition and mobilization. In NAFTA's wake, bilateral negotiations have been the fallback option for every administration—a way to minimize the resistance that multilateral deals generate in the post-NAFTA era. And yet ironically, because bilateral agreements generally have smaller economic benefits and lower political stakes, activists and their legislative allies have often been able to more successfully influence them using institutionalized strategies.

The dynamics that the battle over NAFTA unleashed between activists and the U.S. government had many unintended consequences. Key among them was that trade became politicized in ways it never had before. It is likely that under the Trump administration the dynamics between the state and civil society will experience yet another shift—with no less serious implications for democratic practices and mobilization. And yet, as this chapter shows, each administration tried and generally failed to produce any significant multi-country trade agreement (CAFTA-DR was an exception, but its economic and political impact paled in comparison to NAFTA's). Activists have derailed negotiations of each major multi-country deal since, starting with the FTAA and MAI to the WTO Doha Round, to TPP and TTIP. One could argue that this is a small but meaningful victory for fair trade activists that is largely ignored. NAFTA was the first, and the last major multi-nation trade agreement that any president has been able to pass.

8

Conclusions

THE IMPLICATIONS OF INSTITUTIONAL CLOSURE
FOR DEMOCRACY AND MOBILIZATION

IN APRIL 2008 during a San Francisco fundraiser, a young Barack Obama made one of the most widely reported missteps of his Democratic primary campaign. During his speech, Obama tried to explain the reactions of workers to job losses across the Rust Belt: "They get bitter, they cling to guns or religion or antipathy to people who aren't like them or anti-immigrant sentiment or anti-trade sentiment as a way to explain their frustrations" (Pallasch 2008). When the quote appeared on a political blog a few days later, the media exploded. As reported in the *New York Times*: "The remarks touched off a torrent of criticism from Mrs. Clinton, Mr. McCain and a string of Republican activists and party officials, all of whom accused Mr. Obama of elitism and belittling the working class" (Zeleny 2008a).

The guns and religion aspect of Obama's quote largely eclipsed the anti-trade point. Some progressive bloggers and conservatives, however, noted the slight. As conservative columnist William Kristol observed:

> But Obama in San Francisco does no courtesy to his fellow Americans. Look at the other claims he makes about those small-town voters. Obama ascribes their anti-trade sentiment to economic frustration—as if there are no respectable arguments against more free-trade agreements. This is particularly cynical, since he himself

has been making those arguments, exploiting and fanning this sentiment that he decries. Aren't we then entitled to assume Obama's
opposition to NAFTA and the Colombian trade pact is merely cyn-
ical pandering to frustrated Americans? (Kristol 2008)

At a Building Trades Legislative Conference in DC four days later, Obama
quickly tried to clarify his remarks: "I know that there's been a lot of fuss over
the last couple of days because I said that people were bitter. People seemed
to misunderstand what that means. Yes, people are angry. If you've been fill-
ing up your gas tank you're angry. If you've watched your entire community
decimated because a steel plant is closed, that will make you mad. You've
got to feel some frustration" (Zeleny 2008b). During the primaries, Obama
promised on multiple occasions to renegotiate NAFTA if elected.

Eight years later, Donald Trump, a dark horse Republican presidential candidate, made the same promises even more forcefully. Indeed,
his attacks on NAFTA were scathing. He called NAFTA "the worst, in
my opinion, the worst trade deal in the history of this country. It's not
even close." He used the issue of trade to assail his Democratic opponent
Hillary Clinton (usually with inaccurate information):

"The real Clinton global initiative is their economic plan to shift
America's jobs overseas . . . You're looking here really at the
wreckage of NAFTA and the wreckage of China's entrance into the
World Trade Organization." "America has lost nearly one-third of
its manufacturing jobs since 1997. . . driven by these two—Hillary
Clinton understood and backed, and Bill Clinton certainly as the
president, initiatives. They are a disaster."[1]

More than a quarter century after its passage, NAFTA still serves as a political litmus test; a candidate's position on NAFTA often makes front-page
news—and in 2016 it helped propel Donald Trump to the White House.
Although his margin of electoral victory was small—likely less than
80,000 votes—his laser focus on NAFTA and the loss of manufacturing
jobs in the United States tapped into deep-seated resentment among
some voters who felt left behind by trade and burdened by the economic
anxiety it generated, particularly those in midwestern swing states who
had previously voted for President Obama. The question of NAFTA's real
impact is an important one, however, and too few pundits and politicians
have actually tried to answer it objectively.

The Effects of NAFTA on Jobs, Manufacturing, and Inequality

Assessing NAFTA's impact across a range of different outcomes is very difficult. That is in large part because it is impossible to control for all the variables that statistically could affect outcomes. For example, Mexico experienced an economic crisis and peso devaluation soon after NAFTA went into effect. Disentangling the effects of NAFTA from other economic variables on overall levels of trade and GDP presents thorny statistical problems. Employment levels and job loss and growth (including manufacturing jobs) are also affected by a plethora of variables in addition to NAFTA.

The difficulty of statistically parsing out the effects of NAFTA has resulted in disparate conclusions by academics and policymakers. NAFTA's proponents claim the agreement has helped stimulate trade, investment, and new jobs, whereas its critics contend it has increased poverty and inequality, intensified migration, and killed jobs, particularly in manufacturing. More than two decades after its passage, NGOs and think tanks continue to mark its anniversaries with reports (e.g., "NAFTA at Twenty"), and activists still take to the streets to protest its effects. On January 1, 2008, when all tariffs on corn and beans were finally eliminated under the trade deal, protesters marched on both sides of the border.

At first glance, NAFTA's impact on the continent's economic landscape appears to be astounding. Since NAFTA's passage, trade between the three North American nations increased dramatically; it quadrupled between 1993 and 2016, from approximately $290 billion in 1993 to more than $1.1 trillion in 2016.[2] In 2016, Canada and Mexico accounted for 34 percent of total U.S. exports and 26 percent of U.S. imports (Villarreal and Fergusson 2017). According to the U.S. Department of Agriculture, the value of U.S. agricultural exports to Canada and Mexico more than quadrupled between 1993 and 2015, increasing from $8.9 billion to $38.6 billion.[3] The combined GDP for Canada, the United States. and Mexico was $21.1 trillion in 2016 which represented 28 percent of the world's gross domestic product that year.[4]

After NAFTA's first decade, research on its impact began to accumulate, and, scholars disagreed about a range of outcomes. Hufbauer and Schott (2005) argued that the agreement fostered competition and investment that increased efficiency and productivity, stating: "It has worked.

North American firms are now more efficient and productive. They have restructured to take advantage of economies of scale in production and intra-industry specialization" (Hufbauer and Schott 2005:61). Although they conceded that Mexican growth rates since NAFTA have been "a disappointment," they argued that anemic rates were not due to NAFTA, but rather to a lack of liberalization in those areas of the economy not covered under NAFTA (2005:62).

In contrast, a 2003 Congressional Budget Office (CBO) report found only a small, positive aggregate impact of the agreement for the United States and Mexico. The report concluded that trade had been increasing between Mexico and the United States long before the agreement went into effect and would have continued without NAFTA. The CBO also found that NAFTA had only a small effect on the U.S. labor market, and a positive but small effect on U.S. GDP (CBO 2003).

As NAFTA moved into its second decade, a new round of research emerged. A 2010 study found that "U.S. macroeconomic fluctuations dominate the effects of trade liberalization" with NAFTA (Sunthonkhan 2010:iii). Although many including the CBO found minimal aggregate labor impact, in their National Bureau of Economic Research working paper McLaren and Hakobyan (2010) analyzed the most affected industries and localities in the United States and found evidence of "dramatically lowering wage growth for blue-collar workers in the most affected industries and localities," and added that "[t]hese distributional effects are much larger than aggregate welfare effects estimated by other authors" (2010:1). In a 2014 review of key research, Hufbauer et al. concluded that NAFTA had only modest and localized negative effects on U.S. wages, did not perceptibly affect U.S. unemployment, and did not achieve the growth in Mexico that its proponents predicted (Hufbauer et al. 2014).

There is also little scholarly consensus on NAFTA's impact on Mexican workers. Overall, key economic indicators reflect Mexico's poor economic performance since NAFTA's passage, including Mexico's lackluster GDP growth, high poverty rate, significant underemployment, and low real (inflation-adjusted) wages. Although it is impossible to attribute these outcomes to NAFTA alone, what is clear is that NAFTA did not protect Mexico's economy from them (Weisbrot et al. 2017). Portes painted a dim picture for workers in Mexico in the first decade after the agreement: "More than ten years after the signing of the treaty, economic growth has been anemic in Mexico, averaging less than 3.5% per year or less than 2% on a per capita basis since 2000; unemployment is higher than what it was when the treaty was signed; and half of the labor force must eke out a living in invented jobs in the informal economy, a figure ten percent higher than in the pre-NAFTA years."[5] Polaski pointed out that real wages are lower for many Mexican workers under NAFTA,[6] and unlike previous periods in Mexican history, higher productivity has not resulted in higher wages (Polaski 2006:2). Gordon Hanson (2003), however, found that more skilled workers and those in Mexican states with more exposure to globalization did experience a relative wage increase after NAFTA's passage (see also Garduño Rivera 2010; Hanson 2007).

The outcome around which there tends to be most scholarly agreement is NAFTA's effect on increasing inequality across the continent. As economists at the Economic Policy Institute reported in 2006: "Twelve years later, it is clear that the costs to workers outweighed the benefits in all three nations. . . . In each nation, workers' share of the gains from rising productivity fell and the proportion of income and wealth going to those at the very top of the economic pyramid grew . . . " (Scott, Salas, and Campbell 2006:1). According to Polaski:

Compared to the period before NAFTA, the top 10 percent of households have increased their share of national income, while the other 90 percent have lost income share or seen no change. Regional inequality within Mexico has also increased, reversing a long-term trend toward convergence in regional incomes. But a widening gap between the wages of skilled and unskilled workers is partly attributable to trade, and NAFTA probably accounts for a small portion of the observed growth in wage disparity within the United States.[7]

Even some of NAFTA's original supporters concede its shortcomings when it comes to fomenting inequality. According to economist J. Bradford DeLong:

the gap between [Mexicans'] mean income and that of the United States has widened. And there is worse news: Because of rising inequality the gap between mean and median incomes has risen. The overwhelming majority of Mexicans are no more productive in a domestic market income sense than their counterparts of 15 years ago, although some segments of the population have benefited. Exporters (but not necessarily workers in export industries) have gotten rich. The north of Mexico has done relatively well . . . . Yet success at what neoliberal policymakers like me thought would be the key links for Mexican development has had disappointing results. Success at creating a stable, property respecting domestic environment has not delivered the rapid increases in productivity and working-class wages that neoliberals like me would have confidently predicted when NAFTA was ratified. (DeLong 2006:19)

Economist Dani Rodrik isolates and highlights the problem, as Peter Evans explains: "Rodrik calculates that for every $1 of overall gains in the United States from increased trade, $50 of income is shifted. For working families, any gains from the $1 increase are dwarfed by the negative $50 income shift."[8] His calculation suggests that trade disrupts working class communities irrespective of net gains. This disruption is what Donald Trump was able to articulate and capitalize on in his presidential campaign.

Workers' Perceptions of NAFTA

What many scholars have missed in their own internecine academic battles over NAFTA's economic effects is that most workers base their perceptions of NAFTA on their own experiences—and for those who directly lost jobs to NAFTA, those experiences were grim. The impact of NAFTA losses was also felt by entire communities beyond those losing jobs, and was devastating to local economies. Workers are less concerned with NAFTA's effects on overall trade, GDP, and even consumer prices than on their own jobs (this is also true of Mexican and Canadian workers). Even if NAFTA had created a net gain in jobs across the United States, for a worker who lost his or her job, the fact that someone gained one in a different part of the country is irrelevant. Moreover, the fact that she may be paying less for a variety of goods (from televisions to furniture) is also irrelevant given that without a job, she will have to forgo most purchases.

For the past twenty-five years, politicians, pundits, and scholars have offered too little compassion for the workers dislocated by trade. For workers who lost jobs when their work moved to Mexico (and for Mexican workers whose wages stagnated and whose working conditions deteriorated), NAFTA was *the* problem. And although fluctuations in GDP usually occur below the radar, factory relocations are completely transparent; workers are told that their jobs will be relocated and to where.

Their experience at two Indiana factories illustrates the indignities workers suffer when factories are shuttered—in this case machinists were forced to train the workers who would replace them (or forgo a severance package), as reported in the *Milwaukee Journal Sentinel*:

> [A machinist] said supervisors from the company's Mexico plant have been touring the Indianapolis plant, and the company wants its workers to train their replacements in return for severance packages. "If that's not a slap in the face, I don't know what is," [he] said, adding that the plant is expected to close in 2017. "Right now, the jobs are slated to move to Mexico. What we are in negotiations for is to try and finalize severance packages. Those talks are going very slow," he said. [The machinist] said he was told the move to Mexico would save [the company] $15 million a year. The company, which has about 7,700 employees, had $67.5 million in profit on $1.9 billion in sales in fiscal 2016. The average wage at the Indianapolis plant is about $25 per hour.[9]

Companies only have to threaten to move factories in order to extract union concessions, stop organizing drives dead in their tracks, or ensure relative labor peace (see Bronfenbrenner 1997)—they do not actually have to relocate. This strategy of "whipsawing" undercuts wages and creates actual or threatened competition among workers; it also pits workers from different countries against each other.

Democratic and Republican presidents and members of Congress have generally only offered lip service to the real disruptions that workers face when their work is relocated or disappears due to trade agreements. Indeed, in the years since NAFTA's passage, many Democratic political leaders, especially presidents, have championed free trade, claiming that in the long run it benefits workers by creating more jobs and lowering the cost of consumer goods. This enthusiastic support for trade—culminating in President Obama's promotion of TPP in 2016—undermined support for the Democratic party across the Midwest, and likely eclipsed any possibility that a robust coalition between progressive Democrats and Rust Belt workers left behind by trade would emerge. Activists' strategy of killing trade deals outright by electing anti-trade politicians backfired during the 2016 presidential election. A small but significant number of working class Rust Belt voters ignored Democrats' pleas to vote for Hillary Clinton and did not vote, opted for a third party candidate, or chose the unequivocal anti-trade Republican candidate who promised to punish companies that relocated to Mexico.

Although Republicans (particularly members of Congress) have more consistently supported free trade than Democrats, the implications of each party's trade positions on voter preferences varies, as Peter Evans explains:

> The Republican Party is full of conservative globalists who assid-uously support trade deals precisely in order to strengthen their corporate allies, but liberal globalists pay a more costly price at the ballot box. By acting as apologists for trade agreements, socially lib-eral globalists from Bill Clinton to Barack Obama courted working people's anger and undermined the credibility they needed to build support for social programs. They opened the way for a reactionary nationalist like Trump to pick [up] the banner of defending workers, opening a political Pandora's box.[10]

The big lesson for both parties from the 2016 election is that contin-uing to ignore the impact of trade on workers' lives not only has serious economic and ethical implications —it can also have serious electoral consequences. During the election, Hillary Clinton changed her posi-tion on trade and was forced to renounce her support of TPP, which she had helped craft. A crucial pillar of Bernie Sanders's campaign was a strong anti-free-trade stance that helped him win key Rust Belt states during the Democratic primaries, including West Virginia, Indiana, Michigan, and Wisconsin—all of which Donald Trump later won in the presidential election.

How each party addresses workers' needs, in light of globaliza-tion processes, however, will inevitably diverge, and will have different consequences. Democrats' failure to demand stronger worker and job protections in trade agreements and to renounce ISDS mechanisms has undermined the party's credibility with many in its working class and union base. And Donald Trump's anti-trade position, blended with xenophobia, racism, and nationalism, will place Republicans in a dif-ficult position with their corporate funding base and with moderate Republican voters if they adopt it as their default platform on trade. EU Commissioner for Trade Cecilia Malmström offered a dire prediction—and warning—about the likely outcome of Trump's anti-globalization policies:

In 2016, we saw many trying to reverse the trend of increasing globalisation, and increasing openness. Their reflex was to say "close a border! Build a wall!"—as though that were the solution to all our problems. It isn't. . . . Those who, in the 21st century, think that we can become great again by rebuilding borders, reimposing trade barriers, restricting people's freedom to move, are doomed to fail.[11]

As we write this book the ground is shifting in relationship to trade policy. President Trump is renegotiating NAFTA and threatening to withdraw from it. Mexico and Canada have both stated they will not sign a new deal if terms are not favorable and they are planning for the possibility of NAFTA's demise. In 2018 trade is as contentious a policy issue as it was when NAFTA went into force. Indeed that trade so greatly influenced the 2016 presidential election reflects the enduring impact of NAFTA's negotiation and passage.

NAFTA and the Politicization of Trade

This book attempts to explain the dynamics that drove the backlash against globalization in 2016, resulting in the election of a U.S. president whose campaign centered on opposition to free trade agreements. We argue that these dynamics began to foment over twenty-five years ago during the first trade battle over NAFTA. We examined how those trade politics and policies emerged and developed during NAFTA's negotiation, and how they continued to affect subsequent trade battles, reinforcing resentment among anti-trade activists, including many working class voters. But why was NAFTA so contentious, and how did its negotiation politicize free trade agreements for the first time since WW II?

For decades prior to NAFTA, trade policy was considered something best hammered out with as little popular attention and input as possible. Free trade advocates saw critics as policy losers who simply needed to be challenged to greater efficiencies by competition; the nation was better off when their voices were marginalized. Before NAFTA, trade had been a nonissue politically in the United States. Free trade advocates suggested that grassroots political mobilization around trade was unlikely because North Americans had little understanding of the effect of trade policy on their lives. During the NAFTA struggle environmental and labor activists proved them wrong. They greatly broadened citizens' awareness about the reach and the scope of trade by bringing their message outside of the Beltway and constructing a more populist message about the ubiquity of trade's impact on their lives.

And they offered an alternative for developing and evaluating trade policy based on goals of more widespread, equitable, and sustainable growth. They argued that even if one did not care about dolphins, the health and safety of Mexican workers, or job loss in the United States and Canada, trade vitally affected every part of their lives, from the food they ate, the products they purchased, to even the air they breathed—and that citizens should therefore demand to be heard on trade decisions made in Washington. They argued that the terms under standard trade liberalization exact too high a price in the level of dislocation and inexorable logics for health, the environment, labor, and social welfare. Environmental and labor activists forced citizens to question *how* we globalize. As a result of their efforts, the question of what kind of globalization we want to foster has cemented itself in trade discourse. It can be debated but not ignored.

The NAFTA battle proved to be so contentious because at its core, it was a battle over how the rules governing the global economy would be made. A lot was therefore at stake. In the years leading up to NAFTA's introduction, labor and environmental activists realized that trade policy was beginning to blur distinctions between domestic and international policy issues, infusing many domestic issues with international elements. As trade policy began to shift to include not simply tariff rules, but rules about the movement of capital and corporations' right to profits and states' ability to uphold domestic laws, activists became concerned. Although trade policy field actors and many scholars viewed this shift as creating new interests and activists who came to the trade debate, we show how in fact the opposite occurred: activists viewed this shift as the invasion of trade negotiations and agreements into *their* traditional space. Indeed deals such as NAFTA expanded far beyond traditional trade matters to impose policy constraints on issues that are at the core of labor and environmental activists' and public interest advocates' realm. For decades, however, trade policy had flown below the public's radar. Politicizing trade policy by making it a source of public concern and contention would therefore not be easy.

NAFTA's introduction and subsequent contestation provided a turning point in the politicization of trade politics. Environmental, labor, and other anti-NAFTA activists created both a congressional insurgency and a larger grassroots movement in an effort to promote labor, environmental, and consumer protections. Two distinct outcomes appeared possible at the onset of the NAFTA debates: passage of a standard neoliberal agreement, or failure in the United States as a result of existing tensions among trade policy elites. Instead, what emerged was a dynamic broad-based political movement that made trade a subject of popular contention and resulted in a novel trade arrangement that recognized the linkages between trade policy and labor and environmental rights for the first time in a modern trade agreement.

Labor and environmental activists' mobilization in response to NAFTA was about asserting their democratic interest in the trade arena where they had not previously done so. Activists did not achieve their ultimate goal of either improving NAFTA to the point that they could support it, or killing the agreement in its final and unsatisfactory form. They did not achieve power-over in their NAFTA struggle. They did, however, build power-to during the NAFTA negotiations. What they accomplished was important and unexpected even though it was limited: activists significantly increased the public consciousness on trade issues and turned a previously technocratic concern into a highly visible populist issue, they expanded and mobilized new constituencies and coalitions that had not previously linked their policy goals with trade outcomes, and they exploited (with their congressional allies) vulnerabilities in the rules by which the trade policy field operates. This allowed them to pressure negotiators into changing their position and include labor and environmental protections, however weak, in NAFTA's side agreements. As Pharis Harvey of ILRF explained:

> Even though the mechanisms achieved under NAFTA were inadequate, it was an important turning point. The debate on labor and environmental conditions brought legitimacy to the concept of international environmental and labor standards and rationally looking at the incentives to trade.[12]

Activists ultimately helped shape how the rules governing the North American economy are made. Activists' most significant contribution was

to politicize and democratize trade policy for the first time, and that politicization did not abate during subsequent trade battles.

But activists also shaped the rules governing the *global* economy. What
happened during NAFTA's negotiation mattered by providing a coun-
terbalance to the trade liberalization agenda domestically, which then
shaped a U.S. counter-force in civil society to resist the dominant role the
U.S. government and corporations were playing in promoting the new
NAFTA model for trade agreements around the world. While activists
in developing countries had fought against impositions of similar policy
packages via international agreements such as the International Monetary
Fund and World Bank structural adjustment agreements, NAFTA was
U.S. activists' entrée to the fight. Activists' institutional, network, and
framing impacts legitimized the role of labor, environmental, and other
actors in the trade debate and highlighted the importance of weighing
the externality effects of trade policy. It also legitimized arguments about
collective rights and common goods in a political culture rooted in individual rights, liberties, and individualism. The rhetorical battle activists
waged against NAFTA challenged the privileging of individual rights in
North America, particularly in the United States. It foregrounded the
collective rights and common good of North American citizens. This aspect of their battle against NAFTA was quite radical, and yet it is usually overlooked and under-analyzed. Activists' impact has continued to
resonate; their model of building internationally-linked country-based
campaigns to fight free trade agreements diffused around the world,
and was deployed successfully in the fight against MAI, FTAA, the WTO
Doha Round, and the TPP. Although activists have not won the war, they
changed the trade policy terrain in ways that solidifies their position in
ongoing trade battles.

Understanding How Movements Shape Policy

NAFTA provides an extremely useful case for expanding a vibrant and
burgeoning literature that tries to understand the role of civil society in
shaping state policy. Our theoretical framework centered on field intersection provides the foundation for a truly integrative mapping of routine and
contentious politics that has significant and generalizable implications
for movements beyond those focused on trade. Social movement scholarship largely focuses on disruptive behavior and draws rigid boundaries
around different kinds of activities. It therefore misses the ways in which

collective action often includes both insider and outsider strategies. The extant literature also provides little theoretical guidance about when each of these types of strategies or practices is more advantageous and in what political context. Social movement theorists therefore tend to reify disruptive and insurgent activity and miss its complex relationship with routine institutionalized practices. And as Bloom reminds us, the general focus on who mobilizes rather than on how they mobilize limits our understanding of movement dynamics and outcomes. He urges us to focus on mobilizing practices.[13]

Using the NAFTA case, we show the ways in which routine and contentious practices complement one another and are often used collaboratively to take advantage of different leverage points across fields. The terrain of intersecting fields is sufficiently complex to enable differently positioned actors to employ both "insider" and "outsider" collective action tactics. Using a combination of contentious and routine activity, environmental and labor activists succeeded in bringing new actors into the trade policy field, changing the rules of trade policy, and widening the parameters of the trade debate both within the legislative and trade policy fields and among the public more generally. Every trade policy debate and negotiation that has followed bears the stamp of the NAFTA fight.

In addition, a shift in analysis to field intersection explains a crucial but underexplored component of contentious political activity—how social movements succeed within hostile fields. Social movement scholarship cannot sufficiently explain how social change occurs within a field hostile to it, because it misses the critical leverage points situated where fields intersect. Those who are marginalized within, or excluded from, one field are not inevitably without political advantages or resources. Our framework illuminates the mechanisms by which actors who are constrained within one field can mobilize in others to alter the rules, distribution of influence, conceptual understanding of a problem, or decision-making calculus by which policies are determined. And by illuminating these mechanisms of field overlap, our framework also helps us better understand the processes underlying politicization and how they operate. Indeed politicization can be conceptualized as the processes by which key actors leverage resources across fields "to contest the symbolic framing in which 'routine' decisions had heretofore been made" (Laumann and Knoke 1987:379).

The NAFTA case shows that the outcome of the creation of trade regimes is not predetermined nor path dependent and that change is possible even when the institutional configurations of an individual field or the architecture across multiple fields create difficult constraints and challenges for nonstate actors. It is possible for activists to demand regulatory protections even if they have few resources relative to capital. Structural conditions can affect preferences, increase the political access of some groups over others, and improve the likelihood of attaining international policy goals. But such conditions neither create insurmountable constraints nor inevitably lead to particular policy outcomes.

No matter how restricted policy fields are or how determinative influential field actors remain in privileging particular symbolic conceptions of policy aims, dimensions for change are embedded in every context; actors can mobilize in other fields to agitate for changes in the distribution of influence in a policy arena or more fundamentally in the rules by which policies are determined. Activists are constrained, but not inescapably defined, by the structural conditions and social context in which they operate.

Given those constraints, however, activists can make choices that help or hamper their efforts to pursue their policy ends. The NAFTA case shows that there are often multiple points of leverage that can be exploited across fields, and that activists can be more or less skilled at engaging them. Moreover political entrepreneurship can make a real difference in alliance-building, framing, and resource brokerage strategies, creating opportunities that were not previously visible. Social movements can influence what happens in a hostile field because they can draw on strengths constituted outside that field. This can result in rapid and unexpected disruption, such as with NAFTA, where new issues seem to come out of nowhere and scramble the debate. Or they can emerge gradually, as network alliances expand over time, resource dependency nurtures, or reframings develop.

While a framework centered on field intersection means that we understand environmental and labor activists to be causal agents who are not merely trapped waiting for political opportunity windows to open and close, it also means that they can make more and less effective strategic and tactical choices. Labor leaders would have been better positioned if they had contested NAFTA sooner. Environmental leaders would have been in better shape if they had not been willing to view access as a sufficient core goal. Not everything is possible; activists try to shape new realities while they operate within existing constraints.

The NAFTA case suggests that social movements with routinized access to intersecting fields have better chances to influence policy the less insulated and absolute the power in the field, and the less concentrated the centers of authority. Our analysis, however, only provides the first step in understanding the dynamics of field intersection. More theoretical and empirical work is needed in order to determine whether particular types of field intersections are relatively more important than others, whether they exhibit common patterns, and whether thresholds for successful leverage exist.

The theoretical framework we present provides a rich new terrain for further organizations and social movements research. It offers organizations scholars new ways to expand their analyses of fields, understand the interface with social movements, and conceptually map complex institutional structures and dynamics that may have previously gone unexamined. Our framework also has important implications for organizations research by providing greater conceptual clarity to our understanding of exogenous shocks to organizational fields. Indeed, it may help explain more large-scale or rapid social transformations, as change moves through overlapping fields in "contagion" or "wave" effects, facilitated by linked interactions across multiple fields. Although the NAFTA case illuminates the importance of field overlap mechanisms, additional cases are needed to better explore the ways in which organizational identities, interests, and constraints vary across fields, as well as the implications of different field logics for social action.

Examining field intersections also has critical implications for social movement research by providing a new framework for conceptualizing political opportunity structures and movement success and failure. Our framework reconceptualizes political opportunity structures as dynamic configurations of overlapping fields that can be leveraged strategically to achieve specific policy outcomes, rather than as propitious moments that activists must perceive in order to take advantage of. It is where fields interlock that political opportunity structures are constituted. At these intersections where structural contradictions are highest, key allies, powerful new frames, and resources for disadvantaged actors are found. The institutional characteristics of each field, the relationship between fields, and the social interactions of nonstate actors and decision-makers within them, all affect nonstate actors' calculus of influence in determining their mobilization strategy.

By placing *strategy* at the center of analysis, then, our framework also offers promising avenues for new research on movement success and failure. Success results, in large part, from activists' ability to skillfully use leverage and broker across fields. Our analysis suggests that activists could improve their chances of success by looking for places where significant penetration or intersections with other fields exist, exploiting key points of leverage, and utilizing strategies that take advantage of them. Historical comparative cases of movement success and failure would provide additional analytical leverage for better understanding social movement success, particularly as field overlap changes over time. Comparative social movement research also offers a particularly rich area for exploring more fully how dependencies on grassroots fields can be effectively employed. And further research that analyzed how activists *perceive* the viability of different leverage points, and how this affects their strategic choices, would be invaluable.

Undermining State Institutions, Undermining Democracy

The unexpected ability of labor and environmental activists to influence the nature and scope of international trade policy provides key insights into the relevance of institutional configurations in the pursuit of political goals more generally. Most critically, it illuminates the importance of institutional opportunities for civil society engagement with and influence on state policy. Ironically the most significant lessons from the first free trade battle over NAFTA are not about trade policy itself, but rather about the importance of state institutions for democratic practice. When governments weaken or dismantle state institutions, the consequences to democracy can be severe. As the NAFTA case shows, when governments close citizens' access to state institutions by limiting participation and transparency, they also weaken and undermine democracy.

Trade has been a proxy for the decay of democratic institutions and practices, and an epicenter of the battles to preserve them for over two decades. NAFTA is an important case that allows us to examine how the state tries to thwart democratic interventions in policy formation. But the NAFTA case also shows how activists can develop and deploy strategies that mitigate the effects of state institutional closure and democratic erosion.

The argument therefore resonates regardless of the outcome of the 2016 election. Indeed the decay of state institutions and democracy is relevant not only for international policies, but also for domestic issues, and not just in relation to the executive branch, but to the legislative branch as well. Legislators, for example, often attempt to make legislative processes more opaque, and activists have a narrow range of options for how to respond strategically. In contrast to the Affordable Care Act, which was negotiated with input from many constituencies and interest groups over the course of a year, proponents propelled the American Health Care Act of 2017 to a House vote in a matter of days with no public debate or participation. Even Senator and GOP presidential candidate Rand Paul complained about the lack of transparency when he arrived at the Capitol and was denied access to a copy of a closely guarded draft of the GOP healthcare bill.[14]

Much of the way trade negotiations have played out in the United States minimizes democratic input and involvement, both by institutional design and because they are handled as international agreements. The unique institutional configuration of the trade policy field makes it more impervious to the mobilization of nonstate actors—and perhaps more vulnerable to democratic decay—than other policy fields. Activists have added challenges to surmount—such as fast-track restrictions created to prevent individual members of Congress from packing an agreement with elements that favor narrowly tailored interests, and the rigid structure of the USTR advisory committee—in their efforts to influence trade policy. And the international nature of trade negotiations introduces another layer of complexity in terms of interests, rule parameters and actors with different agendas. These unique characteristics of trade policy formation provide an enormous collective action problem from a trade liberalization perspective. Given the deck stacked against them institutionally, it is surprising that activists influenced NAFTA at all.

And yet, labor and environmental activists gained traction when attempting to influence negotiations whose ground rules were designed to minimize that input. This was possible because activists were privy to information about what the areas of contention were, and what were the bottom-line demands by various stakeholders—they could therefore mobilize around fissures or cleavages across fields. Thus activists' ability to improve NAFTA depended on access and information that came through state channels, which allowed them to develop and deploy specific framing, resource brokerage, and alliance-building strategies at critical junctures in the negotiations.

Activists' access to state channels and level of participation in trade policy has waxed and waned in the years after NAFTA's passage. But in general, the government has continued to try to thwart access and transparency, and load free trade agreements with non-tariff related provisions that threaten domestic policies created to protect citizens. Activists have responded by placing issues of transparency at the center of post-NAFTA trade battles. By focusing fair trade campaigns on transparency and democratic participation in the negotiation process and in the trade agreements themselves, activists brought together even broader constituencies than had been involved in the NAFTA struggle.

At key moments, such as during the Obama administration under USTR Michael Froman, civil society participation in trade policy has been severely eroded, and democratization in relationship to trade has faced serious setbacks. When the government employs democratic closure activists are prevented from leveraging broader cleavages, exploiting networks, and utilizing resources. Their ability to apply pressure across fields is severely constrained. This means that it is very difficult for activists to influence trade policy.

But it also means, perhaps ironically, that while the government undermined one form of pushback based on institutionalized insider strategies, it simultaneously raised the stakes of trade policy, stimulating another form of pushback rooted in disruptive grassroots outsider strategies. In an environment of democratic retrenchment, activists' primary strategic option is to try to kill trade agreements whole cloth. In order to do so they can try to elect political allies, or use disruptive strategies that pose a challenge to authorities and make business as usual impossible. Arguably, by maintaining closed negotiating processes after NAFTA and refusing to address civil society concerns about the content of trade agreements, trade policy elites contributed to the demise of the MAI, FTAA, the WTO Doha Round, the TPP, as well as the election of Donald Trump.

A general decay of democratic policymaking has significant implications for the nature and content of all kinds of policies. In the trade realm, it means that in order to improve NAFTA during its current renegotiation, activists will need some access and information vis-a-vis state institutions. And evidence suggests improving NAFTA would result in better economic and political outcomes than destroying it. Since Donald Trump's election many scholars, activists, and policymakers have warned that a wholesale eradication of NAFTA would have dire consequences for workers, consumers, farmers, and businesses across the continent.[15] An integrated economy and the dense networks created by NAFTA during the last quarter century across supply chains, factories, financial markets, and the harmonization of key standards (in agriculture and food, environment, etc.) have real benefits. As they did during the NAFTA struggle, today activists prefer to improve NAFTA by building on these benefits, while simultaneously strengthening labor and environmental protections and eliminating ISDS mechanisms. It is still unclear whether they will have that opportunity under the Trump administration.

The NAFTA case is extremely relevant for movements and civil society organizations across a wide range of issue areas around the world, from social movements struggling to influence international climate change policy to NGOs advocating for international banking regulation. The NAFTA battle was a potent reminder that institutional opportunities are crucial to activists' efforts to try to shape international policy. It is extremely difficult for civil society organizations to influence and shape state policy when institutional channels are blocked by the state. And when the state closes institutional opportunities for civil society participation—for example, by negotiating climate change agreements secretly—it leaves activists little recourse but to engage in disruptive tactics as the best chance for success.

Thus, the state essentially limits the ways in which individuals and organizations can participate in civil society, changing the nature of both discourse and participation in political issues. This dynamic actually intensifies politicization and polarization. It was on full display during the first week of his presidency, when Donald Trump signed an executive order banning refugees from seven Muslim countries. The public response was swift—activists took to the streets to protest all across the country. Although it remains to be seen how the next trade battles will play out under the Trump administration, if history teaches us anything, it is that each administration—regardless of party—has found ways to undermine the public's ability to democratically intervene in the government's trade policy.

As our analysis shows, the battle over NAFTA was in many ways less a battle over trade policy than a battle over the role of democratic state institutions in policymaking. The first trade battle is therefore still relevant after twenty-five years because it exposes the need for future battles to be waged over protecting democratic participation and engagement across all policy issues, not only trade. Indeed, the primary goal of future progressive movements should be to demand, and through their mobilization *ensure*, that state institutions are open, transparent, accessible, and responsive to all. Only by building alliances and movements across issue areas—from trade, labor, and the environment to immigration and refugee rights, among many others—will progressive activists have any chance to push back against the erosion of democracy and democratic institutions in the United States and around the world.

Notes

CHAPTER 1

1. Corporate supporters and governments rebranded the agreement. It was originally referred to as the Trans-Atlantic Free Trade Agreement (TAFTA).

2. http://www.spiegel.de/international/world/protest-movement-threatens-ttip-transatlantic-trade-deal-a-1091088.html.

3. http://www.bbc.com/news/world-europe-37396796; https://politica.elpais.com/politica/2016/05/15/actualidad/1463343025_306049.html; http://www.lavanguardia.com/local/barcelona/20161015/411029454560/manifestacion-ttip-cepta-barcelona.html

4. http://www.flushthetpp.org/protest-at-white-house-kicks-off-nationwide-days-of-action/

5. http://www.commondreams.org/newswire/2016/04/01/april-fools-protests-nationwide-warn-members-congress-tpps-no-joke-take.

6. Because all citizens of North and South America are "American" and Mexicans are also "North American," we use the adjective "U.S." throughout the book. Because in English there exists no noun except "American" to describe U.S. citizens, we use it only when necessary.

7. Except among Texans living within one hundred miles of the border. http://www.huffingtonpost.com/entry/border-residents-didnt-vote-for-trumps-wall_us_5890e016e4b02772c4e9bc88?4g0z74appfapxo3sor.

8. For ease, we use the term trade throughout the book rather than trade agreements.

9. News from the Citizens Trade Campaign 1993.

10. Of course some unions in developing countries viewed labor standards as hidden protectionism.

11. The strategies themselves were not new. Rather, they were newly deployed by activists to mobilize around trade policy.

12. Labor leaders did not support this option. The AFL-CIO called for Clinton to re-negotiate the agreement instead.

13. The European Economic Community/European Union Treaties have included mechanisms for the enforcement of labor laws since 1957. Its court, how-ever, has dealt with those issues. The European Union therefore did not create adjudicatory bodies dedicated solely to the enforcement of key basic labor rights.

14. Audley 1997:66.

15. Exceptions to the relative paucity of sociological work on trade include: Ayres 1998; Dreiling 2001; Duina 2006; Chorev 2007.

16. The maquiladora program was designed to attract foreign investment and re-duce unemployment, primarily along Mexico's northern border.

17. When we use the term "citizen," we are generally referring to those who re-side in North America and form part of its community, regardless of their legal status.

18. Unionization in the United States is now at low rates not seen in over one hun-dred years and, as scholars such as Francisco Fernando Herrera Lima (2014) have argued, Mexican unions are now in their worst crisis since before the Mexican revolution.

19. These ideas come from Marshall Ganz's notes for his course "Practicing Democracy: Leadership, Community and Power," 17 and Ganz "Leading Change."

20. Ganz "Practicing Democracy," course notes, 17.

21. Cited in Apple 1993.

22. http://www.citizen.org/TPP.

23. *Inside U.S. Trade* is a weekly report on government and industry trade action published by Inside Washington Publishers. Source material was originally col-lected for related projects. See Evans (2002) and Kay (2005; 2011a).

24. A Lexis-Nexis search yielded more than one thousand articles (n = 1083) on NAFTA. Excluding duplication, 202 articles were chosen for closer analysis that collectively covered all the major events of negotiations, grassroots activism, and the political battle in Washington.

CHAPTER 2

1. Bloom cites Bourdieu 1990; Isaac 2008; Joas 1996; Sewell 1992; and Swidler 1986.

2. For other discussions of interest group politics, see Berry 1989; Rauch 1994; Hayes 1981; Wilson 1990; and Thomas 1993.

3. Bloom 2017. Personal communication with author, May 19.

4. Although most organizational theorists highlight the networked component, and Bourdieuian theorists the structural and cultural components of these local social orders, Fligstein 2001 draws from both.

5. Their definition is more akin to Bourdieu's concept of social field, see *Homo Academicus* (1988) and *State Nobility: Elite Schools in the Field of Power* (1996); or Weber's concept of social order. See also Martin 2003.

6. Although theories of community ecology and niche competition come closest to conceptualizing field overlap, they are more limited than the approach we advance here (see Ruef 2000).

7. They use the term "domain."

8. Laumann and Knoke define a policy domain as: "a subsystem identified by specifying a substantively defined criterion of mutual relevance or common orientation among a set of consequential actors concerned with formulating, advocating, and selecting courses of action (i.e. policy options) that are intended to resolve the delimited substantive problems in question" (1987:10).

9. Laumann and Knoke 1987:379.

10. See Davis et al. 2005; Schneiberg and Lounsbury 2008 for other examples.

11. Bourdieu's discussion of structurally homologous groups in *Homo Academicus* (1988) approximates this idea.

12. We could have called the NAFTA fields "subfields" of the larger trade policy field. We decided against using the term "subfields," however, because we feel it inaccurately defines a larger cohesive whole and minimizes the structured integrity of each of the arenas of action.

13. See Martin and Sikkink 1993.

14. The USTR also functions as the U.S. representative in all international trade organizations and has administrative responsibility for the Generalized System of Preferences (GSP), Section 301 petitions against foreign unfair trade practices, and import relief cases.

15. Office of the U.S. Trade Representative (1992).

16. Wallach and Hilliard 1991; Anderson, Cavanaugh, and Gross 1993.

17. For elaborated discussions of the institutional characteristics of trade policy formation in the United States, see Destler 1995; Goldstein 1993; Destler 2005; Kaplan 1996; and Cohen 1988. For a discussion of the institutional limitations on the influence of societal groups in the trade domain, see Haggard 1988; Goldstein 1993; and Destler 1995.

CHAPTER 3

1. Underlying concerns about the burgeoning trade deficits was a sense that trading partners—particularly European countries and Japan—were undercutting the multilateral trading system and hurting U.S. industry by aggressively shielding their domestic markets, subsidizing exports to the United States and dumping goods into the U.S. market below cost.

2. The Bretton Woods system established a monetary policy based on the gold standard among developed nations in 1944. In 1971, the United States ended its linkage of the U.S. dollar with gold, and the Bretton Woods system ended.

3. Salinas faced enormous economic problems that had begun over a decade earlier. In the 1980s rising U.S. interest rates and plummeting world oil prices resulted in a debt-payment crisis and a peso devaluation in 1982. Salinas's predecessor, Miguel de la Madrid, had already initiated the most substantial liberalization reforms, including ending more than five decades of economic policy based on import-substitution industrialization.

4. U.S. trade with Ontario alone in the 1980s surpassed the United States' entire trade relationship with Japan (Closs et al. 1988; Gunter 1988). This interdependence was of a highly unequal nature. In 1985 the United States bought almost 80 percent of Canada's exports and supplied more than 70 percent of its imports, compared to the approximately 20 percent of its imports and exports that the United States traded with Canada (Gunter 1988).

5. Countervail duties are used by countries to offset subsidies by the exporter's government, whereas anti-dumping duties act to prevent foreign companies from selling at prices below their domestic prices.

6. The president could do the former using his power under the escape clause.

7. Union leaders more generally began to criticize the lack of a coherent U.S. industrial strategy. Japan, South Korea, and European countries, they argued, were gaining ground in part because they followed an explicit strategy of market penetration that the United States did not counter. Foreign nations' import dumping, subsidization of industries, and protection of domestic markets led union leaders and other critics to increasingly argue that the playing field was no longer level.

8. The Caribbean Basin Initiative mandated that as a condition for a country's duty-free access to the United States the president would factor in the extent to which "workers in such a country are afforded reasonable workplace conditions and enjoy the right to organize and bargain collectively" (Marshall 1990:74). The agreement had no enforcement mechanisms.

9. During the 1992 United Nations Conference on Environment and Development (The Earth Summit) in Rio de Janeiro, NGOs successfully pushed for a linkage between sustainable development and market mechanisms.

10. Personal Interview with Mark Ritchie of IATP, June 11, 2001.

11. Personal Interview with Mark Ritchie of IATP, June 11, 2001. To make it easier to read, we changed the term he used from "ag" to agriculture in the quote.

12. Personal Interview with Don Weiner of the Fair Trade Campaign, April 5, 2001.

13. Personal Interview with Mark Ritchie of IATP, June 11, 2001.

14. Personal Interview with Craig Merrilees of the Fair Trade Campaign, April 21, 2001.

15. Part of the 1958 Food Additives Amendment (section 409) to the 1954 Federal Food, Drug and Cosmetic Act, the Delaney Clause prohibits the use of any pesticide residues found to cause cancer in animals as a food additive.

16. Personal Interview with Lori Wallach of Public Citizen, May 7, 1998.

17. See Norton 2003 for a critique.

18. Although maquiladoras were originally limited to the border region, the geographical restrictions were loosened in 1972. As of 1990, more than 80 percent of maquiladora plants were located in the border region.

19. By 1990, the number of maquiladora factories increased yet again to nearly 1,900 and employed 450,000 workers (Gereffi 1992).

20. Plants predominately operating in garment production, semiconductor assembly, and light manufacturing are generally characterized by low-wage, labor-intensive operations. A second wave of maquiladora plants engaged in automobile-related manufacturing and advanced electronics assembly tend to use more advanced technology and a higher-skilled labor force, and pay higher wages (Gereffi 1992; Shaiken 1990, 1991; Sklair 1993).

21. Shaiken cites Middlebrook 1991.

22. Personal Interview with David Brooks of U.S.-Mexico Dialogos, May 8, 2001.

23. While the overall Mexican population increased 21 percent between 1980 and 1990, the population in the thirty-nine Mexican municipalities along the border increased by 30 percent. The populations of Tijuana increased by 61 percent and Ciudad Juarez by 41 percent. Tijuana, Ciudad Juarez, and Mexicali contained the largest number of maquiladora factories during this period (Gereffi 1992).

24. One study of maquiladoras in Mexicali found that the biggest environmental problems caused by maquiladoras stemmed from their generation of hazardous waste (Sanchez 1990).

25. *BorderLines* 1993.

26. See June 4, 1988.

27. *AFL-CIO News*, March 4, 1989.

28. See Coalition for Justice in the Maquiladoras (1999).

29. Bustamante 1972 and Frank 1999 explore some of this history.

30. Available at: http://www.nathannewman.org/EDIN/.labor/.files/.archive/.global.union.html.

31. Personal Interview with Alicia Sepúlveda Nuñez of the STRM, August 27, 2000.

32. Personal Interview with AFL-CIO official, 2001.

CHAPTER 4

1. At this early stage Canada was not a party to the agreement and it was not referred to as NAFTA. Canada joined negotiations on January 23, 1991.

2. Personal Interview with Pharis Harvey of ILRF, April 14 1998. At that time, it was called the International Labor Rights Education and Research Fund.

3. See also Personal Interview with Karen Hansen-Kuhn of DGAP, April 22, 1998, for a discussion of the meeting.

4. MODTLE emerged after the Working Group on Trade and Environmentally Sustainable Development split up. In fall 1992, MODTLE became the Alliance for Responsible Trade (ART).

5. Discussions about forming CTWC as an NGO counterpart to the Congressional Fair Trade Caucus occurred in June 1991 (Personal Interview with Pharis Harvey of ILRF, March 2, 2001). CTWC was created in the summer of 1991. It institutionalized the Public-Citizen-led coalition that had helped spearhead the fast-track fight.

6. Personal Interview with Evy DuBrow of ILGWU, May 12 1998. Marge Allen of AFSCME and Segundo Mercado-Llorens of UFCW were central participants in the development of the fast-track legislative coalition and CTCW, even though NAFTA did not affect their union members as directly as industrial textile, electrical, and auto unions.

7. See also Buttel and Taylor 1992.

8. This stems in large part from the "new social movements" literature developed by scholars such as Melucci and Tourraine. See Scott 1990 for an overview.

9. For discussions of the complexity of environmental mobilization and action, see Dobson 1990. For a discussion of the efficacy of environmental action, see Cahn 1995. The widespread development of environmental movements in developing countries in recent years also calls into question whether there is a structural primacy to environmental mobilization. See Martinez-Alier 1994; Buttel 1997; Buttel and Taylor 1992; and Yearley 1994.

10. See Sklair 1994; Yearley 1994. For a discussion of green political theory, see Barry 1999.

11. Schnaiberg 1980 and Schnaiberg and Gould 1994. See Gould et al. 1996 for a discussion of the treadmill of production on an international scale.

12. Testimony of William Barclay 1992.

13. Testimony of William Snape, March 10, 1993, p. 123.

14. Cited in Switzer and Bryner 1998.

15. For a discussion of the history and limitations of international labor organizations, see Stevis 1998; Boswell and Stevis 1997.

16. See Bustamante 1972; Frank 1999.

17. The Confederation of Mexican Workers (CTM) is the major Mexican union federation with historic ties to the ruling party.

18. Personal Interview with AFL-CIO representative Tim Beaty, February 29, 2000, in Washington, DC.

19. Personal Interview with John Audley of the Sierra Club, April 27, 1998.

20. Personal Interview with Tom Donahue of the AFL-CIO, May 23, 2001.

21. See National Wildlife Federation, November 17, 1990, and *Inside U.S. Trade*, November 23, 1990, p. 19.

22. Personal Interview with Craig Merrilees of the Fair Trade Campaign, April 3, 2001.

23. Testimony of Craig Merrilees, May 8, 1991, p. 312. See also testimony of John Audley of the Sierra Club, April 8, 1992.

24. Testimony of Mark Anderson, June 28, 1991, p. 7. See also Stewart Hudson's April 24, 1991, testimony for the NWF and Joseph Sanchez's May 14, 1991, testimony on behalf of the UAW.

25. Testimony of Mark Anderson, June 28, 1991.

26. For discussions of the health consequences of toxic dumping in the border region, see Testimony of Craig Merrilees of the FTC and NTC, April 23, 1991, and testimony of Stewart Hudson of the NWF, March 6, 1991.

27. Testimony of Michael Gregory, April 23, 1991, p. 40.

28. Testimony of Lori Wallach and Tom Hilliard, May 8, 1991, p. 25. See also Mercado-Llorens who testified on behalf of the UFCW, December 9, 1991.

29. Maggs 1991.

30. *Inside U.S. Trade,* January 11, 1991, p. 2.

31. *Inside U.S. Trade,* February 8, 1991, p. 9.

32. Letter dated December 10, 1990, printed in *Inside U.S. Trade,* January 11, 1991, p. 7.

33. Participants included: the NWF, AFL-CIO, UAW, the Family Farm Coalition, Greenpeace, the NRDC, the Community Nutrition Institute, and ILRF, among others (*Inside U.S. Trade,* November 23, 1990, p. 19).

34. Environmental organizations represented included the NWF, FOE, and Greenpeace. ILRF was the primary labor organization, but other labor unions included the UAW, ILGWU, International Union of Food and Allied Workers, and ACTWU. Other organizations included DGAP, Arizona Toxics Information Project, Association of Farmworker Opportunity Programs, Child Labor Coalition, Community Nutrition Institute, Institute for Policy Studies, U.S.-Mexico Dialogos, National Consumers League, National Family Farm Coalition, National Toxics Campaign, United Methodist Board of Church and Society, as well as Mexican academics and people from the Pro-Canada network (see *Inside U.S. Trade,* January 11, 1991, p. 7).

35. See *Inside U.S. Trade,* November 23, 1990, p. 19 and *Inside U.S. Trade,* January 18, 1991, p. 14.

36. See Brecher and Costello 1991 and Roger 1991.

37. Personal Interview with Pharis Harvey of ILRF, March 2, 2001.

38. Personal Interview with Karen Hansen-Kuhn of DGAP, April 22, 1998.

39. *Inside U.S. Trade,* February 8, 1991, p. 5.

40. Audley 1997:52. Audley worked for the Sierra Club during much of the NAFTA struggle.

41. See MacArthur 2000.

42. See Wyden et al. 1991. See also *Inside U.S. Trade,* February 22, 1991, p. 6.

43. National Wildlife Federation, November 17, 1990, and *Inside U.S. Trade,* February 22 1991, p. 5. Other members of Congress also sent letters supporting a linkage between environmental concerns and the trade agreement. See *Inside U.S. Trade,* March 1, 1991, p. 7.

44. See Duncan 1991.

45. Dunne 1991:4.

46. See Otteman, May 24, 1991. *Inside U.S. Trade* also reported that NWF's support for fast track would come as a result of Reilly's letter to Sen. Wirth clarifying the environmental commitments included in President Bush's Action Plan (see Reilly 1991; Hair 1991).

47. Personal Interview with Kathryn Fuller of WWF, May 26, 1998.

48. *Inside U.S. Trade,* February 22, 1991, p. 5.

49. *Inside U.S. Trade,* February 22, 1991, pp. 1, 4, 19.

50. *Inside U.S. Trade,* February 22, 1991, p. 1.

51. See *CQ Weekly,* March 2, 1991, for a discussion of the politics surrounding the official request. Because of the language of the 1988 act, Congress had no way to differentiate between trade agreements that would be affected by the fast-track vote. They therefore had to decide the fate of fast-track authority for both GATT, which had more support in Congress among Democrats, and NAFTA, which was perceived as more problematic. Some members of Congress pushed for splitting the fast-track vote into two separate votes, so that they could support GATT while denying fast-track procedures for NAFTA. The Bush administration opposed the call (Watkins 1991). At the time, Senator Lloyd Bentsen suggested, however, that the linkage of fast track for both GATT and NAFTA actually made passage more difficult, because it allowed the opponents of GATT and the opponents of NAFTA to unite (see Otteman, March 1, 1991, p. 21).

52. See Cloud 1991a.

53. One of the Bush administration's leaders on fast-track claimed the administration arranged for the letter from Rostenkowski and Bentsen to preempt Gephardt (see MacArthur 2000). The two legislators had been scheduled to meet with USTR Hills on March 1 to "begin the process of putting together a coalition" (Cloud 1991a).

54. *Inside U.S. Trade,* May 3, 1991, p. 8.

55. *Inside U.S. Trade,* March 29, 1991, pp. S2 and S3.

56. National organizations such as NWF and NRDC, although outsiders in the trade policy field, were legitimate and influential among environmental policymakers and legislators on issues ranging from land management and energy policy to air pollution. Once decision-makers accepted the linkage between trade and environmental issues, leading environmental organizations did not have to justify their own legitimacy as experts on environmental issues.

57. *Inside U.S. Trade,* April 5, 1991, p. 8.

58. *Inside U.S. Trade,* April 5, 1991, p. 8.

59. *Inside U.S. Trade,* April 5, 1991, p.8.
60. All of the major national environmental organizations, however, embraced the concept of sustainable development.
61. Herein we modify Audley's (1997) terminology by distinguishing between pro-growth and adversarial environmental organizations.
62. Cited in Audley 1997:54.
63. Advisory Committee on Trade Policy Negotiations 1991:7.
64. Otteman, May 3, 1991, pp. S-1, S-5. In February 1992, the Bush budget proposal called for the elimination of the Trade Adjustment Assistance Program. Bush called for worker assistance for those injured by NAFTA under the Economic Dislocation and Worker Adjustment Assistance Act, which provided training assistance but not income support. AFL-CIO representatives called the program inadequate, underfunded, and overly narrow in its criteria for qualification (Kirkland 1991).
65. Bush 1991. See *Inside U.S. Trade,* July 19, 1991, p. 19.
66. Bush 1991. Environmental appointments to each of these committees did not all materialize, and Public Citizen filed lawsuits to demand civil society representation on them. A trade and environmental policy advisory committee was formed that included environmental and industry representatives in equal numbers.
67. Bush 1991. The environmental review came in response to Public Citizen's National Environmental Policy Act (NEPA) lawsuit.
68. Cloud 1991b.
69. Calmes 1991.
70. As in the House, the vote was actually on a resolution to cancel the continuation of fast-track (Bradsher 1991).
71. *Inside U.S. Trade,* May 24, 1991, p. 1. See also Gugliotta 1991.
72. Natural Resources Defense Council, May 8, 1991.
73. Bradsher 1991.
74. Lee, May 23, 1991, p. A21.
75. Lee, May 23, 1991, p. A21.
76. Cited in MacArthur 2000:129.

CHAPTER 5

1. Merrilees and Weiner 1992.
2. Personal interview with Mark Ritchie of the Institute for Agriculture and Trade Policy, June 11, 2001.
3. Personal communication with Lori Wallach, January 2018.
4. Burkholder 1991.
5. Garin-Hart Strategic Research Group (1991). The summary of key findings did not include the sampling error range. See also *AFL-CIO News,* May 1, 1991.
6. Otteman, *Inside U.S. Trade,* August 2, 1991, p. 12.

7. *NAFTA Thoughts*, December 1991.

8. McDonnell 1991.

9. Lindquist 1991. See also Crawley 1991.

10. McDonnell 1991. For stories of protests of Salinas, see *Toronto Star* 1991.

11. See *Inside U.S. Trade*, August 23, 1991, p. 1.

12. Personal interview with Bill Snape of DOW, May 14, 1998. See also Otteman, September 6, 1991, pp. 1, 14, 15. For further congressional action on the matter, see *Inside U.S. Trade*, September 13, 1991, pp. 4–5 and March 13, 1992, pp. 3–5; Otteman, *Inside U.S. Trade*, October 4, 1991, pp. 10–11; and *Inside U.S. Trade*, September 27, 1991, pp. 1–2.

13. Wilson 1994:32.

14. See, for example, *NAFTAThoughts*, February 1992.

15. Wastler 1992, p. 5A; Merrilees and Weiner 1992.

16. Dunne and Bransten 1992.

17. Merrilees and Weiner 1992.

18. Public Citizen Trade Team, August 14, 1992. See also Darling 1992.

19. Staffing for CTWC was provided by Public Citizen. Its staff included activists that had been active in Public Citizen, the Family Farm Coalition, and Public Interest Research Group (Merrilees and Weiner 1992).

20. Merrilees and Weiner 1992. This memo also states that Mark Anderson sent out a letter to labor activists encouraging closer coordination with CTWC and FTC. See *New York Times* 1992 and *News from the New Teamsters* 1992. The activists worked with a budget of no more than $200,000 (Dunne and Bransten 1992).

21. *Inside U.S. Trade*, November 1, 1991, p. 9.

22. *Inside U.S. Trade*, November 1, 1991, p. 9. MODTLE's January paper on the agreement addressed these (MODTLE 1992).

23. *NAFTAThoughts* 1992:2.

24. The AFL-CIO's work with CJM was an exception to this general rule, but CJM operated far outside of Washington.

25. Personal Interview with Mark Anderson of the AFL-CIO, April 3, 2001.

26. Personal Interview with Craig Merrilees of the Fair Trade Campaign, April 3, 2001.

27. See Personal Interview with Barbara Warden, April 30, 1998.

28. Personal Interview with Tom Donahue of the AFL-CIO, May 23, 2001.

29. Personal Interview with Chris Townsend of the UE, April 1, 1998.

30. Shantz and Anderson 1992.

31. Burkholder 1991. The survey asked residents in the United States, Canada, and Mexico which country would benefit the most from a North American free trade zone. Although majorities in both Mexico and Canada stated that the United States would probably benefit the most, 52 percent of those polled in the United States believed that the primary beneficiary would probably be Mexico.

32. NBC News 1993.

33. Otteman, September 13, 1991, p. 7.
34. *Inside U.S. Trade,* June 21, 1991, p. 13.
35. Otteman, *Inside U.S. Trade,* September 13, 1991, p. 7.
36. Cited in MacArthur 2000:129.
37. See Otteman, August 2, 1991, pp. 1, 12; Gregory 1992. Activists won the original suit that was overturned by the District Court and upheld on appeal. For further information about the lawsuit, see *Inside U.S. Trade,* October 4, 1991, p. 7 and November 29, 1991, p. 8.
38. Prickett et al. 1991.
39. National Wildlife Federation 1991.
40. *Inside U.S. Trade,* November 8, 1991, p. 7.
41. For campaign coverage of the resolution, see Citizen Trade Watch Campaign, December 13, 1991.
42. *Inside U.S. Trade,* February 14, 1992, p. 20. See also Riegle 1991. For labor support of the resolution, see Sheehan 1991. Citizen Trade Watch Campaign, September 26, 1991.
43. Citizen Trade Watch Campaign, December 13, 1991.
44. Merrilees and Weiner, October 23, 1991.
45. The bill was criticized for being too complex. See *Inside U.S. Trade,* March, 13 1992, p. 8.
46. *Inside U.S. Trade,* December 13, 1991, p. 7 and Kolbe et al. 1991.
47. *Inside U.S. Trade,* February 28, 1992, p. S-9.
48. Audley 1997:87. NWF began to develop its own consensus position that was more general in scope. NRDC did not endorse it when it was released on May 25.
49. "Too High a Price for Free Trade," 1992.
50. *Inside U.S. Trade,* July 28, 1992, p. S-3.
51. Public Citizen Trade Team, August 14, 1992.
52. Cranford 1992. See also Public Citizen Trade Team, August 14, 1992.
53. Gephardt 1992.
54. *Inside U.S. Trade,* September 11, 1992, p. 7; Audley 1997:83.
55. The margin of error was plus or minus 3.5 percentage points (Time/CNN 1992).
56. Inside U.S. Trade, July 28, 1992, pp. S-2 and S-3.

CHAPTER 6

1. Of course, Mexico and/or Canada always had the option to simply withdraw from negotiations.
2. Cited in *Inside U.S. Trade,* August 21, 1992, p. 5.
3. Personal interview with Greg Woodhead of the AFL-CIO, April 4 1998.
4. Cloud 1992.
5. Feigen 1992:1.
6. Feigen 1992:2.

7. IUE News Release 1992.

8. Audley 1997:81.

9. Reps. Gephardt and Levin did not sign the letter, but other major representatives allied with labor groups did. See *Inside U.S. Trade,* October 16, 1992, pp. 1, 16. See also Kaptur et al. 1992.

10. These organizations included: Public Citizen, Arizona Toxics, BEP, Center for International Environmental Law, DOW, Earth Island, Fair Trade Campaign, Humane Society, Sierra Club, and Friends of the Earth.

11. *Steelworkers Legislative Appeal* 1992.

12. Citizens Trade Campaign, February 1993.

13. Public Citizen Trade Team, December 30, 1992.

14. Perkins 1992. *Inside U.S. Trade,* December 25, 1992, p. 7.

15. ART/CTC 1992; *Inside U.S. Trade,* December 25, 1992, p. 7.

16. *Inside U.S. Trade,* December 18, 1992, p. 10.

17. Durbin and McIlwraith 1993.

18. Wilson 1994:32.

19. AFL-CIO Executive Council, February 17, 1993. See also *NAFTA Thoughts,* February, 1993.

20. Audley 1997:71.

21. The Labor Department's involvement centered on its International Affairs Office.

22. *Inside U.S. Trade,* January 8, 1993, p. 5; *Inside U.S. Trade,* January 15, 1993, p. 18.

23. *Inside U.S. Trade,* April 2, 1993, p. 19.

24. *Inside U.S. Trade,* April 2, 1993, p. 19.

25. Personal interview with Lawrence Katz of the U.S. Department of Labor, March 13, 2001.

26. See Cameron and Tomlin 2000, p. 186. For further discussion, see *Inside U.S. Trade,* January 15, 1993, pp. 6–7.

27. See *Inside U.S. Trade,* April 2, 1993, p. 19.

28. *NAFTAThoughts* 1993a.

29. *Inside U.S. Trade,* April 30, 1993, pp. S-2–S-6; *Inside U.S. Trade,* May 7, 1993, p. 9.

30. See Audley 1997; *Inside U.S. Trade,* April 30, 1993, p. S-1 and *Inside U.S. Trade,* May 7, 1993, p. 9.

31. *NAFTAThoughts* 1993b. A copy of the letter is included in *Inside U.S. Trade,* May 7, 1993, pp. S-2–S-5.

32. Personal Interview with Craig Merrilees, April 3, 2001.

33. *Inside U.S. Trade,* May 7, 1993, p. S-2.

34. *Inside U.S. Trade,* May 7, 1993, p. S-2.

35. *Inside U.S. Trade,* May 14, 1993, p. 7.

36. *Inside U.S. Trade,* May 21, 1993, pp. S-1, S-9.

37. *Inside U.S. Trade,* May 21, 1993, p. S-1.

38. *Inside U.S. Trade,* May 21, 1993, p. S-1. See also *Inside U.S. Trade,* June 11, 1993, pp. S-5–S-8.

39. *Inside U.S. Trade,* June 11, 1993, p. S-2.

40. *News from Citizens Trade Campaign* 1993.

41. *News from Citizens Trade Campaign* 1993.

42. *News from Citizens Trade Campaign* 1993.

43. Crowe 1993.

44. Clinton 1992.

45. Personal interview with Mark Anderson of the AFL-CIO, January 8, 2001.

46. Cited in *Inside U.S. Trade,* June 11, 1993, p. S-1.

47. *New York Times,* July 12, 1993. *Inside U.S. Trade,* July 2, 1993, p. 1.

48. The appeal was successful, and the ruling of the lower court was overturned.

49. *Inside U.S. Trade,* July 16, 1993, p. 2.

50. *Inside U.S. Trade,* July 23, 1993, p. 12. See also *Inside U.S. Trade* July 2, 1993, p. 20 for letter by legislators to Clinton calling for additional pro-environmental provisions.

51. *Citizens Trade Campaign Bulletin,* July 20, 1993.

52. *Citizens Trade Campaign Bulletin,* July 20, 1993.

53. Cited in Cameron and Tomlin (2000:195).

54. *Inside U.S. Trade,* July 23, 1993, pp. 20–21.

55. *Inside U.S. Trade,* July 30, 1993, p. 6.

56. Cited in Apple 1993.

57. *Inside U.S. Trade,* July 16, 1993, p. 5.

58. See Personal Interviews with Bill Cunningham of the AFL-CIO, May 5, 1998, and Greg Woodhead of the AFL-CIO, April 4, 1998.

59. Donahue 1993.

60. Donahue 1993.

61. Anderson 1993.

62. Anderson 1993.

63. Personal interview with Mark Anderson of the AFL-CIO, January 8, 2001.

64. Personal Interview with Steve Herzenberg, U.S. Department of Labor, Assistant to the Chief Negotiator of the labor side agreement to NAFTA, September 27, 2002.

65. *Inside U.S. Trade,* August 13 1993, p. 10.

66. Mexican negotiators' preference for weaker labor oversight reflects government and official union opposition to core labor standards with enforcement mechanisms. Mexico's labor secretary sought to maintain the country's corporatist system of labor relations, and the Confederation of Mexican Workers (Mexico's largest labor federation) supported this negotiating position (Cameron and Tomlin 2000).

67. Workman 1993, p. S-8.

68. USA*NAFTA 1993. See also *Inside U.S. Trade*, July 2, 1993, p. 17. *Inside U.S. Trade*, January 8, 1993, p. 4; see also Anderson, Cavanaugh, and Gross 1993.

69. *Inside U.S. Trade*, May 14, 1993, pp. S-7–S-8; *Inside U.S. Trade*, May 28, 1993, p. 11.

70. Members of these organizations were quite influential in Washington and had strong ties in the trade policy field. For example, forty-six of USA*NAFTA's state captains were members of USTR advisory committees (see Kollman 1998; Anderson, Cavanaugh, and Gross 1993; see also Cameron and Tomlin 2000). They also overwhelmingly represented companies with existing maquiladoras: 91 percent of companies with captains for which company data existed had operations or subsidiaries in Mexico (see Anderson, Cavanaugh, and Gross 1993). And they spent money to promote the agreement; USA*NAFTA and individual corporations with maquiladoras spent $10 million to promote the agreement. Labor, environmental, and other anti-NAFTA organizations ultimately spent just under $10 million on their campaign. It therefore seemed likely that business interests would use their power to ensure that NAFTA had no enforcement mechanisms (see Lewis 1993). USA*NAFTA alone spent $8 million in the final months of the campaign (Kollman 1998).

71. Kollman 1998. For a discussion of other business organizing, see *Inside U.S. Trade*, July 30, 1993, pp. 21–22.

72. *Inside U.S. Trade*, October 29, 1993, p. 11.

73. Cited in Kollman 1998.

74. *Inside U.S. Trade*, October 29, 1993, p. 11.

75. USA*NAFTA captains came from major corporations. See Anderson, Cavanaugh, and Gross 1993.

76. Moreover evidence suggests that in general, business interests were relatively unsuccessful in rallying support for NAFTA. Frustrated by their inadequate efforts to mobilize in support of fast track, Rostenkowski had warned a group of business leaders: "If you want to win this thing, move your ass" (Cameron and Tomlin 2000:74).

77. For Canada, payment would be backed by the courts. The sanctions would remain until fines were paid and laws were enforced based on the findings of the dispute settlement panel. The differential treatment of Canada came in the final hours after Canada refused to accept trade sanctions. Inclusion of the side accords in the Canadian provinces would be entirely voluntary.

78. *Inside U.S. Trade*, August 16, 1993, pp. S-1–S-5. See also *Inside U.S. Trade*, August 20, 1993, pp. 4–5 for discussions of trade policy field members' support of the agreement.

79. Steps for dispute resolution and penalties are equivalent, with maximum fines of US$ 20 million for countries that are found guilty of, and fail to remedy, domestic law violations. As trade levels expand, maximum penalties increase, eventually to exceed no more than .007 percent of total trade in goods. In addition, both supplemental agreements provide a separate penalty procedure

for Canada. Each Canadian province was allowed to decide whether to accept the supplemental agreements. British Columbia, Quebec, and Ontario declined. Canadian courts, rather than the commissions themselves, collect any labor or environmental fines and enforce action plans in summary proceedings without a consideration of the merits. Although Canadian courts had never failed to enforce similar orders in more than 130 years of existence (Grayson 1995), this measure provides a mechanism to minimize infringement of Canadian sovereignty rights.

80. Both supplemental agreements encourage the sharing of technical and legal information between countries and empower the commissions to act as repositories for such data. In 2006 amid scandal, the three countries quietly made the NAALC Secretariat inactive (personal communication with Lance Compa, former Director of Labor Law and Economic Research, Commission for Labor Cooperation. See also http://www.govexec.com/federal-news/2006/10/allegations-of-cronyism-misdeeds-leave-labor-panel-under-cloud/23040/).

81. http://www.cec.org/about-us/NAAEC.

82. http://www.cec.org/about-us/NAAEC.

83. The U.S. Office of Trade and Labor Affairs now handles U.S. submissions.

84. Ironically, the NAALC procedure actually has an unintended benefit by stimulating transnational collaboration among labor unions. The NAALC's procedural rules require that a submission be filed in a country *other* than the one in which the alleged labor law violation occurred. A submission for a violation in the United States must therefore be filed in Mexico and/or Canada. This rule not only makes it extremely difficult for a union to file with a "foreign" NAO without the assistance of a "foreign" union, but also provides an incentive for unions to collaborate on submissions across borders (see Kay 2005; 2011a).

85. Cited in MacArthur 2000, p. 257.

86. Cited in MacArthur 2000, p. 257.

87. Cited in Apple 1993.

88. Hook 1993:3014.

89. Will 1993; see also Citizens Trade Campaign 1993.

90. Lewis 1993. Mexican and U.S. leaders agreed through a separate U.S.-Mexican treaty to create the NADBank and its oversight board, the Border Environmental Cooperation Commission (BECC). NADBank and BECC were charged with funding environmental infrastructure projects along the U.S.-Mexico border. With the agreement on NADBank, Rep. Esteban Torres, who was a vocal critic of NAFTA, the National Council of La Raza, the Southwest Voter Initiative, and the Mexican-American Legal Defense and Education Fund all decided to back the agreement.

91. Lewis 1993; Citizens Trade Campaign, November 12, 1993.

92. Wines 1993. See also Citizens Trade Campaign 1993.

93. The House Ways and Means Committee formally recommended passage of NAFTA by a 25-12 vote on November 4 (*Inside U.S. Trade*, November 12, 1993, p. 8).

94. Ten more Republicans took part in the House vote than expected.

95. Forty-three Republicans voted against the agreement.

96. Personal interview with Tom Donahue of the AFL-CIO, May 23, 2001.

CHAPTER 7

1. Clinton also eliminated annual congressional reviews of China trade status and the related annual opportunity to demand improved access.

2. https://www.globalpolicy.org/globalization/globalization-of-the-economy-2-1/multilateral-agreement-on-investment-2-5.html.

3. Mary Jane Bolle, "U.S.-Jordan Free Trade Agreement," Congressional Research Service Report for Congress, December 13, 2001, at: http://congressionalresearch.com/RL30652/document.php?study=U.S.-Jordan\+Free\+Trade\+Agreement.

4. Robert A. Rogowsky and Eric Chyn, 2007. "U.S. Trade Law and FTAs: A Survey of Labor Requirements." International Trade Commission. *Journal of International Commerce and Economics*.http://www.usitc.gov/publications/332/journals/trade_law_ftas.pdf.

5. United States-Panama Trade Promotion Agreement.

6. http://www.thenation.com/article/obama-needs-keep-promise-rewrite-nafta/.

7. http://www.nytimes.com/2009/04/21/business/21nafta.html?_r=0.

8. http://www.democracynow.org/2009/8/11/obama_reverses_campaign_pledge_to_renegotiate.

9. http://web.archive.org/web/20170307214844/http://www.aflcio.org/Issues/Trade/Colombia/Colombia. Accessed on Internet Archive Wayback Machine from March 2017.

10. AFL-CIO Memorandum on "Ineffectiveness of Colombia's Labor Action Plan," October 4, 2011.

11. http://www.huffingtonpost.com/2014/05/19/trade-fracking_n_5340420.html.

12. http://www.nytimes.com/2015/04/14/opinion/dont-keep-trade-talks-secret.html.

13. http://www.huffingtonpost.com/2014/01/11/fast-track-trade-democrats_n_4580720.html.

14. http://www.huffingtonpost.com/2012/05/23/trans-pacific-partnership-ron-wyden_n_1540984.html.

15. http://www.wyden.senate.gov/news/blog/post/iycmi-wyden-statement-introducing-congressional-oversight-over-trade-negotiations-act.

16. http://www.wyden.senate.gov/news/blog/post/iycmi-wyden-statement-introducing-congressional-oversight-over-trade-negotiations-act.

17. https://www.washingtonpost.com/blogs/the-switch/wp/2013/12/18/obama-administration-sued-over-its-secretive-trade-negotiations/.

18. http://therealnews.com/t2/index.php?option=com_content&task=view&id=31&Itemid=74&jumival=13986.

19. http://www.politico.com/magazine/story/2015/05/tpp-elizabeth-warren-labor-118068.html#.ValCQEXOaTc.

20. http://www.salon.com/2015/02/06/the_depressing_explanation_why_the_trans_pacific_partnership_is_being_kept_secret_partner/.

21. http://www.reuters.com/article/2012/05/14/us-usa-trade-kirk-idUSBRE84C0AQ20120514.

22. http://therealnews.com/t2/index.php?option=com_content&task=view&id=31&Itemid=7v4&jumival=13986.

23. Emphasis in original blog post at: http://elizabethwarren.com/blog/you-cant-read-this.

24. http://www.stuff.co.nz/the-press/opinion/66574397/Academics-condemn-secrecy-over-Trans-Pacific-Partnership-Agreement.

25. http://www.stuff.co.nz/the-press/opinion/66574397/Academics-condemn-secrecy-over-Trans-Pacific-Partnership-Agreement.

26. http://www.dw.com/en/german-frustration-builds-over-ttip-secrecy-from-us/a-18819097.

27. https://www.citizen.org/documents/TRADEActFactSheet-HILL020210.pdf.

28. http://www.citizen.org/pressroom/pressroomredirect.cfm?ID=2912.

29. http://www.wsj.com/articles/unions-to-fight-trade-pact-by-freezing-donations-1426029735.

30. http://www.nystateofpolitics.com/2015/06/afl-cio-assails-rep-rices-fast-track-flip-flop/.

31. http://www.politico.com/story/2015/06/labor-attack-ads-kathleen-rice-trade-118753.

32. This group included labor unions and organizations such as EPI and ILRF.

33. http://www.theglobeandmail.com/globe-debate/time-for-keystones-nafta-option/article23232598/.

34. Public Citizen research, including polling and focus groups, showed it resonated with the public.

35. http://www.aflcio.org/Issues/Trade/What-Is-ISDS.

36. http://opinionator.blogs.nytimes.com/2014/03/15/on-the-wrong-side-of-globalization/.

37. http://www.yesmagazine.org/blogs/john-cavanagh-and-robin-broad/taking-on-the-trade-laws-of-the-1-percent.

38. Declaration of Joint Principles ETUC/AFL-CIO, "TTIP Must Work for the People, Or It Won't Work at All," May 21, 2014.

39. http://teamsternation.blogspot.com/2015/01/hundreds-of-protesters-in-nyc-tell-tpp.html.

40. http://teamsternation.blogspot.com/2015/01/hundreds-of-protesters-in-nyc-tell-tpp.html.

41. http://trade.ec.europa.eu/doclib/docs/2017/january/tradoc_155261.pdf.

CHAPTER 8

1. https://www.cfr.org/backgrounder/naftas-economic-impact.

2. https://www.fas.usda.gov/data/free-trade-agreements-and-us-agriculture.

3. http://international.gc.ca/trade-commerce/trade-agreements-accords-commerciaux/agr-acc/nafta-alena/fta-ale/facts.aspx?lang=eng.

4. http://www.wmur.com/article/rank-and-file-republican-activists-hear-trump-rail-against-clinton-on-trade/5212614.

5. Portes 2006 at: http://borderbattles.ssrc.org/Portes/.

6. Which she acknowledges are "mainly attributable to the peso crisis of 1994–1995" (Polaski 2006).

7. Polaski 2006:21.

8. http://bostonreview.net/forum/globalization-blame/peter-evans-peter-evans-responds-dean- baker.

9. http://www.jsonline.com/story/money/business/2016/12/08/rexnord-workers-caught-trump-vs-union-war-words/95165642/.

10. http://bostonreview.net/forum/globalization-blame/peter-evans-peter-evans-responds-dean-baker.

11. http://trade.ec.europa.eu/doclib/docs/2017/january/tradoc_155261.pdf.

12. Personal interview with Pharis Harvey of ILRF, March 2, 2001.

13. Joshua Bloom, 2017, Personal communication with author, May 19.

14. http://www.politico.com/story/2017/03/rand-paul-blocked-gop-obamacare-bill-235613.

15. See, for example, http://www.wbur.org/hereandnow/2016/04/27/economist-gordon-hanson-nafta.

Bibliography

Advisory Committee for Trade Policy and Negotiations (The) (ACTPN). 1991. *A Report to the U.S. Congress Concerning the President's Request for the Extension of Fast-Track Procedures Implementing Legislation for Trade Agreements.* Washington, DC. March.

AFL-CIO. 2011. "Memorandum on Ineffectiveness of Colombia's Labor Action Plan." October 4.

AFL-CIO Executive Council. 1993. "Statement by the AFL-CIO Executive Council on the North American Free Trade Agreement." February 17.

AFL-CIO News. 1989. "Maquiladora Toxics." March 4.

AFL-CIO News. 1991. "AFL-CIO Secretary-Treasurer Thomas R. Donahue on the Garin-Hart Poll Results." May 1. Department of Information.

Amenta, Edwin et al. 2010. "The Political Consequences of Social Movements." *Annual Review of Sociology* 36:287–307.

Anderson, Mark. 1991. "Statement Before the Subcommittee on Trade, Committee on Ways and Means U.S House of Representatives on U.S.-Mexico Economic Relations." June 28.

Anderson, Mark. 1993. "NAFTA Campaign." Letter to Thomas Donahue. June 24.

Anderson, Sarah, John Cavanaugh, and Sandra Gross. 1993. "NAFTA's Corporate Cadre: An Analysis of the USA *NAFTA State Captains." July.

Apple, R.W. 1993. "The Free Trade Accord: News Analysis; A High-Stakes Gamble Paid Off." *New York Times*, November 18.

Armstrong, Elizabeth A. 2002. *Forging Gay Identities: Organizing Sexuality in San Francisco, 1950–1994.* Chicago: University of Chicago Press.

ART/CTC. 1992. Letter to President-Elect Clinton. December 15.

Audley, John. 1992. Testimony on Behalf of the Sierra Club Before the House Agriculture Committee. "Review of Issues Related to the North American Free Trade Agreement—NAFTA." April 8.

Audley, John. 1993. "Why Environmentalists Are Angry about the North American Free Trade Agreement." In *Trade and Environment: Law, Economics and Policy,* edited by Durwood Zaelke, Paul Orbuch, and Robert Housman. Washington, DC: Island Press, 191–202.

Audley, John. 1997. *Green Politics and Global Trade: NAFTA and the Future of Environmental Politics*. Washington, DC: Georgetown University Press.

Ayres, Jeffrey M. 1998. *Defying Conventional Wisdom: Political Movements and Popular Contention against North American Free Trade*. Toronto: University of Toronto Press.

Baer, M. Delal and Sidney Weintraub. 1994. *The NAFTA Debate: Grappling with Unconventional Trade Issues*. Boulder, CO: Lynne Rienner.

Barclay, William. 1992. Testimony on Behalf of Greenpeace International Before the House Committee on Agriculture. April 8. Pp. 241–245.

Barry, John. 1999. *Rethinking Green Politics*. London: Sage.

Baum, Jeeyang R. 2011. *Responsive Democracy: Increasing State Accountability in East Asia*. Ann Arbor: University of Michigan Press.

Bayard, Thomas and Kimberly Elliott. 1994. *Reciprocity and Retaliation in U.S. Trade Policy*. Washington, DC: Institute for International Economics.

Beck, Ulrich. 1992. *Risk Society: Towards a New Modernity*. London: Sage.

Bernstein, Mary. 1997. "Celebration and Suppression: The Strategic Uses of Identity by the Lesbian and Gay Movement." *American Journal of Sociology* 103(3):531–565.

Berry, Jeffery. 1989. *The Interest Group Society*. New York: Harper Collins.

Bertrab, Hermann von. 1997. *Negotiating NAFTA: A Mexican Envoy's Account*. Westport, CT: Praeger.

Bloom, Joshua. 2014. *Pathways of Insurgency: Black Freedom Struggle and the Second Reconstruction, 1945–1975*. Dissertation, Department of Sociology, University of California-Los Angeles.

Bloom, Joshua. 2015. "The Dynamics of Opportunity and Insurgent Practice: How Black Anti-colonialists Compelled Truman to Advocate Civil Rights." *American Sociological Review* 80(2):391–415.

Bloom, Joshua and Waldo E. Martin Jr. 2013. *Black against Empire: The History and Politics of the Black Panther Party*. Berkeley: University of California Press.

Bognanno, M.F. and Kathryn J. Ready, eds. 1993. *The North American Free Trade Agreement: Labor, Industry, and Government Perspectives*. Westport, CT: Quorum Books.

Bolle, Mary Jane. 2001. "U.S.-Jordan Free Trade Agreement." *Congressional Research Service Report for Congress*.

BorderLines. 1993. "Arizona and Sonora Get It Together." 1(3):1–5.

Boswell, Terry and Dimitris Stevis. 1997. "Globalization and International Labor Organizing: A World-System Perspective." *Work and Occupations* 24(3):288–308.

Bothwell, Robert. 1992. *Canada and the United States: The Politics of Partnership*. New York: Twayne.

Bourdieu, Pierre. 1988. *Homo Academicus*. Translated by Peter Collier. Stanford, CA: Stanford University Press.

Bourdieu, Pierre. 1990. *The Logic of Practice*. Stanford, CA: Stanford University Press.

Bourdieu, Pierre. 1996. *State Nobility: Elite Schools in the Field of Power*. Translated by Lauretta C. Clough. Oxford: Polity Press.

Bourdieu, Pierre and Loïc Wacquant. 1992. *An Invitation to Reflexive Sociology*. Chicago: University of Chicago Press.

Bradsher, Keith. 1991. "House Vote Backs Bush's Authority on Trade Accords." *New York Times*, May 24. P. 1.

Brecher, Jeremy and Tim Costello. 1991. "Labor Goes Global II: A One-World Strategy for Labor." *Z Magazine*, March:90–97.

Bronfenbrenner, Kate. 1997. "Final Report: The Effects of Plant Closing or Threat of Plant Closing on the Right of Workers to Organize." Dallas, TX: Secretariat of the Commission for Labor Cooperation.

Bronfenbrenner, Kate. 2007. *Global Unions: Challenging Transnational Capital through Cross-Border Campaigns*. Ithaca, NY: Cornell University Press.

Browne, William. 1998. "Lobbying the Public: All-Directional Advocacy." In *Interest Group Politics*, edited by Allan Cigler and Burdett Loomis. Washington, DC: CQ Press, 342–364.

Browne, Harry and Beth Sims. 1993. "Global Capitalism, Global Unionism." *Resource Center Bulletin*, Winter. Albuquerque, NM: Resource Center.

Brulle, Robert J. and Craig J. Jenkins. 2008. "Fixing the Bungled U.S. Environmental Movement." *Contexts* 7(2):14–18.

Burkholder, Richard. 1991. "Americans and Mexicans Support North American Free Trade Zone, Canadians Opposed." The Gallup Organization. April 4.

Bush, George. 1991. Letter to Chairman Lloyd Bentsen. Washington, DC. May 1.

Bustamante, Jorge A. 1972. "The 'Wetback' as Deviant: An Application of Labeling Theory." *American Journal of Sociology* 4:706–718.

Buttel, Frederick. 1997. "Social Institutions and Environmental Change." In *The International Handbook of Environmental Sociology*, edited by Michael Redclift and Graham Woodgate. Cheltenham, UK: Edward Elgar, 33–47.

Buttel, Frederick and Peter Taylor. 1992. "Environmental Change: A Critical Assessment." *Society and Natural Resources* 5:211–230.

Cahn, Matthew. 1995. *Environmental Deceptions: The Tension between Liberalism and Environmental Policymaking in the United States*. Albany: State University of New York Press.

Calmes, Jackie. 1991. "House Extends 'Fast Track'." *Wall Street Journal*, May 24. P. A3.

Cameron, Maxwell and Brian Tomlin. 2000. *The Making of NAFTA: How the Deal Was Done*. Ithaca, NY: Cornell University Press.

Caulfield, Norman. 2010. *NAFTA and Labor in North America*. Champaign: University of Illinois Press.

CBO. 2003. "The Effects of NAFTA on U.S.-Mexican Trade and GDP." Congressional Budget Office, May.

Charnovitz, Steve. 1993. "Environmental Harmonization and Trade Policy." In *Trade and the Environment: Laws, Economics and Policy*, edited by Durwood Zaelke, Paul Orbuch, and Robert Housman. Washington, DC: Island Press, 267–286.

Chorev, Nitsan. 2007. *Remaking US Trade Policy: From Protectionism to Globalization.* Ithaca, NY: Cornell University Press.

Chorev, Nitsan. 2009. "International Trade Policy under George W. Bush." In *Assessing the George W. Bush Presidency*, edited by Andrew Wroe and Jon Herbert. Edinburgh: Edinburgh University Press, 129–146.

Citizen Trade Watch Campaign. 1991. Letter to U.S. Senators. September 26.

Citizen Trade Watch Campaign. 1991. "News Release." December 13.

Citizens Trade Campaign. 1993. "Draft Talk Points: CTC Team Congressional Visits February 17–24, 1993." February.

Citizens Trade Campaign. 1993. "NAFTA Vote 'Buying' to Cost Taxpayers Billions." November 12.

Citizens Trade Campaign Bulletin. 1993. "NAFTA's Hot This July: Capitol Hill Update." July 20. P. 1.

Clemens, Elisabeth S. 1993. "Organizational Repertoires and Institutional Change: Women's Groups and the Transformation of U.S. Politics, 1890–1920." *American Journal of Sociology* 98:755–798.

Clinton, Bill. 1992. "Expanding Trade and Creating American Jobs." Speech given at North Carolina State University, Raleigh, NC, October 4.

Closs, M.J. 1988. "Canada: The Neighbouring Auto Industry." In *Canada at the Crossroads: Essays on Canadian Political Economy*. Edited by Robert J. Thorton, Thomas Hyclak, and J. Richard Aronson. Greenwich, CT: JAI Press.

Cloud, David. 1991a. "Congress Wary of Bush Plan to Open Doors to Mexico (charts)." *CQ Weekly.* February 23. Pp. 451–458.

Cloud, David. 1991b. "Hill Gives Bush Green Light to Negotiate Trade Pacts." *CQ Weekly.* May 25. Pp. 1358–1361.

Cloud, David. 1992. "Warning Bells on NAFTA Sound for Clinton." *Congressional Quarterly*, November 28.

Coalition for Justice in the Maquiladoras. 1999. "Coalition for Justice in the Maquiladoras 1989–1999."

Cohen, Stephen. 1988. *The Making of United States International Economic Policy*: Principals, Problems, and Proposals for Reform. New York: Praeger.

CQ Weekly. 1991. "Trade: Bush Asks to Stay on Fast Track." March 2. P. 531.

Cranford, John. 1992. "Trade: House Signals Concerns on Free-Trade Pact." August 8.

Crawley, James. 1991. "Border Waste Plan Is Vague, Critics Charge." *San Diego Union-Tribune.* September 24. Pp. AA-1.

Crowe, Kenneth. 1993. "1,100 March in Favor of Free Trade Pact." *Newsday*, May 2. P. 48.

Darling, Juanita. 1992. "Dynamite Deal; Environmental, Labor Groups Make Their Voices Heard." *Los Angeles Times.* August 7. P. D2.

Davis, Gerald F., Doug McAdam, W. Richard Scott, and Mayer N. Zald. 2005. *Social Movements and Organization Theory*, edited by G.F. Davis, D. McAdam, W. Richard Scott, and M.N. Zald. New York: Cambridge University Press.

DeLong, Bradford J. 2006. "Afta Thoughts on NAFTA." *Berkeley Review of Latin American Studies*. Center for Latin American Studies, University of California, Berkeley.

DeLuca, Kevin. 1999. *Image Politics: The New Rhetoric of Environmental Activism*. New York: Guilford Press.

Destler, I.M. 1995. *American Trade Politics*. 3rd Edition. Washington, DC: Institute for International Economics.

Destler, I.M. 2005. *American Trade Politics*. Fourth Edition. Washington, DC: Institute for International Economics.

Dewey, Scott. 1998. "Working for the Environment: Organized Labor and the Origins of Environmentalism in the United States, 1948–1970." *Environmental History* 3:45–63.

De Ville, Ferdi and Gabriel Siles-Brügge. 2015. *TTIP: The Truth about the Transatlantic Trade and Investment Partnership*. Cambridge: Polity Press.

Diamond, Larry. 1999. *Developing Democracy: Toward Consolidation*. Baltimore: Johns Hopkins University Press.

DiMaggio, Paul and Walter Powell. 1991. *The New Institutionalism in Organizational Analysis*. Chicago: University of Chicago Press.

Dobson, Andrew. 1990. *Green Political Thought*. New York: HarperCollins Academic.

Donahue, Thomas. 1993. Letter to Ambassador Kantor. June 17.

Dreiling, Michael C. 2001. *Solidarity and Contention: The Politics of Security and Sustainability in the NAFTA Conflict*. New York: Garland.

Duffy, Meghan, Amy Binder, and John Skretny. 2010. "Elite Status and Social Change: Using Field Analysis to Explain Policy Formation and Implementation." *Social Problems* 57:49–73.

Duina, Francesco. 2006. *The Social Construction of Free Trade: The European Union, NAFTA, and MERCOSUR*. Princeton, NJ: Princeton University Press.

Duncan, Cameron. 1991. "Re: More on the US-Mexico-Canada FTA." Memo to Tani, Sergio, Marcie. February 13.

Dunne, Nancy. 1991. "Fears over US-Mexico Free Trade Pact." *Financial Times* (London). January 30. P. 4.

Dunne, Nancy and Lisa Bransten. 1992. "NAFTA Foes Campaign on a Shoestring." *Financial Times* (London). August 2. P. 4.

Durbin, Andrea and Atlanta McIlwraith. 1993. CTC Memorandum. "Subject Summary of Organizers Strategy Meeting." Memo. April 7.

Eagleton-Pierce, Matthew. 2013. *Symbolic Power in the World Trade Organization*. Oxford: Oxford University Press.

Erne, R., B. Agathonos-Mähr, and O. Gauper. 1998. "Social Democracy in the Age of Internationalisation Transfer." *European Review of Labour and Research* 4(2): 371–375.

Evans, Peter B. 1985. "Transnational Linkages and the Economic Role of the State: An Analysis of Developing and Industrialized Nations in the Post-World War II Period." In Peter B. Evans, Dietrich Rueschemeyer, and Theda Skocpol. *Bringing the State Back In.* New York: Cambridge University Press, 192–226.

Evans, Peter B. 1995. *Embedded Autonomy: States and Industrial Transformation.* Princeton, NJ: Princeton University Press.

Evans, Peter B., Dietrich Rueschemeyer, and Theda Skocpol. 1985. *Bringing the State Back In.* New York: Cambridge University Press.

Evans, Rhonda. 2002. *The Rise of Ethical Trade Advocacy: NAFTA and the New Politics of Trade.* PhD dissertation, Department of Sociology, University of California, Berkeley, Berkeley, CA.

Evans, Rhonda and Tamara Kay. 2008. "How Environmentalists 'Greened' Trade Policy: Strategic Action and the Architecture of Field Overlap." *American Sociological Review* 73(6):970–991.

ETUC/AFL-CIO Declaration of Joint Principles. 2014. "TTIP Must Work for the People, Or It Won't Work at All," May 21.

Fairbrother, Malcolm. 2006. "Neoliberal Mercantilism and North American Free Trade: A Study of the Political Causes of Globalization." PhD Dissertation. Department of Sociology. University of California, Berkeley.

Fairbrother, Malcolm. 2007. "Making Neoliberalism Possible: The State's Organization of Business Support for NAFTA in Mexico." *Politics & Society* 35(2):265–300.

Feigen, Ed. 1992. "Re: Grass Roots Anti-NAFTA Action Plan." Memo to Mark Anderson. August 25.

Fligstein, Neil. 2001. *The Architecture of Markets: An Economic Sociology of Twenty-First-Century Capitalist Societies.* Princeton, NJ: Princeton University Press.

Fligstein, Neil and Doug McAdam. 2012. *A Theory of Fields.* New York: Oxford University Press.

Frank, Dana. 1999. *Buy American: The Untold Story of Economic Nationalism.* Boston: Beacon Press.

Frieden, Jeffry A. and Ronald Rogowski. 1996. "The Impact of the International Economy on National Policies: An Analytical Overview." In *Internationalization and Domestic Politics,* edited by Robert O. Keohane and Helen V. Milner. New York: Cambridge University Press, 25–47.

Galenson, Walter. 1996. *The American Labor Movement.* Westport, CT: Greenwood Press.

Gamson, William A. and David S. Meyer. 1996. "Framing Political Opportunity." In *Comparative Perspectives on Social Movements: Political Opportunities, Mobilizing Structures, and Cultural Framings,* edited by D. McAdam, J. D. McCarthy, and M. N. Zald. Cambridge: Cambridge University Press, 275–290.

Ganz, Marshall. 2000. "Resources and Resourcefulness: Strategic Capacity in the Unionization of California Agriculture, 1959–1966." *American Journal of Sociology* 105(4):1003–1062.

Garduño-Rivera, Rafael. 2010. "Effect of NAFTA on Mexico's Income Distribution in the Presence of Migration." Unpublished paper prepared for the Agricultural & Applied Economics Association Meeting. July.

Garin-Hart Strategic Research Group. 1991. "The Mexican Trade Agreement Survey: A Summary of Key Findings."

Gephardt, Richard. 1992. "Prepared Statement in Support of House Concurrent Resolution 246." News From the House Majority Leader. August 6.

Gereffi, Gary. 1992. "Mexico's Maquiladora Industries and North American Integration." In *North America without Borders?*, edited by Stephen Randall with Herman Konrad and Sheldon Silverman. Calgary: University of Calgary Press, 135–152.

Giddens, Anthony. 1994. *Beyond Left and Right: The Future of Radical Politics.* Stanford, CA: Stanford University Press.

Goldstein, Judith. 1993. *Ideas, Interests, and American Trade Policy.* Ithaca, NY: Cornell University.

Goodwin, Jeff and James M. Jasper. 1999. "Caught in a Winding, Snarling Vine: The Structural Bias of Political Process Theory." *Sociological Forum* 14:27–54.

Gottlieb, Robert. 2005. *Forcing the Spring: The Transformation of the American Environmental Movement, Revised Edition.* Washington, DC: Island Press.

Gould, Kenneth et al. 1996. *Local Environmental Struggles.* Cambridge: Cambridge University Press.

Graubart, Jonathan. 2008. *Legalizing Transnational Activism: The Struggle to Gain Social Change from NAFTA's Citizen Petitions.* University Park, PA: Penn State University Press.

Grayson, George. 1995. *The North American Free Trade Agreement: Regional Community and the New World Order.* Lanham, MD: University Press of America.

Greenwood, Justin. 2011. *Interest Representation in the European Union*, 3rd ed. London: Palgrave Macmillan.

Gregory, Michael. 1991. Testimony on Behalf of Arizona Toxics Information Before the Senate Committee on Environment and Public Works and the Subcommittee on Labor of the Committee on Labor and Human Resources. "Economic and Environmental Implications of the Proposed U.S. Trade Agreement with Mexico." April 23.

Gregory, Michael. 1992. "Environment, Sustainable Development, Public Participation and NAFTA: A Retrospective. *Journal of Environmental Law and Litigation* 7(1):99–174.

Gugliotta. 1991. May 24. "House Votes Backs on Trade; President Seeking 'Fast Track' for Pact with Mexico." *Washington Post.* P. A1.

Guisinger, Alexandra. 2009. "Determining Trade Policy: Do Voters Hold Politicians Accountable?." *International Organization* 63.03:533–557.

Gunter, Frank. 1988. "In Bed with the Elephant: Canadian-US Economic Relations." In *Canada and the Crossroads: Essays on Canadian Political Economy*', edited by Robert Thornton et al. Contemporary Studies in Economic and Financial Analyses, 64.

Haggard, Stephen. 1988. "The Institutional Foundations of Hegemony: Explaining the Reciprocal Trade Agreements Act of 1934." *International Organization* 42(1):91–119.

Haines, Herbert. 1988. *Black Radicals and the Civil Rights Mainstream*. Knoxville: University of Tennessee Press.

Hair, Jay. 1991. "An Environmental Vote." *Washington Post*. May 22. P. A20.

Hamilton, Daniel S. 2014. *The Geopolitics of TTIP: Repositioning the Transatlantic Relationship for a Changing World*. Center for Transatlantic Relations SAIS.

Hannah, Erin. 2016. *NGOs and Global Trade: Non-state Voices in EU Trade Policymaking*. London: Routledge.

Hannah, Erin, James Scott, and Silke Trommer, editors. 2015. *Expert Knowledge in Global Trade*. London: Routledge.

Hanson, Gordon H. 2003. *What Has Happened to Wages in Mexico since NAFTA?*. No. w9563. National Bureau of Economic Research.

Hanson, Gordon H. 2007. "Globalization, Labor Income, and Poverty in Mexico." 2007. In *Globalization and Poverty*, edited by Ann Harrison. National Bureau of Economic Research. Chicago: University of Chicago Press.

Hart, Michael. 1991. "Dispute Settlement and the Canada-United States Free Trade Agreement." In *The Economic Impact and Implications of the Canada-US Free Trade Agreement*, edited by Fakhari Siddiqui. Lewiston, NY: Edwin Mellen Press, 113–146.

Hayes, Michael. 1981. *Lobbyists and Legislators: A Theory of Political Markets*. Brunswick, NJ: Rutgers University Press.

Herrera Lima, Fernando. 2014. "El aislamiento internacional del sindicalismo mexicano en su crisis actual." Latin American Studies Association Annual Meeting, Chicago, May.

Hook, Janet. 1993. "Special NAFTA Report: The Uphill Battle for Votes Produces a Whirl of Wooing and Wheedling." *CQ Weekly* 51 (November 6):3014.

Howell, Thomas and Alan Wolff. 1992. "Introduction." In *Conflict among Nations: Trade Policies in the 1990s*, edited by Thomas Howell et al. Boulder, CO: Westview Press, 1–44.

Hudson, Stewart. 1991. Testimony on Behalf of the National Wildlife Federation Before the House Subcommittee on International Economic Policy and Trade and on Western Hemisphere Affairs of the Committee on Foreign Affairs. "The North American Free Trade Agreement." March 6.

Hudson, Stewart. 1991. Testimony on Behalf of the National Wildlife Federation Before the House Committee on Agriculture. "Proposed United States-Mexico Free-Trade Agreement and Fast-Track Authority." April 24.

Hudson, Stewart. 1991. Testimony on Behalf of the National Wildlife Federation Before the House Subcommittee on International Economic Policy and Trade and on Western Hemisphere Affairs of the Committee on Foreign Affairs. "The North American Free Trade Agreement." March 6.

Hufbauer, Gary, Cathleen Cimino, and Tyler Moran. 2014. "*NAFTA at 20: Misleading Charges and Positive Achievements.*" In "NAFTA 20 Years Later." PIIE Briefing No. 14-3, November. Washington, DC: Peterson Institute for International Economics.

Hufbauer, Gary and Jeffrey Schott. 1992. *North American Free Trade: Issues and Recommendations.* Washington, DC: Institute for International Economics.

Hufbauer, Gary and Jeffrey Schott. 2005. *NAFTA Revisited: Achievements and Challenges.* Washington, DC: Institute for International Economics.

Hurst, William J. forthcoming. *The South China Sea: What Everyone Needs to Know.* New York: Oxford University Press.

Inside U.S. Trade. 1990. "USTR Official Says Mexico Accord Should End before U.S. Presidential Campaign." November 23. Pp. 1–3.

Inside U.S. Trade. 1990. "Citizen Groups to Press Inclusion of Social Issues in U.S.-Mexico Trade Accord." November 23. P. 19.

Inside U.S. Trade. 1991. "Hill Says FTA Agenda Not Closed; Pledges Close Consultation with Congress." January 11. Pp. 6–7.

Inside U.S. Trade. 1991. "Official Warns of Mandatory Adjustment Aid in Trade Pact with Mexico, Canada." January 11. Pp. 1–2. January 15, 1991.

Inside U.S. Trade. 1991. "Chamber Officials See Easing of Investment Rules as a Priority in Mexico FTA." January 18. P. 14.

Inside U.S. Trade. 1991. February 8. Pp. 5 and 9.

Inside U.S. Trade. 1991. "Hills Tells Panel USTR Willing to Consult on Drugs, Environment, and Labor." February 22. Pp. 1, 19–20.

Inside U.S. Trade. 1991. "House Members Warn Hills on NAFTA, Extension of Fast-Track Authority" February 22. P. 4.

Inside U.S. Trade. 1991. "House Members Tie Fast-Track Support to Inclusion of Environment in FTA." February 22. Pp. 5–6.

Inside U.S. Trade. 1991. "Panel Chairman Tells USTR to Expand Range of Issues in Free Trade Talks. March 1. Pp. 7–8.

Inside U.S. Trade. 1991. "Gephardt Adds to Pleas for Non-trade Issues to Be in North America Trade Pact." March 29. Pp. S-1–3.

Inside U.S. Trade. 1991. "Environment Group Said to Inform USTR of Principles for Mexico Talks." April 5. P. 8.

Inside U.S. Trade. 1991. "Rostenkowski Sees Floor Vote on Measure to Disapprove Fast-Track Authority." May 3. P. 8.

Inside U.S. Trade. 1991. "Administration Wins Fast Track in House; Senate Approval Expected by Today." May 24. Pp. 1, 18–19.

Inside U.S. Trade. 1991. "House Letter on Fair Trade Caucus." June 21. P. 13.

Inside U.S. Trade. 1991. "White House Said to Approve All but One Nominee for Environment Advisor Posts." July 19. Pp. 1, 19.

Inside U.S. Trade. 1991. "GATT Dispute Settlement Panel Rules against U.S. on Ban of Mexican Tuna." August 23. Pp. 1, 20.

Inside U.S. Trade. 1991. "House Members to Call for U.S. to Reject GATT Landmark Tuna Ruling." September 13. Pp. 4–5.

Inside U.S. Trade. 1991. "Mexico Opts to Foresake [*sic*] GATT for Bilateral Resolution of Tuna Dispute." September 27. Pp. 1–2.

Inside U.S. Trade. 1991. "Administration Misses Second Deadline for Draft NAFTA Environment Report." October 4. Pp. 6–7.

Inside U.S. Trade. 1991. "Opponents of NAFTA Present Their Alternative Plan to Top Trade Negotiators." November 1. Pp. 9–10.

Inside U.S. Trade. 1991. "Forty 'Fast-Track' Democrats Warn Bush to Present Early Environment Accord." November 8. Pp. 7–8.

Inside U.S. Trade. 1991. "Judge Close to Ruling on Need for Environment Statement for NAFTA, GATT." November 29. Pp. 8–9.

Inside U.S. Trade. 1991. "Gejdenson Charges U.S. Separation of Environment, Trade Talks Risks Leverage." December 13. P. 7.

Inside U.S. Trade. 1992. "Administration under Rising Pressure from Citizens Groups on GATT, NAFTA." February 21. Pp. S-1–2.

Inside U.S. Trade. 1992. February 14. P. 20.

Inside U.S. Trade. 1992. "Bush Unveils Three-Year, $1-Billion Environmental Plan for U.S.-Mexico Border." February 28. Pp. S-9–S-11.

Inside U.S. Trade. 1992. "Environmentalists Oppose Administration Tuna Plan, But Will Negotiate." March 13. Pp. 3–5.

Inside U.S. Trade. 1992. "House Bill Would Make Violations of Labor, Environmental Laws Actionable." March 13. P. 8.

Inside U.S. Trade. 1992. "Mexican Groups Call for Halt to NAFTA Talks, Other Groups Vow Fight. July 28. Pp. S-3–S4.

Inside U.S. Trade. 1992. "Political Opposition to North American Trade Pact Mounts in Canada." August 21. Pp. 5–6.

Inside U.S. Trade. 1992. "House Democrats Press Clinton to Reject NAFTA and Renegotiate Pact." October 16. Pp. 1, 16.

Inside U.S. Trade. 1992. "Defenders of Wildlife Say Environmental Side Deal Could Bring Support for NAFTA." December 18. P. 10.

Inside U.S. Trade. 1992. "NAFTA Opponents Urge Clinton to Tackle Fundamental Flaws in Trade Pact." December 25. P. 7.

Inside U.S. Trade. 1993. "Clinton, Salinas to Meet Today as Stage Set for Further Talks on NAFTA." January 8. Pp. 4–5.

Inside U.S. Trade. 1993. "Clinton Says U.S., Mexico Must Examine New Models to Ensure Beneficial NAFTA." January 15. Pp. 6–7.

Inside U.S. Trade. 1993. "Transition Trade Official Says NAFTA Might Take Back Seat to Domestic Agenda." January 15. Pp. 1, 18.

Inside U.S. Trade. 1993. "Initial U.S. Presentation on NAFTA Labor Accord Is Silent on Trade Sanctions." April 2. Pp. 1, 19–20.

Inside U.S. Trade. 1993. "U.S. Environment, Labor Proposals Are Silent on NAFTA Dispute Mechanisms." April 30. Pp. S-1–S-6.

Inside U.S. Trade. 1993. "Environmental Groups Offer to Support NAFTA if Demands Are Met." May 7. P. S-2–S-5.

Inside U.S. Trade. 1993. "Mexican Official Acknowledges Possibility of Environmental Dispute Panels." May 7. P. 9.

Inside U.S. Trade. 1993. "U.S. Chamber Backs Limited Role for NAFTA Environment, Labor Commissions." May 14. P. S-7–S-8.

Inside U.S. Trade. 1993. "Mexican NAFTA Labor Draft Excludes Use of Sanctions, Proposes I.L.O. Role." May 21. P. S-1, S-9.

Inside U.S. Trade. 1993. "Chamber Criticizes NAFTA Side Deals, Alleges Failure to Consult Business." May 28. Pp. 11–12.

Inside U.S. Trade. 1993. "NAFTA Negotiators Make Conceptual Progress, Yet Fail to Break Deadlock." June 11. P. S-1–S-2.

Inside U.S. Trade. 1993. "Composite Drafts of NAFTA Side Pacts Show Sparse Progress in Ottawa." June 11. P. S-5–S-8.

Inside U.S. Trade. 1993. "Administration to Appeal Ruling Mandating NAFTA Environment Study." July 2. P. 1; P.17.

Inside U.S. Trade. 1993. "Legislators Call for Expanded Environmental Agenda In NAFTA." July 2. P. 20.

Inside U.S. Trade. 1993. "Senate Passage of NAFTA No Sure Thing, Bradley Aide Warns NAM." July 16. P. 5.

Inside U.S. Trade. 1993. "NAFTA Negotiators Make Limited Headway on Regional Secretariat." July 16. P. 1–2.

Inside U.S. Trade. 1993. "NEC Narrows Options for Financing of NAFTA Environment Initiatives." July 23. P. 1; July 23. P. 12; July 23. Pp. 20–21.

Inside U.S. Trade. 1993. "Bonior, Kaptur Claim Comfortable Vote Count for NAFTA Defeat." July 30. P. 6.

Inside U.S. Trade. 1993. "101 Farm Groups Form Coalition to Fight for NAFTA Passage." July 30. Pp. 21–22.

Inside U.S. Trade. 1993. "Gephardt, Baucus Call for Stronger Enforcement in NAFTA Side Deals." August 13. P.10.

Inside U.S. Trade. 1993. "Kantor Highlights Enforcement Provisions of NAFTA Side Accords." August 16. P. 1; August 16. Pp. S-4 and S-5.

Inside U.S. Trade. 1993. "De La Garza Says NAFTA Support Is in National Interest." August 20. P. 4–5.

Inside U.S. Trade. 1993. "Pro-NAFTA Republicans Criticize Business Lobbying for Trade Pact." October 29. P. 11.

Inside U.S. Trade. 1993. "As House Vote Nears, NAFTA Endorsements Outpace New Opponents." November 12. P. 8.

Isaac, Larry W. 2008. "Movement of Movements: Culture Moves in the Long Civil Rights Struggle." *Social Forces* 87(1):33–63.

IUE News Release. 1992. September 30.

Joas, Hans. 1996. *The Creativity of Action.* Chicago: University of Chicago Press.

Kaplan, Edward. 1996. *American Trade Policy, 1923–1995.* Westwood, CT: Greenwood Press.

Kaptur, Marcy et al. 1992. "Letter to Governor Bill Clinton." *Inside U.S. Trade,* October 3. P. 13.

Kay, Tamara. 2004. *NAFTA and the Politics of Labor Transnationalism.* PhD dissertation, Department of Sociology, University of California, Berkeley, Berkeley, CA.

Kay, Tamara. 2005. "Labor Transnationalism and Global Governance: The Impact of NAFTA on Transnational Labor Relationships in North America." *American Journal of Sociology* 11(3):715–756.

Kay, Tamara. 2011a. *NAFTA and the Politics of Labor Transnationalism.* New York: Cambridge University Press.

Kay, Tamara. 2011b. "Legal Transnationalism: The Relationship between Social Movement Building and International Law." *Law & Social Inquiry* 36(2):419–454.

Kay, Tamara. 2015. "New Challenges, New Alliances: The Politicization of Unions in a Post-NAFTA Era." *Labor History* 56(3):246–269.

Kazis, Richard and Richard L. Grossman. 1982. *Fear at Work: Job Blackmail, Labor, and the Environment.* New York: Pilgrim Press.

Kingdon, John W. 1995. *Agendas, Alternatives and Public Policies.* New York: HarperCollins.

Kirkland, Lane. 1991. Letter to Representative Dan Rostenkowski. May 2.

Kitschelt, Herbert P. 1986. "Political Opportunity Structures and Political Protest: Anti-Nuclear Movements in Four Democracies." *British Journal of Political Science* 16(1):57–85.

Klandermans, Bert. 1988. "The Formation and Mobilization of Consensus." In *From Structure to Action: Comparing Movement Participation across Cultures,* edited by Bert Klandermans, Hanspieter Kriesi, and Sidney Tarrow. Greenwich, CT: JAI Press, 173–196.

Kolbe, Jim et al. 1991. Letter to President Bush. November 26.

Kollman, Ken. 1998. *Outside Lobbying: Public Opinion and Interest Group Strategies.* Princeton, NJ: Princeton University Press.

Kopinak, Kathryn. 1993. "The Maquiladorization of the Mexican Economy." In *The Political Economy of North American Free Trade,* edited by Ricardo Grinspun and Maxwell Cameron. New York: St. Martin's Press, 141–161.

Kristol, William. 2008. "The Mask Slips." *New York Times,* April 14.

Laumann, Edward and David Knoke. 1987. *The Organizational State.* Madison: University of Wisconsin Press.

Lederman, Josh. June 9, 2015. "For Dems who vote yes on trade, Obama officers help in 2016." Associated Press.

Lee, Gary. 1991. "'Fast Track' Sprint: Frenzied Lobbying on a Treaty Not Yet Written." *Washington Post.* May 23. P. A21.

Lewis, Charles. 1993. "The NAFTA-Math; Clinton Got His Trade Deal, but How Many Millions Did It Cost the Nation?" *Washington Post,* December 26.

Lindquist, Diane. 1991. "Border Pollution Plans Hit; Ecology, Business and Government Objections Heard." *San Diego Union-Tribune.* September 24. P. A-3.

Loomer, B. 1976. "Two Conceptions of Power." *Process Studies* 6(1):5–32.

Lounsbury, Michael. 2007. "A Tale of Two Cities: Competing Logics and Practice Variation in the Professionalizing of Mutual Funds." *Academy of Management Journal* 50:289–307.

MacArthur, John. 2000. *The Selling of Free Trade: NAFTA, Washington, and the Subversion of American Democracy.* New York: Hill and Wang.

Maggs, John. 1991. "US Labor Fights Mexico Trade Pact." *Journal of Commerce.* February 6. P. 1A.

Marshall, Ray. 1990. "Trade-Linked Labor Standards." *Proceedings of the Academy of Political Science* 37(4):67–78.

Martin, John Levi. 2003. "What Is Field Theory?." *American Journal of Sociology* 109:1–49.

Martin, Isaac W. 2010. "Redistributing toward the Rich: Strategic Policy Crafting in the Campaign to Repeal the Sixteenth Amendment, 1938–1958." *American Journal of Sociology* 116(1):1–52.

Martin, Lisa and Kathryn Sikkink. 1993. "U.S. Policy and Human Rights in Argentina and Guatemala, 1973–1980." In *Double-Edged Diplomacy,* edited by Peter Evans, Harold Jacobson, and Robert Putnam. Berkeley: University of California Press, 330–362.

Martínez-Alier, J. 1994. "Commentary: The Environment as a Luxury Good or 'Too Poor to Be Green.'" *Ecological Economics* 13:1–10.

Mayer, Frederick W. 1998. *Interpreting NAFTA: The Science and Art of Political Analysis.* New York: Columbia University Press.

Mayer, Brian. 2009. *Blue-Green Coalitions: Fight for Safe Workplaces and Healthy Communities.* Ithaca, NY: Cornell University Press.

McAdam, Doug. 1982. *Political Process and the Development of Black Insurgency, 1930–1970.* Chicago: University of Chicago Press.

McAdam, Doug, Sidney Tarrow, and Charles Tilly. 2001. *Dynamics of Contention.* Cambridge: Cambridge University Press.

McCallum, J.K. 2013. *Global Unions, Local Power: The New Spirit of Transnational Labor Organizing.* Ithaca, NY: Cornell University Press.

McCammon, Holly J. 2012. *The U.S. Women's Jury Movements and Strategic Adaptation.* New York: Cambridge University Press.

McDonnell, Patrick. 1991. "Environmental Fears Voiced on Free-Trade Plan; Border: Critics Say Proposals to Protect the Border Environment after a U.S.-Mexico Free-Trade Accord Are a Farce." *Los Angeles Times.* September 24. P. B1.

McLaren, John and Shushanik Hakobyan. 2010. *Looking for Local Labor Market Effects of NAFTA.* No. w16535. National Bureau of Economic Research.

Melucci, Alberto. 1988. "Getting Involved: Identity and Mobilization in Social Movements." In *International Social Movement Research.* Vol. 1, edited by Bert Klandermans. Greenwich, CT: Jai Press, 329–348.

Melucci, Alberto. 1989. *Nomads of the Present: Social Movements and Individual Needs in Contemporary Society.* Philadelphia: Temple University Press.

Mercado-Llorens, Segundo. 1991. Testimony on Behalf of the United Food and Commercial Workers Before the House Subcommittees on International Economic Policy and Trade and the Western Hemisphere Affairs of the Committee on Foreign Affairs. "North American Free Trade Agreement: American Jobs and Environmental Protection." December 9.

Merrilees, Craig. 1991. Testimony on Behalf of the Fair Trade Campaign and also the National Toxics Campaign Before the Senate Committee on Environment and Public Works and the Subcommittee on Labor of the Committee on Labor and Human Resources. "Economic and Environmental Implications of the Proposed U.S. Trade Agreement with Mexico." April 23.

Merrilees, Craig. 1991. Testimony on Behalf of the Fair Trade Campaign and also the National Toxics Campaign Before the House Committee on Energy and Commerce. "North American Free Trade Agreement." May 8.

Merrilees, Craig and Don Weiner. 1992. "Re: Advisor Update #1." Memo to Bob Kingsley. June. October 10.

Meyer, David S. 2004. "Protest and Political Opportunities." *Annual Review of Sociology* 30:125–145.

Meyer, John W. and Richard W. Scott. 1983. *Organizational Environments: Ritual and Rationality.* Beverly Hills, CA: Sage.

Middlebrook, Kevin J. 1991. "The Politics of Industrial Restructuring." *Comparative Politics* April:275–297.

Milner, Helen. 1988. *Resisting Protectionism.* Princeton, NJ: Princeton University Press.

Minchin, Timothy J. 2003. *Forging a Common Bond: Labor and Environmental Activism during the BASF Lockout.* Gainesville: University Press of Florida.

MODTLE. 1992. "Development and Trade Strategies for North America." January 3.

MODTLE and CTWC. 1992. "Too High a Price for Free Trade: Citizens' Analysis of the February 21 Draft of the North American Free Trade Agreement." April 6.

Montrie, Chad. 2008. *Making a Living: Work and Environment in the United States.* Chapel Hill: University of North Carolina Press.

Morgan, Kimberly J. and Ann Shola Orloff, eds. 2017. *The Many Hands of the State: Theorizing Political Authority and Social Control.* New York: Cambridge University Press.

Morin, Jean-Frédéric et al. 2015. *The Politics of Transatlantic Trade Negotiations: TTIP in a Globalized World.* New York: Routledge.

Murphy, Hannah. 2010. *The Making of International Trade Policy: NGOs, Agenda-Setting and the WTO.* Northampton: Edward Elgar.

NAFTAThoughts. 1991. "Trade Concerns and Alternatives Aired at Zacatecas." December.

NAFTAThoughts. 1992. "Progress and Secrecy in Negotiations." February.

NAFTAThoughts. 1993a. "NAFTA Debate Broadens amidst New Controversy." February.

NAFTAThoughts. 1993b. "NAFTA Supporters and Critics Jockey for Position in Anticipation of Negotiated Package." May.

Natural Resources Defense Council. 1991. "Environmentalists Discuss North American Free Trade Agreement with President Bush." May 8.

National Wildlife Federation. 1990. "Environmental Concerns Related to a United States-Mexico-Canada Free Trade Agreement." November 17.

National Wildlife Federation. 1991. "Key Environmental Commitments Made by the Bush Administration Regarding NAFTA." July 9.

NBC News. 1993. "Poll Results." April 20.

Nelson, Douglas. 1996. "The Political Economy of U.S. Automobile Protection." In *The Political Economy of American Trade Policy*, edited by Anne Kreuger. Chicago: University of Chicago Press, 133–196.

New York Times. 1992. "For America's Common Wealth." August 13. P. 22.

New York Times. 1993. "NAFTA, Meet the Environment." July 12. P. A16.

News from the Citizens Trade Campaign. 1993. "National Week of Action for Fair Trade to Be Held May 1–9." April 21.

News from the New Teamsters. 1992. "Los Angeles City Council Passes Unanimous Resolution Opposing Bush Administration's 'Free Trade' Policy." June 17.

Nonet, Philippe and Philip Selznik. 2017. *Law and Society in Transition: Toward Responsive Law*, 3rd ed. New York: Routledge.

Norton, Paul. 2003. "A Critique of Generative Class Theories of Environmentalism and of the Labour-Environmentalist Relationship." *Environmental Politics* 12:96–119.

O'Brien. 1998. "Shallow Foundations: Labour and the Selective Regulation of Free Trade." In *The Economics and Politics of International Trade*, edited by Gary Cook. London: Routledge, 105–124.

Obach, Brian. 2004. *Labor and the Environmental Movement: The Quest for Common Ground.* Cambridge, MA: MIT Press.

Office of the United States Trade Representative. 1992. *1992 Trade Policy Agenda and 1991 Annual Report of the President of the United States on the Trade Agreements Program.*

Orme, William A. 1993. *Continental Shift: Free Trade and the New North America.* Washington, DC: Washington Post Company.

Orme, Jr., William A. 1996. *Understanding NAFTA: Mexico, Free Trade, and the New North America.* Austin: University of Texas Press.

Otteman, Scott. 1991. "Bentsen Backs Fast-Track Extension, Will Allow Floor Vote for Opponents." *Inside U.S. Trade.* March 1. Pp. 1 and 21.

Otteman, Scott. 1991. "Administration Plan for Mexico Would Reopen Canada FTA on Autos." *Inside U.S. Trade.* May 3. Pp. S-1; S-5.

Otteman, Scott. 1991. "Administration Gains Slight Environmental Endorsement for Fast Track." *Inside U.S. Trade.* May 24. P. 7.

Otteman, Scott. 1991. "Administration Trade-Environment Policy Yields Draft Plan, Lawsuit." *Inside U.S. Trade.* August 2. P. 12.

Otteman, Scott. 1991. "GATT Tuna Ruling Spawns Environmentalist, Congressional Backlash." *Inside U.S. Trade.* September 6. Pp. 1, 14, 15.

Otteman, Scott. 1991. "USTR Reveals Assumptions for NAFTA Environmental Review to Congress. *Inside U.S. Trade.* September 13. Pp. 7–8.

Otteman, Scott. 1991. "Administration Pressed to Forego Attempt to Change Dolphin Protection Act." *Inside U.S. Trade.* October 4. Pp. 10–11.

Pallasch, Abdon M. 2008. "Obama: God, Guns Are Only Refuge of Bitter Pennsylvanians." *Chicago Sun-Times.* April 12. P. 2.

Pastor, Robert. 1992. "NAFTA as the Center of an Integration Process: The Nontrade Issues." In *North American Free Trade: Assessing the Impact,* edited by Nora Lustig, Barry Bosworth, and Robert Lawrence. Washington, DC: The Brookings Institution, 176–209.

Pastor, Manuel and Carol Wise. 1994. "The Origins of Sustainability of Mexico's Free Trade Policy." *International Organization* 48(3):459–489.

Pearson, Charles. 1993. *The Trade and Environment Nexus: What Is New since '72?* In *Trade and Environment: Law, Economics and Policy,* edited by Durwood Zaelke, Paul Orbuch, and Robert Housman. Washington, DC: Island Press, 23–32.

Perkins, Jane. 1992. "Statement of Jane Perkins, President of Friends of the Earth, On the Launching of National Campaign to Fight Bush's NAFTA." *Friends of the Earth,* December 16.

Polaski, Sandra. 2006. "The Employment Consequences of NAFTA." Carnegie Endowment for International Peace. February 26.

Portes, Alejandro. 2006. "NAFTA and Mexican Migration." July 31. Border Battles the U.S. Immigration Debates. The Social Science Research Council.

Preeg, Ernest. 1995. *Traders in a Brave New World.* Chicago: University of Chicago Press.

Prickett, Glenn et al. 1991. "Re: Environmental Review of NAFTA." Letter to Charles Ries. July 9.

Public Citizen Trade Team. 1992. "Update Packet Including News on H. Con. Res. 246 Victory (8/6), NAFTA Announcement and More . . . " Memo. August 14.

Public Citizen Trade Team. 1992. "Update Packet: Official Launch of Citizens' Campaign against Bush's NAFTA; Print and Media Campaign; International Efforts; and More . . ." Memo to People Interested in Citizens' Campaign on International Trade. December 30.

Rauch, Jonathan. 1994. *Demosclerosis*. New York: Times Books.

Reilly, William. 1991. Letter to Senator Timothy E. Wirth. Reprinted in *Inside U.S. Trade*. May 24. Pp. 8–9.

Riegle, Donald. 1991. "S.Res. 109—Modify Fast Track for N. American Free Trade." Letter to Senators. October 21.

Roberts, J. Timmons and Nikki D. Thanos. 2003. *Trouble in Paradise: Globalization and Environmental Crises in Latin America*. London: Routledge.

Roett, Riordan, editor. 1999. *MERCOSUR: Regional Integration, World Markets*. Boulder, CO: Lynne Rienner.

Roger, Michael. 1991. "More on the US-Mexico-Canada FTA." Memo. February 13.

Rogowsky, Robert A. and Eric Chyn. 2007. "U.S. Trade Law and FTAs: A Survey of Labor Requirements." *Journal of International Commerce and Economics*. International Trade Commission.

Rose, Fred. 2000. *Coalitions across the Class Divide: Lessons from the Labor, Peace, and Environmental Movements*. Ithaca, NY and London: Cornell University Press.

Rosenberg, Jerry. 1994. *Dictionary of International Trade*. New York: John Wiley and Sons.

Rosner, David and Gerald Markowitz, editors. 1987. *Dying for Work: Workers' Safety and Health in Twentieth Century America*. Bloomington: Indiana University Press.

Ruef, Martin. 2000. "The Emergence of Organizational Forms: A Community Ecology Approach." *American Journal of Sociology* 106:658–714.

Rupert, M. 1995. "(Re) Politicizing the Global Economy: Liberal Common Sense and Ideological Struggle in the US NAFTA Debate." *Review of International Political Economy* 2(4):658–692.

Samuel, Terrance. 2009. "A Good Working Environment". *The American Prospect*. Online Edition. http://www.prospect.org/cs/articles?article=a_good_working_environment. Accessed on March 19, 2013.

Sanchez, Roberto. 1990. "Health and Environmental Risks of the Maquiladora in Mexicali. *Natural Resources Journal* 30:163–186.

Sanchez, Joseph. 1991. Testimony on Behalf of the Hotel Employees & Restaurant Employees Union Before the House Task Force on Economic Policy, Projections and Revenues of the Committee on the Budget. May 14.

Schnaiberg, Allan. 1980. *The Environment: From Surplus to Scarcity*. New York: Oxford University Press.

Schnaiberg, Allan and Kenneth Gould. 1994. *Environment and Society*. New York: St. Martin's Press.

Schneiberg, Marc and Michael Lounsbury. 2008. "Social Movements and Institutional Analysis." In *Handbook of Organizational Institutionalism*, edited by

R. Greenwood, C. Oliver, K. Sahlin-Andersson, and R. Suddaby. Thousand Oaks, CA: Sage, 650–672.

Schneiberg, Marc and Sarah Soule. 2005. "Institutionalization as a Contested, Multilevel Process: The Case of Rate Regulation in American Fire Insurance." In *Social Movements and Organization Theory*, edited by G.F. Davis, D. McAdam, W. Richard Scott, and M.N. Zald. New York: Cambridge University Press, 122–160.

Scott, Alan. 1990. *Ideology and the New Social Movements*. London: Unwin Hyman.

Scott, W. Richard, Martin Ruef, Peter Mendel, and Carol Caronna. 2000. *Institutional Change and Healthcare Organizations: From Professional Dominance to Managed Care*. Chicago: University of Chicago Press.

Scott, Robert E., Carlos Salas, and Bruce Campbell 2006. "Revisiting NAFTA: Still Not Working for America's Workers." Economic Policy Institute Briefing Paper #173. Washington, DC: Economic Policy Institute.

Sewell, William, Jr. 1992. "A Theory of Structure: Duality, Agency, and Transformation," *American Journal of Sociology* 98(1):1–29.

Shaiken, Harley, 1990. *Mexico in the Global Economy: High Technology and Work Organization in Export Industries*. San Diego: Center for U.S.-Mexican Studies, University of California.

Shaiken, Harley. 1991. "The Universal Motors Assembly and Stamping Plant: Transferring High Tech Production to Mexico." *Columbia Journal of World Business* 26(2):125–137.

Shaiken, Harley. 1994. "Advanced Manufacturing and Mexico: A New International Division of Labor?" *Latin American Research Review* 29(2):39–71.

Shaiken, Harley. 1995. "The NAFTA, a Social Charter, and Economic Growth." In *NAFTA as a Model of Development: The Benefits and Costs of Merging High- and Low-Wage Areas*, edited by Richard Belous and Jonathan Lemco. Albany: State University of New York Press, 23–31.

Shantz, Joseph and Mark Anderson. 1992. Letter to All State Federations and Major Central Labor Councils. June 1.

Sheehan, Jack. 1991. "Subject: NAFTA." Memo to District Directors and Legislative Representatives. November 7.

Shrybman, Steven. 1991. "Trading Away the Environment." *World Policy Journal* 9(1):93–110.

Sklair, Leslie. 1993. *Assembling for Development: The Maquila Industry in Mexico and the United States*. Boston: Unwin Hyman.

Sklair, Leslie. 1994. "Global Sociology and Global Environmental Change." In *Social Theory and the Global Environment*, edited by Michael Redclift and Ted Benton. London: Routledge, 205–227.

Snape, William. 1993. Testimony on Behalf of the Defenders of Wildlife. "Impacts of Trade Agreements on U.S. Environmental Protection and Natural Resource Conservation Efforts." March 10. Washington, D.C. in front of the One Hundred and Third Congress.

Snow, David and Robert Benford. 1988. "Ideology, Frame Resonance, and Participant Mobilization." *International Social Movement Research* 197–218.

Snow, David and Robert Benford. 1992. "Master Frames and Cycles of Protest." In *Frontiers in Social Movement Theory*, edited by Aldon Morris and Carol McClurg Mueller. New Haven, CT: Yale University Press, 133–155.

Speck, Paul. 1990. July 26. "Letter to Andrea Durbin." Durbin worked for Friends of the Earth and Speck worked for NWF.

Starr, Paul. 2007. *Freedom's Power: The History and Promise of Liberalism.* New York: Basic Books.

Steelworkers Legislative Appeal. 1992. October 27.

Stevis, Dimitris. 1998. "International Labor Organizations, 1864–1997: The Weight of History and the Challenges of the Present." *Journal of World-Systems Research* 4:52–75.

Stevis, Demitris. 2002. "Agents, Subjects, Objects, or Phantoms? Labor, the Environment, and Liberal Institutionalization." *Annals of the American Academy* 581:91–105.

Sunthonkhan, Duangkamol. 2010. "The Impact of NAFTA on the U.S. Labor Market." Ph.D. Dissertation, Department of Economics. University of Utah.

Swedberg, Richard. 2006. "The Toolkit of Economic Sociology." In *The Oxford Handbook of Political Economy*, edited by D. Wittman and B. Weingast. New York: Oxford University Press, 937–950.

Swidler, Ann. 1986. "Culture in Action: Symbols and Strategies." *American Sociological Review* 51(2):273–286.

Switzer, Jacqueline and Bryner, Vaughn. 1998. *Environmental Politics.* New York: St. Martin's Press.

Tarrow, Sidney. 1994. *Power in Movement.* Cambridge: Cambridge University Press.

Thomas, Clive. 1993. "The American Interest Group System: Typical Model or Aberration?" In *First World Interest Groups: A Comparative Perspective*, edited by Thomas, Clive. Westport, CT: Greenwood Press, 27–52.

Tilly, Charles. 2000. "Processes and Mechanisms of Democratization." *Sociological Theory* 18(1):1–16.

Time/CNN. 1992. "Grapevine." July 9.

"Too High a Price for Free Trade: Citizens' Analysis of the February 21 Draft of the North American Free Trade Agreement." 1992. April 6.

Toronto Star. 1991. "Opponents of Free Trade Heckle Speech by Salinas." October 1. P. C2.

Trommer, Silke. 2014. *Transformations in Trade Politics: Participatory Trade Politics in West Africa.* New York: Routledge.

USA*NAFTA. 1993. "USA*NAFTA Statement on Judge Richey's District Court Decision." June 30.

Villarreal, M. Angeles and Ian F. Fergusson. 2015. *The North American Free Trade Agreement (NAFTA).* Washington, DC: Congressional Research Service.

Voss, Kim and Rachel Sherman. 2000. "Breaking the Iron Law of Oligarchy: Union Revitalization in the American Labor Movement." *American Journal of Sociology* 106:303–349.

Walker, Edward T., Andrew W. Martin, and John D. McCarthy. 2008. "Confronting the State, the Corporation, and the Academy: The Influence of Institutional Targets on Social Movement Repertoires," *American Journal of Sociology* 114(1):35–76.

Wallach, Lori and Hilliard, Tom. 1991. "The Consumer and Environmental Case against Fast Track." *Public Citizen*, May.

Wallach, Lori and Tom Hilliard. 1991. Testimony on Behalf of Public Citizen Before the House Subcommittee on Commerce, Consumer Protection and Competitiveness of the Committee on Energy and Commerce. "North American Free Trade Agreement" May 8.

Wastler, Allen. 1992. "Inside Talk—Allen Wastler This All-Star Game Had a Different Type of Trading." *Journal of Commerce.* July 21. P. 5A.

Wathen, Tom. 1992. *A Guide to Trade and the Environment.* New York: Environmental Grantmakers Association.

Wathen, Tom. 1993. "A Guide to the Environment." In *Trade and Environment: Law, Economics and Policy*, edited by Durwood Zaelke, Paul Orbuch, and Robert Housman. Washington, DC: Island Press, 3–22.

Watkins, Steven. 1991. "Hills Strongly Urges Congress Not to Split 'Fast-Track' Approval Vote." *Inside U.S. Trade.* March 15. Pp. 1, 16, and 17.

Weisbrot, Mark, Lara Merling, Vitor Mello, Stephan Lefebvre, and Joseph Sammut. 2017. "Did NAFTA Help Mexico? An Update after 23 Years." Washington, DC: Center for Economic and Policy Research. March.

Wilkinson, Rorden. 2014. *What's Wrong with the WTO and How to Fix It.* Malden: John Wiley & Sons.

Will, George. 1993. "TV Greases the Skids under a Very Slippery Performance." *Times-Picayune.* November 12. P. B07.

Wilson, Rand. 1994. "Winning Lessons from the NAFTA Loss." *Labor Research Review* 13(1):28–37.

Wilson, Graham. 1990. *Interest Groups.* Cambridge, MA: Basil Blackwell.

Wines, Michael. 1993. "The Free Trade Accord; A 'Bazaar' Way of Rounding Up Votes." *New York Times.* November 11. P. A23.

Workman, Willard A. 1993. "Letter to USTR Kantor." April 29.

Wyden, Ron, Bruce Vento, James Bilbray, Arthur Ravenel, Jr., Richard Durbin, Dan Glickman, Paul Henry, Dennis Eckart, Nancy Pelosi, Byron Dorgan, and Bernard Sanders. 1991. "Letter to the President." February 22. Reprinted in *Inside U.S. Trade.* "House Letter to Bush on Mexico FTA." February 22. P. 6.

Yearly, Steven. 1994. "Social Movements and Environmental Change." In *Social Theory and the Global Environment*, edited by Michael Redclift and Ted Benton. London: Routledge, 150–168.

Zeleny, Jeff. 2008a. "Obama Slams Critics on Middle-Class Comments." *New York Times*, April 11.

Zeleny, Jeff. 2008b. "In Labor Speech, Obama Revisits Bitterness." *New York Times*, April 15.

Interviews

Personal Interview with Chris Townsend of the UE, April 1, 1998.

Personal Interview with Greg Woodhead of the AFL-CIO, April 4, 1998.

Personal Interview with Greg Woodhead of the AFL-CIO, April 7, 1998.

Personal Interview with Mark Anderson of the AFL-CIO, April 7, 1998.

Personal Interview with Pharis Harvey of ILRF, April 14, 1998.

Personal Interview with Karen Hansen-Kuhn of DGAP, April 22, 1998.

Personal Interview with John Audley of the Sierra Club, April 27, 1998.

Personal Interview with Barbara Warden of the UAW, April 30, 1998.

Personal Interviews with Bill Cunningham of the AFL-CIO, May 5, 1998.

Personal Interview with Lori Wallach of Public Citizen, May 7, 1998.

Personal Interview with Bill Snape of DOW, May 14, 1998.

Personal Interview with Evy DuBrow of ILGWU, May 12, 1998.

Personal Interview with Kathryn Fuller of WWF, May 26, 1998.

Personal Interview with AFL-CIO representative, February 29, 2000.

Personal Interview with Tim Beaty of the AFL-CIO, February 29, 2000.

Personal Interview with Alicia Sepúlveda Nuñez of the STRM, August 27, 2000.

Personal Interview with Mark Anderson of the AFL-CIO, January 8, 2001.

Personal Interview with Anonymous official of the AFL-CIO, January 12, 2001.

Personal Interview with Pharis Harvey of ILRF, March 2, 2001.

Personal Interview with Lawrence Katz of the U.S. Department of Labor, March 13, 2001.

Personal Interview with Craig Merrilees of the Fair Trade Campaign, April 3, 2001.

Personal Interview with Don Weiner of the Fair Trade Campaign, April 5, 2001.

Personal Interview with Craig Merrilees of the Fair Trade Campaign, April 21, 2001.

Personal Interview with David Brooks of U.S.-Mexico Dialogos, May 8, 2001.

Personal Interview with Tom Donahue of the AFL-CIO, May 23, 2001.

Personal Interview with Mark Ritchie of IATP, June 11, 2001.

Personal Interview with Steve Herzenberg, U.S. Department of Labor, Assistant to the Chief Negotiator of the labor side agreement to NAFTA, September 27, 2002.

Index